# LEAN ENTREPRENEURSHIP

## INNOVATION IN THE MODERN ENTERPRISE

*George Watt*

*Howard Abrams*

To Dennis:

Keep Innovating !

CA Press

**Apress®**

*Lean Entrepreneurship: Innovation in the Modern Enterprise*

George Watt
Kanata, ON, Canada

Howard Abrams
San Mateo, CA, USA

ISBN-13 (pbk): 978-1-4842-3941-4
https://doi.org/10.1007/978-1-4842-3942-1

ISBN-13 (electronic): 978-1-4842-3942-1

Library of Congress Control Number: 2018962003

Managing Director, Apress Media LLC: Welmoed Spahr
Acquisitions Editor: Susan McDermott
Development Editor: Laura Berendson
Coordinating Editor: Rita Fernando

Distributed to the book trade worldwide by Springer Science+Business Media New York, 233 Spring Street, 6th Floor, New York, NY 10013. Phone 1-800-SPRINGER, fax (201) 348-4505, e-mail orders-ny@springer-sbm.com, or visit www.springeronline.com. Apress Media, LLC is a California LLC and the sole member (owner) is Springer Science + Business Media Finance Inc (SSBM Finance Inc). SSBM Finance Inc is a **Delaware** corporation.

For information on translations, please e-mail rights@apress.com, or visit http://www.apress.com/rights-permissions.

Apress titles may be purchased in bulk for academic, corporate, or promotional use. eBook versions and licenses are also available for most titles. For more information, reference our Print and eBook Bulk Sales web page at http://www.apress.com/bulk-sales.

Any source code or other supplementary material referenced by the author in this book is available to readers on GitHub via the book's product page, located at www.apress.com/9781484239414. For more detailed information, please visit http://www.apress.com/source-code.

Printed on acid-free paper

*To Mom, Adrienne, Lila, and Carter:*
*Thank you so much for your unwavering love*
*and support over these many years, without*
*which this book would not exist.*
*To Dad: Sorry you missed this.*

*—h*

*To Lee Anne, Heather, and James. You were there*
*for me throughout the entire journey that led*
*to this book and always smiled when I said,*
*"Sorry, I can't right now" as I wrote it. Thank you*
*for a lifetime of unconditional love and support.*

*—George*

# Contents

# About the Authors

**George Watt** became passionate about technology and innovation at a very early age and built his first "computer" out of cardboard boxes somewhere around age 5. George led the design workshops for the Accelerator program described in this book and created and deployed its foundation artifacts and ceremonies. Throughout his career, George has delivered innovations of his own, such as a knowledge base for a neural network-based predictive performance management solution, one of the earliest private clouds (2005), and a lightweight event management agent. A transformative leader, George has spearheaded initiatives that have enabled organizations to address complex technology problems, deliver new business benefits, and drive millions of dollars in savings and productivity gains. George began his technical career as a systems programmer/sysadmin and systems engineer. He has held many national and global leadership positions, and has led global teams spanning North America, Europe, Asia, and Australia. As VP of Strategy for CA Technologies Office of the CTO, he is passionate about helping budding intrapreneurs turn great ideas into viable businesses, and he is responsible for the global scientific research, worldwide innovation initiatives, and the ongoing evolution of the Accelerator program. George is co-author of The Innovative CIO and tweets as @GeorgeDWatt.

**Howard Abrams** has worn many hats throughout his career, taking on diverse technical and leadership roles—from software architecture to user experience, and from mobile apps to enterprise software. Howard is currently a Distinguished Engineer and Senior Vice President at CA Technologies. He is responsible for CA's internal incubator, CA Accelerator, where incubations function like lean startups and internal innovators receive the support and funding they need to develop and test new products. Prior to joining CA, Howard held technical positions in organizations, including Muse Corporation, the US Navy, Paradigm Simulation, MITRE Corporation, and Jeppesen Sanderson. Howard has been granted 10 patents and has several additional pending. He holds a PhD in Computer Science from the Naval Postgraduate School as well as a BSc in Aerospace Engineering from Embry-Riddle University. Although he began coding at age seven in the Chicago suburbs, Howard now enjoys spending his free time with his wife and two children in the San Francisco Bay Area.

# About the Technical Reviewer

**K. Scott Morrison** is a Senior Vice President and Distinguished Engineer at CA Technologies. He joined CA as part of its acquisition of Layer 7 Technologies, where he served as CTO. Scott is a passionate, entertaining, and highly sought-after keynote speaker. His quotes appear regularly across media, including in *The New York Times, The Wall Street Journal,* and on CNN. He has co-authored academic papers in medical, physics, and engineering journals, and holds 10 US patents. Scott lives with his family in Vancouver BC.

The name of the game was taking market share rather than establishing a new market. Furthermore, the game console market could not realistically be disrupted by some small, nascent startup. Establishing a meaningful foothold would require massive investment. For this reason, the first green-light funding check for Xbox was a billion dollars—not to deliver the first generation of a new console entrant, but simply to get started with the effort in earnest.

HBO GO and Time Warner's investment in building video streaming capabilities was also not an exploratory "what if" incubation. The company's efforts were in response to the traction that Netflix and other players were making in distributing content via the Internet and consumer devices, including Xbox. The fact that the Internet would disrupt media and video distribution and consumption of content was no longer in dispute. The question was what the company's response would be not only to survive digital disruption, but also to use it as an engine of growth. Again, building a video streaming service for millions of customers required a commitment of significant resources; customer demand had moved well beyond what a small-scale startup effort could deliver.

While they were innovative, both Xbox and HBO GO were large enterprise "big bet" responses to large, proven markets and clearly evident technology trends. Although innovation is never easy, large enterprises are well-suited to making deep investments. They have the resources, and operating at scale is in their DNA. In fact, not operating at scale is what seems foreign to a large, established business. How does an enterprise explore new business opportunities when the market doesn't yet exist or is too nascent to be meaningful in the short term?

Large enterprises can easily miss opportunities in new markets. I vividly remember a meeting with Steve Ballmer presenting a next-generation tablet concept—a 10.4-inch display, touch, and pen enabled, less than half an inch thin—that today you would recognize as a modern tablet. The meeting was over a year before the iPad launched, and although the meeting generally went well, Steve's summary was, "If there were a tablet market, it would exist already." It is of course easy to be too early or too late, but recovering from "too late" in today's fast-moving market is virtually impossible.

So how then can an enterprise create and support an efficient, repeatable framework for small, startup-style incubations exploring high-risk green field opportunities? As I examined the projects underway on my desk that first week, it occurred to me that if we could bring that startup mentality into the large enterprise, but temper it with the rigor and process that is a typically a large enterprise's strong suit, we might have a magic formula for transforming great ideas into real businesses.

There is nothing new about efforts to drive innovation inside the enterprise. "Skunkworks" have been around for decades, where people can experiment away from the intense pressure to immediately add to the bottom line that most businesses demand. As one of the four original Xbox founders, I can attest to Xbox having gotten its start as an unapproved skunkworks effort. In retrospect, we were amazingly lucky to have been able to get traction for the idea within the company. The reality is that skunkworks typically carry the seeds of their own destruction in a lack of discipline around customer focus and an inability to answer the fundamental question: Is there a need for what my idea will do?

Today, the marketplace itself is driving the need for companies to constantly be inventing new products and services. As I wrote in my recently published *Digitally Remastered: Building Software Into Your Business DNA* book, a new world is taking shape. It's a world dominated by digital engagement. The convergence of the Internet, mobile devices, and pervasive connectivity has fundamentally changed the relationship between business and digital technology.

Most importantly, digital engagement changes the relationship with customers and is a powerful mechanism for sensing and responding to unmet needs. This "feedback loop" is a powerful force underpinning a new kind of customer intimacy that is 24/7, deeper than ever before, and requires a constant stream of continuously improving products and services to be satisfied.

This new operating environment has critical implications for how innovation and product development is done today. In the old days, this work could be done in a vacuum and then rolled out to customers, along with expensive marketing and sales models. But today, we live in a world of a fully digital customer journey—from discovery, to trial, to fulfillment—and the ways customers both buy and behave has changed forever. Not only that, but for products to truly meet market needs, they need to be developed in partnership with customers, and through ongoing iteration, constantly improved. This is the new landscape that enterprises face in driving innovation. It is not easy, but as you will read in the pages that follow, it can be done in a repeatable and very efficient way.

The CA Accelerator takes the best of the nimble, flexible startup and Lean principles and marries those with the processes and operating framework of the enterprise. Importantly, it is deployed within the context of a venture-capital style gating process and utilizes the modern approach to developing products that matter: engaging with customers early, and often, at every stage of an idea's realization and transformation into a business.

Howard Abrams and George Watt have laid out the methodology whereby any enterprise can incorporate productive innovation that can drive the bottom line, but also serve as a way of connecting with customers and other stakeholders around the problems they are trying to understand and solve in the digital world.

With this book as a guide, it's possible to see innovation come to life in a way never thought possible in medium- or large-scale organizations. The end result is a tool for not just customer engagement but employee engagement and talent retention. Starting with just a single-page "Lean Canvas," the founders in the CA Accelerator program bring their ideas to market in distinctly unique ways, but what they all share is a passion for innovation and making things that matter.

—Otto Berkes

Chief Technology Officer, CA Technologies

# Acknowledgments

It takes a village to create an accelerator. We are grateful to the many people who worked tirelessly to build the CA Accelerator program. Thank you to Erin Bank, Ginee Berardi, Otto Berkes, Debra Danielson Ryan Martens, David McNierney, Richard Philyaw, Connie Smallwood, Craig Vosburgh, and Jacquelyn O'Neill-Walsh. Thank you to the incubating teams who leaned in early and experienced all of our initial wins, and every one of our early mistakes. Andrew Homeyer, Joav Bally, your contributions as founders were invaluable and your patience much appreciated. We learned so much together. Thank you Dave Mell, master unblocker and operations lead extraordinaire. Thank you to our fellow Angel Team members, past and present, who helped us to inspect and adapt, and who willingly looked in the mirror.

To all of the CA Technologies teams to whom we have said, "we need your help," thank you for being patient, flexible, and creative; and for creating new, innovative approaches that enable incubating teams to move fast and learn fast. Thank you to the people from our Applied Research, Benefits, Branding, Communications, Compensation, Corporate Development, Corporate Strategy, Corporate Travel, Finance, GIS (Global IT), Information Engineering, Internal Audit, Investor Relations, Legal, Marketing, People (Human Resources), Pricing, Procurement, Risk Management, Sales, Sales Accounting, Strategic Research, Talent Acquisition, Talent Development, and User Experience teams, without whom this program would not be possible. A special thank you to Barbara Baldwin, Kyle Curry, Trillium Fox, Anna Griffin, Chris Herbst, Matt Mcclendon, Eric Nintzel, John Ormond, Bill Talbot, Cameron Van Orman, and Anna Xanthos, for your assistance, patience, and contributions to the program.

We would also like to offer a special thank you to the many people who called us in frustration and were willing to be open and candid. Our accelerator is infinitely better because you had the courage to voice your concerns and the trust that we would respect your confidentiality and candor.

Thank you to all the people who pitched ideas to the accelerator. Even when they were not accepted, your hard work improved the program for everyone. We would also like to thank the many others who helped make our program better, perhaps without even realizing they had done so. There are far too many of you to mention.

Just as it takes a village to build an accelerator, it takes a village to write a book. We would like to thank all of the people who helped us as we wrote this book. We had an incredibly aggressive schedule and could not have written it without the kind assistance of Andrew Homeyer, David McNierney, Scott Morrison, and Jacquelyn O'Neill-Walsh. We would also like to thank Rita Fernando, Susan McDermott, and Kezia Endsley from Apress, and Karen Sleeth from CA Press, for your guidance and support.

Finally, there have been so many people who have helped shape our thinking and incubation program, and who have supported and guided us along the way, that we are nearly certain that we have unintentionally left someone out. Thank you. We are confident you know who you are, though we apologize for leaving you out nonetheless.

# Introduction

## If innovation was easy, everybody would be doing it

*"Genius is 1% inspiration and 99% perspiration."*

—Thomas Edison

"Forget it!" "It's just not worth it!"

Phrases like this have long replaced "Eureka!" in established organizations. We have all heard the legends of two garage-dwelling masterminds who had an amazing idea that started with "Eureka!" and became an "overnight success". If a small team, with almost no resources, experience, capital—not much of anything—can deliver such compelling value, why do we hear so often that innovation in established organizations is impossible? Mature organizations should have an enormous advantage. They have access to capital, experience, skills, channels, network, lawyers, marketers… it makes no sense that they cannot outperform those tiny teams.

The truth is that both positions are inaccurate. Innovation in established organizations is not impossible, and innovation in small teams is not always easy. Thomas Edison said, "Opportunity is missed by most people because it is dressed in overalls and looks like work." Who would know better than he? Edison had been working on his battery technology for 16 or more hours every day, seven days a week, for five straight months when his friend, W.S. Mallory, visited his laboratory. When Mallory learned Edison had made over 9,000 attempts at the battery without a single result that showed promise, he asked, "Isn't it a shame that with the tremendous amount of work you have done, you haven't been able to get any results?" With a smile, Edison shot out a reply that delivers great insight into the mind of a successful inventor and innovator, "Results! Why, man, I have gotten a lot of results! I know several thousand things that won't work."[1] With more than 1,000 patents to his name,

---

[1] *Edison: His Life and Inventions*, Frank Lewis Dyer and Thomas Commerford Martin, Harper & Brothers, 1910

Edison taught the world a lot about innovation. He eventually produced his battery after more than 10,000 attempts. Some say it was tens of thousands of attempts in total before he perfected it.

# The Dirty Little Secret of the Overnight Success

Whether in a small team or the largest enterprise, bringing a great idea to life requires time and sweat. Just ask any self-made entrepreneur what life "in the early days" of their idea was like. While there are some exceptions, most often you will hear stories of hard work and hardship.

Consider well-known vacuum inventor, Sir John Dyson. It took him 5,127 prototypes and 15 years to get his cyclone technology working properly. In a column for *Wired*,[2] he describes his journey, and how penny-pinching eventually evolved into his wife giving art lessons to keep his dream alive. The "Sir" he can now place in front of his name is evidence his hard work and determination were worthwhile. By the time of that article's publication, Dyson was on the 35th commercially available version of the vacuum. He never stopped working—or learning.

So the dirty little secret of those instant successes is that they are not normally so instant, and they are usually stories of toil and sacrifice. Though that still begs the original question. "Why does innovation in established organizations seem impossible?" Or at least harder than going it alone. Certainly harder than it should be. Is success or failure in innovation simply a matter of luck? No! Nor should it be. My (George's) father used to say, "I'd rather be lucky than good—at anything". While we would never suggest you should turn down good fortune—a lucky break is great when it happens—luck is not a sound strategy.

Great ideas sometimes fail for fairly obvious reasons. For example, the Six Degrees social network, the Dodgeball.com location-based social service, and tablet pioneer GO corporation simply launched products that were too far ahead of their time. That can happen in established organizations or in stand-alone startups. This is not what we are referring to. The root causes of innovation failure in established companies are much broader and more insidious than this. Sometimes innovation fails in successful companies because the very process that drives their success creates massive innovation antibodies.

In his seminal book, *The Innovator's Dilemma*, Clayton Christensen explored this in depth. In the book, Christensen explained how the very processes that made companies successful were themselves antibodies to disruptive innovation.

---

[2]"No Innovator's Dilemma Here: In Praise of Failure," *Wired* Online, April 8, 2011 https://www.wired.com/2011/04/in-praise-of-failure/

We agree. Throughout our careers we have experienced this. Many times. We have had our own successes and failures. We have slain the dragons of bureaucracy and process and been slain by them. In addition, we have studied this phenomenon many times and even conducted our own research. We can tell you that, while Christensen's point is valid, there is even more to consider.

Whether you are alone in your garage or innovating in a large enterprise, there are several other, critical items that must be addressed deliberately in order to successfully bring new ideas to life in impactful ways, and to ensure they bring value to those who use them. We will guide you through other key risks that, left unaddressed, significantly reduce the chance of an idea's success. They can even damage the mature business. More importantly, we will explain what can be done to address these risks and challenges so your idea has the best possible chance to succeed.

In the next two chapters we will leverage our experience and research to expand on why attempts at innovation fail in established organizations. Understanding these traps and impediments can help you to avoid them and help ensure your ideas are successful. Though that understanding is not enough on its own.

Throughout our careers—in order to survive, and thrive, under these circumstances ourselves—we have had to develop specific strategies and tools for addressing these issues head on. Of course there were also failures, though we learned even more from those. Recently we put all of these things together to create a unique program, CA Accelerator, which we built specifically to give innovative ideas the best possible chance to succeed in an established organization.

In the remainder of the book we will share these strategies, tools, and approaches so you can use them to bring your own ideas to life; ensure you are building something worthwhile; and ensure neither you nor your organization impedes your progress or becomes the reason your idea fails. We will also share our program structure, ceremonies, and detailed artifacts so you can use them to create a program of your own.

# What's in This Book?

Chapter 1, "Their Own Worst Enemy," explores the key reasons innovation fails in established businesses. We will share our personal experiences, hard-learned lessons, and stories of failure. We will also discuss key differences between new and established businesses, why they matter, and share the results of our research on innovation impediments in established organizations.

Chapter 2, "Unintended Consequences," explores the impact of the problems that are discussed in Chapter 1. It also examines how those problems lead to new and exacerbated issues and impediments that result in a not so virtuous cycle of failure, which impacts morale and leads to a self-reinforcing culture of bad behavior. This behavior makes successful innovation much less likely, perhaps impossible, not only for those perpetuating those bad practices, but potentially for others inside and outside the incubating team. Ironically, the employees typically engage in these innovation-killing practices because they have, usually unwittingly, been incented to do so by the organization that would benefit most from their success. We will also discuss what can be done to address these unproductive behaviors by tackling their root causes.

Chapter 3, "Lean Acceleration," introduces a framework for continuous innovation and new business incubation. While innovation in isolation—without the support of the organization and its leadership—is possible in an established organization, it is much less probable. Innovators are likely to give up as they push against the momentum of corporate process and culture. The skills required to both accomplish this and be a successful innovator are rare, and those rare individuals will waste much of their time in a clandestine activity that does not advance their idea. This chapter introduces a framework for repeatable success and describes how we developed, deployed, and evolved our own program. This framework will enable intrapreneurs to move much faster than their standalone entrepreneur counterparts, providing the intrapreneurs with the freedom of a standalone startup as well as the resources and benefits of an established organization.

Chapter 4, "Inside the Accelerator," discusses the inner workings of key aspects of the program and describes the elements required in order to build a successful business incubation program of your own. This chapter discusses project ceremonies and structure, and key tools and foundational artifacts for driving speed and consistency. In addition, this chapter discusses several strategies for preparing the mainstream business executives who will govern the program for the key differences between their mainstream businesses and the nascent businesses they will govern.

Chapter 5, "Innovation Support Structure," explores the creation of innovation support infrastructure in your large organization. It discusses how the program elements created for new incubations can take advantage of your established business to drive speed, agility, and better decision making. It also introduces some of the innovative programs created by our Accelerator incubation program team, and by others who saw the value in our initiative. In addition, it discusses how to ensure new businesses created in your program are not eradicated by corporate culture and innovation antibodies after they "graduate" from your program and join the mainstream organization.

Chapter 6, "Benefits Beyond Revenue," describes how a program of this nature can help drive the long-term viability of your business beyond the obvious creation of new businesses. We have learned that our program can help improve the operation of mainstream businesses, develop employee skills, build new leaders, and drive a culture of innovation far beyond the

# Their Own Worst Enemy

## Why Innovation Fails in Established Organizations

*"Life's real failure is when you do not realize how close you were to success when you gave up."*

—Anonymous

Bringing new ideas from "eureka!" to a point where they are bringing value to people every day is hard. Doing so in established organizations, especially large ones, can be even harder. But why? Why is it not *easier* for people working in these large organizations—with scores of talented people, massive resources, and hundreds of years of experience—to breathe life into great new ideas? That is a question we have pondered for many years. Understanding the answer is key to successfully conquering the problem. So let's begin our journey there.

© CA 2019
G. Watt and H. Abrams, *Lean Entrepreneurship*,
https://doi.org/10.1007/978-1-4842-3942-1_1

# Project Sisyphus: A Study of Innovation in Established Business Organizations

A few years ago I (George) was asked to lead a research project to determine whether new business ideas that were generated in a large, well established organization had a decent chance of success (Sisyphus was not its real name). We assembled a core team that consisted of successful entrepreneurs, strategists, general managers, and people who had innovated in large, well-established organizations (successfully, unsuccessfully, and both). Our terms of reference for this research included investigating:

1. Whether new business ideas had any chance of succeeding

2. Whether *all* new business ideas were consistently afforded the *same* probability of success

3. The root causes of the failure of any businesses that had not succeeded and identification of any common patterns among those failed business ideas

In order to drive consistency in our analysis we studied all aspects of the business design of each new business idea we investigated. We used a fairly common business design model that analyzed key elements that must be present in order for any business to succeed, including:

- **Customer Selection:** Did the business target specific, high-value customer opportunities? Was this done explicitly? Were specific groups explicitly ruled out as target customers?

- **Value Proposition:** What was the businesses' unique and differentiated customer proposition? What unmet customer needs could the business address well that its competitors could not address—or not address *as* well? Was this an explicit choice? Was the business team aware of this choice?

- **Value Capture/Profit Model:** How did, or would, the business create and grow profit?

- **Scope of Activities:** What, specifically, did/would the business sell (e.g., software, services…)? What work was to be done by the business team? What work would be done elsewhere (e.g., outsourced work, purchase of pre-built inputs, use of open source, leverage of platform services…)? Which key components of production and operations must be owned in order to maintain appropriate control over strategic elements of the business?

Edison taught the world a lot about innovation. He eventually produced his battery after more than 10,000 attempts. Some say it was tens of thousands of attempts in total before he perfected it.

# The Dirty Little Secret of the Overnight Success

Whether in a small team or the largest enterprise, bringing a great idea to life requires time and sweat. Just ask any self-made entrepreneur what life "in the early days" of their idea was like. While there are some exceptions, most often you will hear stories of hard work and hardship.

Consider well-known vacuum inventor, Sir John Dyson. It took him 5,127 prototypes and 15 years to get his cyclone technology working properly. In a column for *Wired*,[2] he describes his journey, and how penny-pinching eventually evolved into his wife giving art lessons to keep his dream alive. The "Sir" he can now place in front of his name is evidence his hard work and determination were worthwhile. By the time of that article's publication, Dyson was on the 35th commercially available version of the vacuum. He never stopped working—or learning.

So the dirty little secret of those instant successes is that they are not normally so instant, and they are usually stories of toil and sacrifice. Though that still begs the original question. "Why does innovation in established organizations seem impossible?" Or at least harder than going it alone. Certainly harder than it should be. Is success or failure in innovation simply a matter of luck? No! Nor should it be. My (George's) father used to say, "I'd rather be lucky than good—at anything". While we would never suggest you should turn down good fortune—a lucky break is great when it happens—luck is not a sound strategy.

Great ideas sometimes fail for fairly obvious reasons. For example, the Six Degrees social network, the Dodgeball.com location-based social service, and tablet pioneer GO corporation simply launched products that were too far ahead of their time. That can happen in established organizations or in stand-alone startups. This is not what we are referring to. The root causes of innovation failure in established companies are much broader and more insidious than this. Sometimes innovation fails in successful companies because the very process that drives their success creates massive innovation antibodies.

In his seminal book, *The Innovator's Dilemma*, Clayton Christensen explored this in depth. In the book, Christensen explained how the very processes that made companies successful were themselves antibodies to disruptive innovation.

---

[2] "No Innovator's Dilemma Here: In Praise of Failure," *Wired* Online, April 8, 2011 https://www.wired.com/2011/04/in-praise-of-failure/

# Introduction

## If innovation was easy, everybody would be doing it

*"Genius is 1% inspiration and 99% perspiration."*

—Thomas Edison

"Forget it!" "It's just not worth it!"

Phrases like this have long replaced "Eureka!" in established organizations. We have all heard the legends of two garage-dwelling masterminds who had an amazing idea that started with "Eureka!" and became an "overnight success". If a small team, with almost no resources, experience, capital—not much of anything—can deliver such compelling value, why do we hear so often that innovation in established organizations is impossible? Mature organizations should have an enormous advantage. They have access to capital, experience, skills, channels, network, lawyers, marketers... it makes no sense that they cannot outperform those tiny teams.

The truth is that both positions are inaccurate. Innovation in established organizations is not impossible, and innovation in small teams is not always easy. Thomas Edison said, "Opportunity is missed by most people because it is dressed in overalls and looks like work." Who would know better than he? Edison had been working on his battery technology for 16 or more hours every day, seven days a week, for five straight months when his friend, W.S. Mallory, visited his laboratory. When Mallory learned Edison had made over 9,000 attempts at the battery without a single result that showed promise, he asked, "Isn't it a shame that with the tremendous amount of work you have done, you haven't been able to get any results?" With a smile, Edison shot out a reply that delivers great insight into the mind of a successful inventor and innovator, "Results! Why, man, I have gotten a lot of results! I know several thousand things that won't work."[1] With more than 1,000 patents to his name,

---

[1] *Edison: His Life and Inventions*, Frank Lewis Dyer and Thomas Commerford Martin, Harper & Brothers, 1910

program's metaphoric walls. We share our experience and describe how you can leverage your program to improve the reputation of your business and improve your organization in other surprising ways.

Chapter 7, "Bootstrapping an Incubation Program," provides guidance regarding how to get your incubation program up and running. It goes into details about why it is important to get buy-in early and from a deep and broad set of stakeholders, many of which may not be obvious, as well as the need to make sure those stakeholders clearly understand what they have signed up for. These stakeholders need to understand all of the risks, the potential rewards, and the time it takes for businesses to incubate. The chapter also explores ways to prime your program not only to start working on the future of your company, but also to shake down your program itself. We share the benefits of taking existing skunkworks and unmanaged projects and using them to not only as a source of initial ideas, but also as a source of budget and a selling point to financial stakeholders. In addition, we describe a financial model you can use to estimate the cost of your program and measure its performance.

Chapter 8, "Inspiring Lean Innovation," shares some examples of how our strategies and approaches have been adopted outside our accelerator program, the benefits they bring to other parts of the company, and how you can drive those same benefits into your organization. It also provides examples of how other groups have extended the tools, techniques, and artifacts we use to create new, innovative approaches to their own domains.

Chapter 9, "Conclusion," summarizes our program and findings and provides some final tips for driving these practices into your business.

Innovation and breakthrough business incubation in established organizations does not have to be an exercise in futility. Though it often can be. Some would say it usually is. So let's begin our journey by examining why they might feel that way.

- **Strategic Control:** How was/would the business be built so that it cannot easily be copied by others? How was/would market share and revenue be protected?

- **Organizational Alignment:** How did the business organize for efficient and effective execution and success? What was its approach to leadership, structure, infrastructure…?

Evaluating each of the businesses we investigated in the context of *every* aspect of its business design led us to some valuable insights that may not otherwise have been discovered. Each business design should have represented specific choices that were made explicitly by a business team. Simply learning that specific choices were *not* made was often as valuable as learning about any specific choices that *were* made.

When we completed this research we determined that while new, innovative ideas did have a chance to succeed in large organizations, the odds were not great. This was hardly surprising to us given the experience of the team. Though what this research gave us, that the many articles and books we had read had not, was deep insight into the root causes of failure—and a path toward addressing them.

Over and over we learned there were two primary reasons innovation was failing in established organizations:

1. New businesses were being managed like mature businesses

2. Established organizations did not have a consistent approach to helping new businesses succeed

These two anti-patterns were everywhere. While we discovered pockets of brilliance during our research, there were generally no deliberate, consistently applied best practices to ensure next generation business ideas had an equal chance to succeed. In brief:

- There were no guidelines for best-in-class business design, business designs were not consistently practiced, and when they were created they were usually incomplete

- Teams incubating new ideas were often entirely technology focused, at times performing customer and market analysis only after a product had been brought to market

- Mature businesses tended to see the world through the lens of their existing business models

- Established businesses were only able to understand their own existing licensing models, often limiting their alternatives to "classic" perpetual and/or on-premise license schemes

- When new businesses did not fit into a mature business model, the mature business force-fit them into the model, or made them "disappear"

- Mature business culture, processes, and organization models impeded the execution of new, innovative businesses

- Teams incubating new ideas often lacked the resources and skillsets required in order to bring their ideas to life

- Back-office systems and processes were not designed for breakthrough business and go-to-market models

Analysis of the root causes of these challenges gave us much deeper insight, and clues regarding how to address them. So let's take a look at those.

# Why New, Innovative Business Ideas Are Crushed by Mature Processes and Measures

For decades we have understood that managing everything the same way is a clear path to failure. I can even recall reading about it in the context of leading people in a book entitled, *13 Fatal Errors Managers Make and How You Can Avoid Them*,[1] which was published more than 30 years ago. Yet we found again and again that new, innovative businesses were managed the same way mature businesses were managed. When you view it in this context, it screams "why would anyone even begin to believe that would work?!" Of course, it is way more insidious than that. Though the impact is nonetheless severe.

As a result, new business ideas are crushed under the weight of processes and measures that were created for established mainstream businesses. Mature businesses are measured by income and market adoption rates that are grossly unachievable by a business in its first quarter of exploration. (Or its first year. Or…) As a result people either become disheartened and do not even try to pursue their ideas, or they adopt some very unhealthy behavior and become good at gaming the system. (We dive deeper into issues of this nature in Chapter 2.) We see it all the time, a business that has $10 in annual revenue needs only to obtain one additional $10 customer to claim 100% revenue growth. Though even if they do not game the system, applying the wrong measures at the wrong time can kill a new idea with amazing speed. New business ideas require different measures and targets, especially very early in their life.

---

[1]W. Steven Brown, *13 Fatal Errors Managers Make and How You Can Avoid Them*, Berkley, 1985

Essentially, the corporate tax on new business ideas—the cost of these heavy processes and incorrect, unhelpful measures—is too high. The new businesses are unable to absorb them, and they consume an inordinate amount of the time the incubating team should be spending on bringing their idea to life in a way customers will be compelled to consume it.

You may be thinking, "It cannot all be downside, can it? What about things like funding? Mature businesses have access to large amounts of funding that they can apply to innovative ideas." Sure, it's not all downside. Though we discovered that, without a deliberate and thoughtful approach to incubation, things like this—which should give new business that are incubating inside an established business a great advantage over their garage-resident counterparts—can become a disadvantage. For example, applying too much funding and too many people to an idea too early in its lifecycle can actually slow it down, or kill it. We call this a committed bet. It is a common, resource-squandering trap, and we will discuss it in further detail later.

So, where do we begin? We found that the frustration and dysfunction that prevents many great ideas from succeeding begins very early in their life, often even before a team is assembled or funded. So let's start there.

## Friction, Frustration, Fiction

Very early in our investigation we learned that the root causes of failure began at the very beginning of the innovation process. We learned that the amount of friction facing people with innovative ideas was enormous. Just getting an idea in front of someone was often more work than coming up with the idea or, in some cases, bringing it to the next step in its life. This was true whether or not there was a formal "innovation program". In fact, we learned that formal innovation programs had often added to the amount of friction experienced by budding *intrapreneurs* (the people with the idea, the organization's innovators).

Whether or not there was a formal program the intrapreneur was often asked to prepare a "business case" for their idea. These business cases were quite—okay, almost always—enormous. We found that a requirement of 70 or more pages was not uncommon. In fact, when discussing this root cause with others, we often receive the response, "only 70!"

The size of the case would be enough to give most of us a migraine, but what makes this worse is that the people who often come up with these great, innovative ideas are not usually people who enjoy creating business cases of any size. They have different skills and interests. Building a case of this nature takes them way out of their comfort zone.

If an early over emphasis on these business cases did not stop potential intrapreneurs from trying, this myopic inflexibility in execution might eventually prevent them from succeeding.

## Unconscious Bias Toward Current Business Models

The art of treating new businesses like mature businesses goes beyond processes, procedures, formats, and forms. It begins with a state of mind. An unconscious bias toward current norms. As the saying goes, the biggest problem with unconscious bias is that it is unconscious. The impact of this can begin even before someone starts to communicate their idea.

Our research discovered that *quite often people who came up with new ideas tended to be mesmerized by the core, historical value proposition of the mature business.* This led to their unconsciously putting a huge set of constraints on their deliberate ideation. What may be worse, when they did come up with an idea outside the existing core business, they often discarded it with the belief nobody would be interested in it.

Adding insult to injury, when innovators made it a step further and socialized ideas that were outside the mature business' obvious core value proposition to someone else, those people were often blinded by the current business context. They were sometimes unable to even understand the new idea, and they would resist it. It was as if it was just too much effort to think about anything outside their existing business context. Sometimes the idea died there, though this often evolved into attempts by the intrapreneur at force-fitting the new idea into the business' existing value proposition.

Furthermore, this bias prevented business leaders inside and outside the incubating business from recognizing when a new *business model* might be the key to success. While new business models like subscription licensing and freemiums were disrupting industries, many successful businesses lost share because they were unable to see the value in those changes. Even worse, while those new business models were gaining traction, intrapreneurs were unsuccessfully proposing their use, and the use of other emerging business models, as vehicles for disruption. Sadly, they were often not understood. Many opportunities were missed as a result, and many mainstream businesses suffered as they lost share to others who had leveraged these new models.

The damage this bias can cause is not limited to early business lifecycle activity such as ideation and business model design. It can impact almost any stage of the development of a business. For example, many years ago we encountered a business in a market where they, and the other incumbent leaders, used an on-premise, perpetual licensing scheme to deliver their software (users paid up-front for software, and then a yearly support fee). The market was being disrupted by new entrants who offered Software-as-a-Service (SaaS) solutions using subscription-based licenses (flexible monthly or yearly fees). Though SaaS delivery was just beginning to emerge, leaders in this business understood that they had to create a new solution to respond to this threat. Even though this company had many more years' experience in the domain, and a much more feature-rich product than their new challengers, the challengers were beginning to win in a significant way. The business leaders realized they had to change, and they came up with an idea for a new SaaS-based offering.

However, what was created was essentially exactly the same as their on-premise offering. In fact, much of the code from the original product was simply moved to the new environment without change. The result of their bias was a patchwork that did not deliver the experience the innovative people who conceived the idea had envisioned, and it was not what customers wanted. As a result, their new offering was never widely adopted and eventually was shut down.

We saw this type of thing happen more than once, in more than one market, from more than one business. In one extreme case a team created software in order to solve a serious problem they were facing. While they intended only to use software themselves, it turned out that this new software was potentially disruptive to the market of one of the other businesses in their company. Customers who saw this new solution began to demand it, and they lost interest in the commercially available product. The innovative team turned their software over to the disrupted group so it could be productized and brought to market. Though the product team had access to the idea, the people who created the solution, and working code, they were constrained by their bias. Eventually they delivered a patchwork solution based on their existing products, very similar to the one described in the previous example. It also failed. Though competitive offerings that eventually emerged did not.

These are just two examples that demonstrate this bias must be kept in check during every stage of the business lifecycle. Unconscious bias is pervasive and has a way of insidiously creeping in, even when it has initially been conquered.

## Value Proposition Conflict

Those building, evaluating, influencing, and/or funding new business ideas can fall victim to value proposition conflict. Breakthrough businesses can often have more than one potential value proposition, or their stated value proposition can conflict with existing value propositions. Our research discovered that, when that happened, often the value proposition most like the current business would win, without any experimentation on which was most viable or most valuable.

This myopic approach to value proposition limited the solution's potential customers and markets, and even viability. What may be even more critical is that this, potentially healthy and helpful conflict could have been a signal that one of the company's existing businesses was ripe for disruption. While this discovery could have led to exploration of a business that would have disrupted not only that existing business, but also a competitor's, that avenue of exploration was often brutally closed. In these cases, not only was the opportunity for disruption taken away from the incubating business, it also left the potential for disruption of the company's mature business open to competitors or new entrants.

Value proposition conflict can be generated by customers as well. When an incubating business is targeting a segment that includes customers of the mature business, those customers often have pre-conceived ideas about the company's value propositions and capabilities. As a result, those customers sometimes assume the new product delivers a specific value proposition that it does not actually deliver. Alternatively, those customers sometimes have difficulty understanding a different value proposition than they already associate with the company.

## Overlapping Business Models

New businesses sometimes had business models and/or value propositions that were adjacent to those of mature businesses, or that had some level of overlap with them. Though this should have been an opportunity for synergy, it often became a point of friction. For many of the other reasons that are discussed in this section, efforts to develop an approach that was acceptable to both groups were often onerous and time consuming. This was much more damaging to the new business team, which was typically smaller and had more pressure to move quickly and be nimble.

Simply dealing with this has the potential to consume enough of an incubating team's resources to put it in jeopardy, especially very early in its life. Sometimes when this conflict occurred, a reorganization in the mature business often impeded progress even further, as intrapreneurs had to either start over or wait for the reorganized team to digest the changes.

## Turf Wars

There were times when someone came up with an innovative idea that fell within a broad domain that was owned by a mature line of business where the intrapreneur was not a member. Sometimes when this happened the mature line of business welcomed the new innovation into their domain. After all, if someone from their company wasn't doing it, a competitor might be. While sometimes friction and creative differences arose, the new and old teams were able to drive the idea to a fruitful conclusion, usually with the mature business absorbing the new, innovative business.

However, sometimes the political demons triumph and a turf war ensues. Though we did not find too many cases of this, when it happened its impact was enormous. To begin with, an existing business is always much larger, has broader and more well established personal networks, and enjoys far more resources than a new incubation—so it's hardly a fair fight. Lines of business with unhealthy cultures are extremely well skilled at tactics that can delay or derail competing businesses. They lose sight of the fact that when one group within the company wins, everyone in the company wins. Some turned passive aggression into a fine art.

The irony in the counterproductive cases we studied was that, while the mature business prevented the new incubation from delivering on the new idea, they did not usually execute on the idea themselves. At least not as designed by the new business, or not with their full commitment. In some cases it was pure pageantry, designed to placate proponents of the idea until they became interested in something else. Instead of embracing the new, disruptive technologies, those unhealthy teams dug in on their legacy systems. In one case a team missed markets totaling billions of dollars. While there is no guarantee the new business would have captured a large share of that market, the established business' approach guaranteed $0 in revenue in that market, and eventually loss of share in their legacy business.

## Intractable Systems

"Sorry. I don't care how big you think it will be. Our systems just can't handle a business like that." I'll give you another moment to let that sink in...

That statement may seem shocking. We suppose it is. Sometimes it is more insidious, and less obvious than stated here. Other times the people and teams responsible for the systems stated it, more or less, exactly that way.

Our research discovered that a fairly *common* reason new business ideas failed, or were shut down, was that existing processes and/or (back-office) systems were not capable of dealing with it. When the incubating business had a new business model (or a new target customer, or a new delivery model, or a new go-to market model, or...) that was different than the mature business', those systems—which were built for, and evolved with, the mature business for years—were unable to deal with the needs of the new business. In other cases the people in charge of those systems were either unable, or unwilling, to *make* the necessary changes. They often put pressure on intrapreneurs to move to an existing, supported model, unwittingly eroding the new business' value and advantage.

Often the decision to not even investigate whether the new business' needs could be accommodated was based solely on the amount of revenue the new business was generating. Their revenue was compared either to the revenue

applied to experiments with new digital marketing channels that cost hundreds of dollars. In one case, we discovered there were as many people red-lining a partner's contract as that partner had employees. The partner told the incubating team that they would not be able to continue doing business with them because just responding to the heavy processes was consuming all of their employees' time.

Adding to the frustration of incubating teams were the issues and challenges inherent in all complex processes and systems of this nature. Approvers take time off, email gets lost, and systems break down. The more complex the system, the more likely this is to happen and, often, the more severe the impact of a disruption. And there are always those edge cases that the systems were not designed to address. Shoehorning those into existing systems can require a Herculean effort. To make matters worse, the nature of breakthrough businesses is such that they quite often find themselves trying to shepherd one of those edge cases through a complex processes for which it was not designed.

There is some good news here. We also learned that in many cases the reason that these lightweight experiments were subject to the same processes and rigor as their colossal cousins was simply that nobody had thought to do otherwise. It had not occurred to the people responsible for the processes. Why would it? They are not the ones trying to operate these new businesses. And the intrapreneurs assumed that these systems and processes could not be changed, so they never tried. Or they tried but did not find the right outlet for their request and ceased their efforts in frustration.

## Solution Focus Meets Builder Mindset

There is much written about the fact that entrepreneurs, intrapreneurs, and innovators of all kinds can become too focused on, even enamored with, their solution to the detriment of their idea. There is a great reason for that. It is extremely common, and it can kill great ideas and opportunities. In fact, you will find reference to this in other sections of this chapter because it impacts incubating ideas in so many ways.

We will focus on a very specific manifestation of it in this section. That is, the intersection of solution infatuation with the builder mindset. Let's face it, innovators instinctively love to build things. It's less instinctive for them to love figuring out whether they are building the right things. As a result, once they believe they are on the right track—often once they get the smallest semblance of a signal their idea resonates with someone—they double down on building and stop customer sensing. We also found another, quite different, manifestation of this.

Teams ideating in established businesses tended to analyze customer needs and markets only after they designed, or sometimes developed, a solution. Because of this, they did not proactively explore new and emerging customer needs and markets. This, of course, severely constrained their thinking and ideation and either reinforced, or led them straight into, many of the other constraints and traps we discuss in this chapter such as unconscious business model bias, customer myopia, or building things that nobody wants.

## Emphasizing Revenue Too Early

The performance of mature businesses is typically measured by things such as revenue, gross margin, and market share. Business leaders in established organizations have these measures imprinted in their DNA. We found that they can have a hard time thinking about other measures. We have been in new idea pitch meetings in mature organizations where leaders repeatedly asked for three-year revenue projections only moments after being reminded that the pitches were in the early stages of ideation and that kind of measure would not be available. This way of thinking is a very hard habit to break.

In their formative years, new business ideas have no chance hitting the kind of revenue and margin measures leaders come to expect from mature businesses. Expecting millions of dollars of revenue in the first year of the life of a product that does not yet exist is irrational, yet we saw that expectation time and again. In fairness, it was not as much an expectation of the new product as it was a habitual comparison with mature products and newly introduced product features and extensions.

We encountered countless stories of businesses being shuttered way too early in their life because they had not made their revenue targets. (Those works of fiction found in the business cases we referred to earlier.) We have even seen cases where other companies later brought the same solution to market and drove a strong, profitable business.

In addition to resulting in premature shutdowns, this laser focus on revenue while ignoring other measures can result in perpetuating businesses that should not survive. For example, we have seen reports of outstanding revenue growth from incubating businesses. Triple-digit growth. Impressive, right? Except when you dig deeper and learn that the business grew from $100 of monthly revenue to $200. The growth itself is not a bad thing, nor is the total revenue, depending on the stage a business is in. In these cases it was the use of growth percentage *only* to give the impression the business had begun to achieve its market fit that was the issue.

# Failure to Consider the True Cost of New Businesses

Mature businesses often have common services that are not always directly charged back to their consumers. Sometimes those costs are allocated to a parent unit, or spread across an organization based on headcount or the amount in a specific budget line. When this was the case, the true costs of incubating businesses were not always included in their expense reporting. Furthermore, services of this nature were often disproportionately consumed by incubating businesses.

The net result was that the incubating businesses appeared to be performing better than they were actually performing. Sometimes significantly better. This led to decisions to continue businesses that would otherwise be declared not viable. Perpetuating a bad idea is just as bad as shuttering a viable one. Doing so takes focus and resources from other initiatives. When something like this is discovered, it can cast a shadow on any incubation program where the business is a member. We found it could also have a demoralizing effect on other potential intrapreneurs, especially those waiting for funding.

# Resource Constraints

Ironically, allocation of common services, as described in the previous section, can have the opposite impact on a new incubation. When allocation of common services and expertise is based on a business' total budget or revenue projection, new incubations are so small they often receive none of these services. Sometimes these allocations include services that a new business may actually require even more of than a mature business (e.g., marketing). When this happens, new businesses can be starved for essential resources and their progress can be severely impacted, while some of the most mature businesses may receive an abundance of resources they do not require. (e.g., A product at the end of its life does not really need marketing resources.)

# Skill Deficiency

Creating breakthrough businesses often required skills that the mature organization did not possess, or did not have enough of to be capable of allocating any to the new business. This challenge presented itself along a very broad range of disciplines, including:

- Modern engineering tools, techniques, and technologies

- New and emerging business and delivery models

- New and emerging go-to-market approaches

- Sales approaches (when different from the mature business)

- Ability to interact with new customers in new markets

- Sales, field, and marketing personnel with requisite "permission to play" in specific fields (e.g., evangelists)

Finding the new skills required by breakthrough businesses can be hard. It can take months to find people with skills in high demand. That is an eternity for a business whose life might be measured in mere months. Furthermore, people with skills of this nature can be very expensive. In addition, early on it is critical to find people with broad skillsets and a willingness to do things outside their comfort zones and traditional job descriptions. Scott Morrison, a colleague of ours and former CTO at Layer7, recounted his experience with this in the early days of his startup. He explained, "We used to say 'everyone took out the garbage' at Layer 7, meaning we all did things outside of our usual jobs and comfort zones. You want full stack devs, not JavaScript specialists."

In some cases where incubating teams were able to bring in people with the skills they required, the new people were forced to operate within the constraints of the mature business (as described throughout this chapter). This devalued their skillset and undermined the value they brought to the incubation. It can also put the new employee's skillset at risk of atrophy or result in the development of bad habits. Consequently, this creates a risk that these high-value employees will resign.

## Mature Business Budget Pressure

As was mentioned earlier, mature business measures normally include aggressive targets for revenue and margin (the amount by which the revenue exceeds the cost of running the business). The more mature the business, the higher these targets usually are. In contrast, new businesses will usually have very low margins, or even negative margins as business costs often exceed revenues in the early years.

When mature businesses (or departments, or lines of business…) incubate new businesses, any negative margins from a new business must be offset by increases in margin by the mature business. Consider this simple example. If a mature line of business has a $100 margin target (revenue must exceed costs by $100 for their portfolio), and an incubating business spends $25 more than its revenue (-$25 margin), the mature businesses in the portfolio will have to achieve $125 in margin in order to meet the $100 margin target ($125 - $25).

While the margin erosion caused by an incubating business is not usually such a large percentage of the overall margin target, it does make things more challenging for established businesses by eroding the bottom line while not contributing to the top line. When these lines of business are faced with any budget pressure, the incubating businesses become tempting and easy targets. They can be shut down without damaging the existing core business, and immediately free up cash and other resources. It's a short-term gain that, without careful analysis, can deliver long-term loss.

We found one case where a new, breakthrough product team had been transferred into a mature business organization. Shortly thereafter, that business unit was looking for a way to address a looming funding shortage. Unfortunately for the breakthrough product team, their budget allocation was exactly the same as the amount of funding the mature business was looking for. The new business was shut down to solve the budget puzzle. Hindsight being the greatest teacher of all, years later they learned how far ahead of the market their groundbreaking solution was—when someone else delivered it.

## Intrapreneurial Fear

Stories like the previous one do not take long to make their way through even the largest businesses. In addition, teams that were pursuing breakthrough ideas that, after incubation, were discovered to be legitimately not viable were often penalized. For example, when incubation initiatives were shut down some team members were given difficult, unglamorous assignments that would not contribute to their career growth or advancement. Those were referred to as "doghouse" assignments because people receiving them could put their careers back on track if they accepted their hardship assignment and were successful. Some were laid off. In some cases even people widely known to be companywide top performers were treated this way.

As a result, would-be intrapreneurs were often reluctant to join teams incubating new ideas, or to even *suggest* their own ideas. With rumors that the reward for being innovative was a shorter career it was, for some, difficult to convince even the entrepreneurially-minded to join an innovation program or project. This high level of risk, and the absence of any reward for taking it, made the hunt for talent more difficult and reduced the chances that a team of "A players"—table stakes for new business incubation—could be assembled to pursue an innovative idea.

Even when funded, individual intrapreneurs were often left alone to face the challenges and frustrations so frequently encountered by those innovating in established organizations. There was no support structure to mitigate the many risks they faced, nor to address their inevitable frustration. Which was, of course, the next major category of findings.

# Why New Ideas Fail Without a Consistent Approach to Innovation and Incubation

So, you've made it this far. You have triumphed over heavy processes and measures that were never designed for breakthrough businesses. Unfortunately, your battle is not yet won.

We learned that if our intrapreneurs managed not to be crushed by the processes and measures we just discussed, there was no consistent approach to helping them bring their ideas further and ensure they had at least some chance of succeeding. Incubation of new business ideas was not deliberate— or at least not consistently deliberate. This was often the case not only companywide, but often not even within smaller organizations and groups inside the company.

## Inconsistent Idea Triage

In many cases whether a business was even given an initial chance depended upon where someone resided in the organizational framework, and it often depended upon whom they knew. Whether someone was even afforded the opportunity to spend some minimal amount of time working on an idea, let alone was awarded bespoke funding for it, was often entirely a function of their personal network. It was often highly and entirely political. In other cases the root cause of failure was even simpler. There was no place to bring new ideas, or if there was, it was not widely known. People simply did not know where to take their ideas.

## Organizational Myopia

Even when organizations within a company were able to somewhat mitigate the previously mentioned root causes of failure, they were often unable to see the benefit of a proposed new idea beyond the context of their own organization or team's mission. For example, one business unit would either not see the value of an idea that did not benefit their own business, would not know what to do with the idea (e.g., not know whom to bring it to), or simply would not care about it (i.e., decide not to invest time in even trying to figure out if the idea had a place somewhere else). At times, even when they realized the idea might benefit another organization within their company, they did not know how to proceed.

Not recognizing new ideas for what they are and not knowing where to take them was a common theme. Not understanding what to do with new, innovative ideas is *very* common with newer employees and newer, more low-level managers. Sadly, a large portion of new idea generation happens at this level and can be lost as managers at this level are laser-focused on their mission. (George previously wrote about a strategy for addressing this at `https://wp.me/p1uKi4-ie`.)

Even when a company, or group within a company, had an "innovation process," we discovered that their innovation process itself could be a primary reason new ideas failed. Especially breakthrough or disruptive ideas. These programs and processes were often optimized for core extensions to existing businesses and inherently contained innovation antibodies of their own. As a result, processes and governance were often way too heavy for new, breakthrough ideas, or even disruptive or breakthrough extensions to their existing business. In fact, inappropriately focused or sized processes was a common flaw of innovation programs, even when they were not intended to be focused on a single line of business.

## Failure to Set Realistic Executive Expectations

Even when business leaders had managed to conquer the political and organizational antibodies that commonly annihilate innovative ideas, they did not adequately understand the time that is required to bring a very young idea to life. The executives were working in the context of delivering new features or product extensions. Breakthrough business incubation does not normally happen in weeks, or even quarters. Furthermore, not every breakthrough idea will become a viable business. Most of them will not.

Leadership teams that did not understand this often ran out of patience and withdrew investment way too early. It was not uncommon for leaders to expect profitability within a quarter or two of the start of an initiative. Most expected a return by the end of the fiscal year in which the initiative started at the very least.

Investing too much in an incubation too early increased the odds of this happening. Large investments that were not producing a return hit the executives' radar quickly and funding was often moved to more immediate projects that the leadership team better understood.

We often describe the length of time we expect a leadership team to be able to tolerate investment in a new idea as their "attention span". In this context, executive attention spans were typically very short. Those who did not invest sufficient time influencing, and appropriately setting, expectations at the highest level often found their ideas were shuttered in fairly short order.

In an interesting twist, we also found that sometimes the most senior executives had not achieved sufficient buy-in and support from their subordinates. While the highest-level executive was enthusiastic about incubating breakthrough ideas—and may have even allocated funding for one—their close subordinates (one or two levels below them in the organizational hierarchy) did not share that enthusiasm. In some cases this even led to their, consciously or unconsciously, working across their superior's purposes and hindering the progress of new business teams.

## Failure to Focus on Customers Early

Businesses that managed to get past these not so insignificant impediments often became enamored with their own solutions. There was often no deliberate customer focus early on, arguably when it was needed most. If they thought about customers early, that focus did not continue throughout the life of the business. Often it never happened at all. The result was often a large investment in something that—while often technically elegant, even to the point of artistry—had no practical use. Like the so many entrepreneurs, they built something nobody wanted. In fact, this is often cited as the number one reason startups fail[2].

We had an interesting conversation with one entrepreneur regarding his experience with this. Several times he had tried to launch a new idea by first building a solution and then looking for people who would buy it. He focused on the customer only after he had created a product. None of those initiatives were successful. In contrast, his successful startup idea began with his wondering whether anyone would even be interested in it. Without any work on a product or technology, he created a sign-up page where people with the problem could register. He explained that by the next morning he had around 5,000 sign-ups, and within a week or two he had 10,000. He told us he had built "10,000 things nobody wanted" and the one time he didn't build anything, 10,000 people wanted it.

## Absence of Deliberate Customer Selection and Experimentation

Our research discovered a number of customer-selection related deficiencies were consistently key contributors to failure. What was interesting, though not surprising, was that sometimes customer selection itself was an afterthought. Teams did not spend sufficient time figuring out exactly whom they were building their solution for, and which of those people needed it yesterday (early adopters). Some spent no time at all on this. Ignoring the customer early on was a surprisingly common area of failure, often resulting in a large investment in something that, while being technically elegant, was completely useless. Or at least not worth paying for.

---

[2]"The Top 20 Reasons Startups Fail," *CB Insights,* February 2, 2018, https://www.cbinsights.com/research/startup-failure-reasons-top/

In many cases there was no deliberate and/or consistent process in customer identification, selection, and verification. Failure to consider the customer at all often happens when the inventor falls in love with their solution and loses sight of the reason they are building it. (i.e., to solve someone's problem.) This often results in building the wrong thing, building something nobody wants, or building something relevant that cannot be sold (at least not by you).

# Customer Myopia

A second common customer-related misstep was making the assumption that existing customers of the company's other products and/or services would also be customers for the new idea. Failure to perform customer validation in these cases usually resulted in not finding the right customer, building a product for the wrong customer, or even building a product for one specific (usually very large and important) customer. We have seen that a number of times. The innovation graveyard is full of products that work extremely well for just one customer.

If a prospective intrapreneur brings you a pitch with a list of potential customers that mirrors all of your company's existing customers, it's time to pull on this thread (what are the odds *every* customer you already have will want this new thing?). One symptom we often see is that the names of the customer segments match your company's standard customer segment names. This can be an omen that not enough thought and analysis has gone into customer identification and selection.

Focusing on a company's existing customers can lead to another innovation-killing scenario. If the innovative, new product does not solve problems that the company's current customers have, that can lead business teams—or the senior managers who are funding them—to the conclusion that they have built something that nobody wants. "If these people don't want it, who will?" What a great question! Too bad they ask it rhetorically and do not pursue an answer.

It may simply be that the company's current customers do not have the problem that is solved by the new product or service. Many other people may have the problem, and their market may be even larger than the company's current markets. This unconscious bias toward existing customers of the mature business can kill great ideas that subsequently become very successfully brought to market by new startups or existing competitors.

Some of the businesses we analyzed got into trouble by going in the opposite direction. They adopted an approach that sales people often refer to as "spray and pray," and attempted to sell the product to anyone who would listen. While the lyrics to "Love the One You're With" make for a great song, it is not usually an effective sales strategy. Those who used this approach typically wasted a lot of time and energy and were, essentially, relying on brute force and luck.

David McNierney, who provides marketing guidance and education to our Accelerator teams, sums both aspects of this section up nicely when he says, "If your product is for everybody, it's for nobody." (And he says it often.)

## Tactical Misalignment

Our research also discovered that attempts to bring innovative ideas to life failed when businesses tried to reuse and repurpose resources and tactics that were designed for the organization's mature businesses and customers. On the surface, that is a very logical approach. The availability of resources and tactics should offer a great advantage to a business incubating in an established organization that a standalone startup would not have. That is true, and we discuss how to capture that advantage later in the book. Though we learned that, applied incorrectly, these tactics and resources can become a disadvantage that can contribute to, or be a primary cause of, failure.

Sadly, this type of failure can occur even when businesses successfully avoid the most common customer-related pitfall and are able to successfully and specifically identify their target customers. What often happens next is that they try to repurpose existing processes and approaches that were not designed for those customers. When they do that, the use of those processes becomes onerous and uncomfortable for the incubating business team, and sometimes for their customers. Ironically, what often happens next is that, rather than design new processes to serve their new customers, businesses shift their focus to the customers for which those processes were originally designed. This subjects their business to that most common trap. They begin trying to sell their product or service to mature business' customers who are not the target segment for their product.

Another tactic that often failed was an attempt to leverage the mature business' customer-facing field teams to sell a new, breakthrough product. While this can sometimes work, what often happens is that the field teams are unable to act optimally outside their existing customer demographic. They are exceptional at dealing with a specific persona, but unable to communicate effectively with other personas. For example, they may have an IT operations background but no experience with modern application development, or UX design, or personnel management. If your product is designed to solve a problem outside the IT operations realm, the existing field team may not be able to help, and it may actually be harmful to have them engage with your customers.

Even if the expertise of the mature business' customer-facing teams aligns perfectly with your target personas, there may be other potential causes of failure when engaging them. Keep in mind that these people are typically compensated and measured based on the performance of their existing business. Assisting a new, innovative business can be an unwanted distraction for these

people, and could hamper their ability to deliver on their own objectives. Even the perception that an incubating business is becoming a distraction can attract the attention of the mature business' senior management, and that can lead to political fire-drills that can slow down, or even kill, an incubating business.

That's if you can even engage the field teams. Remember that these teams are usually measured and incented based on sales of mature products, not your incubating product. While promoting your incubation might be "the right thing to do" for the company's long-term future, unless the field teams' measures are changed obtaining a critical mass of traction from field and sales personnel could be an uphill battle. In fact, we have even seen cases where newly developed product line extensions for mature businesses struggled or failed due to these pressures, or because the personal financial incentive to sell the new product was not as attractive as other products available to the sales team. Though don't lose hope. We discuss tactics and approaches to leveraging these teams later.

The final alignment issue we discovered was much more basic. In those (fairly rare) cases where explicit customer choices were made, those explicit choices were not always effectively communicated to everyone in the organization. This, of course, often led to a focus on the wrong customers. For example, when that happened focus sometimes turned back to customers of the mature business (and we have already discussed why that might not always be a path to success). What was worse was that this also led to executives and teams from other parts of the organization working across purposes, potentially damaging other areas of the mature business as well as the company's overall reputation.

## Mature Business Model Gravity

Access to an established customer base, that a team incubating in a garage could not possibly have access to, can be a huge advantage for those incubating within an established enterprise. Though we also found cases where it can be a disadvantage. For example, there were times when an incubating business performed textbook customer selection and identified target customers and early adopters that were not their parent organization's existing/established customers. Sometimes when this happened there was pressure from within the mature business organization to adapt the incubating business' solution to the demands of the company's existing customers (which may or may not have been legitimate needs of those customers). This often resulted in the new business pivoting to a solution that was ultimately not as innovative and, in some cases, had a very limited market. Sometimes even a market of one. The new business was essentially sucked into the gravity well of the old one.

There were some cases where a new, breakthrough solution was positioned to solve a mature customer's problem that it was not created to solve. This was usually the result of someone's misinterpretation of the new product's capability or value proposition. They had unconsciously looked at the solution through the lens of the existing business they supported and made assumptions based on that. Regardless of the cause, this can lead to political and reputational damage that can spell the end of viability for a product. It can also result in the need to drop the original, breakthrough idea and build the item the customer was promised in order to repair customer relationships or meet legal obligations.

Pivoting to a mature customer need is not always a bad thing. There were cases when those pivots toward existing customers was the right, and more lucrative, move. Though often it was not. A conscious pivot is a good thing. Being sucked into the existing business due solely to political pressure, without exploring and experimenting, is not.

These gravity wells can be massive, and we have both been witness to good ideas coming to an abrupt end due to a blind pivot of this nature. We have even seen a case when a team incubating an idea pivoted to design their offering entirely based on one very large customer's demands and, though the team invested many months and millions of dollars to build exactly what the customer demanded, in the end nobody bought their product. Not even the customer for whom it was built.

## Failure to Effectively Capture or Communicate the Value Proposition

Succumbing to business model gravity is not always due solely to the existence of the mature business or its culture. It can actually be the result of intrepreneur inaction.

Sometimes, when intrapreneurs get an idea for a solution, they can become mesmerized by it. They can lose sight of the problem they originally built it to solve, the people who have the problem (their customers), and the value it brings to those people. Our research found that, as a result, a product would sometimes be given to established field and sales teams without communication of its intended value proposition. This left those teams to figure out the value proposition for themselves. It should be no surprise that they usually did so through the lens of the mature businesses they served and understood well. You know where that can lead.

This is more common than you might think. We have even seen it occur in the case of product line extensions with the same basic value proposition as the existing businesses. In one case, a product line brought functionality similar to their existing products to new operating system platforms in a new business

context. Without confirmation, early sales representatives made assumptions about what the new product's capabilities and features were based on what they knew about the more mature products they sold. A lot of the time they were right. Some of the time they were wrong. Some of the time that difference was significant and really mattered. Fortunately, the field engineering team spotted that early on. Eventually training, and great collateral, addressed that issue and the product became an amazing success. Had the field engineering team not recognized that this was happening as early as they did, it could have ended very differently.

We have even seen this happen when new *features* were introduced into a very mature product. Deliberate consideration and explicit statement of the product's value proposition is a must. If you don't know it, your customers won't likely figure it out. If they don't understand it, they won't be your customers.

## Failure to Consider Existing Alternatives

It was surprising how often new businesses gave no thought to the alternatives to their solution. When we mention this, most people think about existing competitors. Certainly, it was surprising how often the competition was not considered. That was likely another symptom of an innovator loving their solution, and it remains a common issue. Even today when people initially bring their ideas to our Accelerator, we learn they have not given careful consideration to their competition. Though "existing alternatives" goes beyond the obvious active competitor.

Sometimes the "competition" is missed in the initial analysis because they are competing on the same problem statement, but with a much different solution. This may be overlooked by those searching only for similar *solutions*. In addition, manual workarounds, home-built tools and processes, or even freeware or community-created solutions will often satisfy a potential customer's need. And we must not forget that "doing nothing" may also be a viable solution. Your solution competes with all of these, and you need an answer for each.

Finally, even when you may not be battling a competitor in a problem or a solution context, you may be competing against other customer priorities and/or budget demands.

We worked with a startup that had captured the passion of a major financial institution. They developed a fantastic relationship, and all signals were that once the startup built their minimum viable product (MVP)—their first release with just enough functionality to delight early adopters—this customer would be breaking down their door to get it. But that did not happen. In fact, it eventually became difficult for the team to get a return phone call. Why? The problem they were solving was never near the top of their customer's priority list. It was never the most important thing for the customer to spend their time and money on.

Since then we have seen similar cases, where customers were excited about a product but did not act when the MVP was released. Their reasons were similar. Among the most common:

- The problem was not a high priority, and resources and budget were focused on other, higher priority issues

- The problem was worth solving, but not worth paying for (or not worth paying enough to create a viable business)

- It was a problem the customer needed to solve only once, and that was not worth the investment (e.g., "manual" solutions were a better approach)

## Insufficient Attention to Strategic Control

Many of the businesses we studied had failed to consider how they were going to acquire and defend market share. Often innovators assume they are the first and only person to recognize a problem and design a workable solution for it. Obviously, that is not always the case. Furthermore, thinking of it first does not mean you will create your business in a way that cannot be easily copied by others. In fact, we now hear the tongue-in-cheek term, *first mover disadvantage* quite often. This references the fact that often the first to a market have to solve all of the hardest problems themselves. The engineering decisions they make early, and subsequent pivots, often leave them with a suboptimal solution or heavy technical debt. That opens the door for others to learn from their experience and come to market with a solution in less time at a lower cost.

Failure to be deliberate about strategic control means your strategy for defending your market is luck.

Our research discovered other common errors related to strategic control. It was very common for innovators to assume that the size of the mature business or the company's current customer base were guarantees of control. While they might be, that is often not the case. It should never be an assumption. In fact, there are cases where a large organization's position in specific markets can be an impediment. When a company is known to be a leader in one market, it often comes with the belief they are not skilled in another. The company may not yet have brand permission to participate in a specific new market.

In addition, we frequently discovered cases where assumptions were made that the strategic control the mature business held in one market would be equally applicable to the incubating business in its markets. While that may be the case, it's a risky assumption and is not necessarily so.

Finally, some incubating businesses failed to review and update the strategic control aspect of their business model regularly. Market conditions change, and competitors evolve. Business models need to keep pace with them.

## Failure to Focus on a Profit Model Early Enough

Though they do need time to develop and grow, new businesses eventually have to capture value. That is usually in the form of profit.

We found that some new businesses did not begin to develop their profit model until their product was long on the market. We have been in more than one meeting where someone stated gleefully that their revenue was (legitimately) growing at an amazing rate. Then, upon further analysis, we discovered that the business was actually losing money on every customer when things like customer acquisition cost and lifetime value were considered. Stated differently, they were growing their losses at an impressive rate.

It is important to have a profit model hypothesis early in the life of a business, and to keep updating it as you learn. Though in many cases profit model was discovered to be an afterthought. It is not always easy to address this if it is discovered too late. Contractual obligations may make shutting down the business, or even stopping sales, difficult. When customers of the new business are also customers of the mature business, this can be even more difficult.

## Absence of Business Model Discipline

Finally, we found that many of the issues discussed previously in this section arose because new business teams did not consistently consider and/or plan in the context of all aspects of a good business model or business design. Some teams did not do any deliberate business design planning whatsoever. Even when those teams had a good, viable idea, absence of business model planning made their execution inefficient, made their business more susceptible to external threats, and reduced the odds of the business delivering to its potential.

We found that there were typically no procedures, templates, measurements, and funding models that were created specifically for next generation businesses. As a result, new intrapreneurs were often rudderless and at risk.

## The Bottom Line

Though incubating within an established organization should be, and can be, a tremendous advantage, we found that it was often a colossal disadvantage. The metaphoric lien the mature organization had on the incubating businesses, the resulting influence the mature culture had on them, and the inherent corporate antibodies often spelled the demise of breakthrough ideas—even viable ones.

Breakthrough business ideas are different. Transformational businesses have different needs than mature businesses, especially very early in their life. They:

- Require exploration and experimentation versus execution at scale

- Necessitate different metrics and measures of progress

- Call for different skills than mature businesses

- Can be too far ahead of well understood customer needs to be understood through the lens of mature, successful businesses

- Often require incubation of new business models

Treating new business ideas as you would treat mature businesses is likely a path toward failure and misery. If your intrapreneurs manage to survive these, they will often adopt some very undesirable behaviors in order to cope with them. We discuss the consequences of that next.

# Unintended Consequences

## The Lone Intrapreneur

*"If you want to go fast, go alone. If you want to go far, go together."*

—African Proverb

Whether it is mismatched corporate processes, measuring the wrong things, or the lack of a consistent approach to help new business ideas succeed, there are a multitude of often undiscovered or undiscussed causes of failed corporate innovation—all of which can have dire consequences for your business. The wreckage that this failed innovation leaves behind goes beyond a few failed projects and can have ripple effects that negatively impact your entire company for years or even decades. Some of these impacts are tangible and obvious, but others are more hidden and insidious. Some of the most damaging consequences are from an intrapreneur and their team, acting alone, outside of any formal structure the larger company has in place. As this lone intrapreneur stays isolated and works to keep their new business off executive radars, they potentially cause issues beyond simply wasting money and other resources.

© CA 2019
G. Watt and H. Abrams, *Lean Entrepreneurship*,
https://doi.org/10.1007/978-1-4842-3942-1_2

One challenge when discussing intrapreneurs and their roles within large and established businesses, is the term "intrapreneur" itself. If you are new to corporate innovation, you may have assumed that the word "intrapreneur" came about with the dot-com bubble and the hype around startups, but it had been around for decades prior to the irrational exuberance that defined that boom and bust period. In fact, the term was originally coined by Gifford and Elizabeth Pinchot in their 1978 whitepaper titled "Intra-Corporate Entrepreneurship," where they predicted that it would "prove useful in establishing employee entrepreneurs who work within the corporation".[1]

Over the years, there have been different interpretations of what an intrapreneur really is and does. Today, the Oxford dictionary defines it as a "manager within a company who promotes innovative product development and marketing".[2] We do not know about you, but in the company that we work for, we hope that everyone is always being as innovative as possible in how they approach their work. Regardless of whether employees are developing new products or answering customer support calls, innovation can and should happen everywhere in an organization. So why are intrapreneurs special? Why can they not innovate like everyone else in the company? Are intrapreneurs even a good thing to have within a company? As with most things in life, it is never cut and dry. In our view, the definition is closer to Pinchot's original: An intrapreneur is someone who leads an effort to create a new business within a larger company. In the context of this book, we often talk about innovative or breakthrough businesses, but in our opinion, that is not a prerequisite. Intrapreneurs in and of themselves are neither good nor bad, but depending on how they operate, they can have good or bad effects on a company. Let's illustrate with a story.

We have all heard some version of this story before: the lone employee has an amazing new product idea they simply know will be a big hit. This intrapreneur, through sheer determination and grit, figures out how to get through tremendous corporate red tape to bring their idea to life. There are two major flavors of this fable you may have heard or perhaps even witnessed first-hand.

In the first version of the story, the intrapreneur battles against all odds, and of course, seemingly endless and entrenched corporate bureaucracy. They overcome these hurdles to secure funding for their new project by staying under the radar and stealing budget and resources from other teams. They manage to pull together a large and amazingly talented team that builds an exciting new product that quickly catches customers' attention and, soon after, revolutionizes the market. This intrapreneur becomes a legend, a true hero who nearly single handedly revitalizes the company.

---

[1] Gifford Pinchot III and Elizabeth S. Pinchot, 1978, *Intra-Corporate Entrepreneurship*, Tarrytown School for Entrepreneurs, Fall 1978, https://drive.google.com/file/d/0B6GgwqtG-DKcSlpsbGRBZkZYSlk/view

[2] *Oxford Living Dictionaries*, s.v. "Intrapreneur," accessed August 20, 2018, https://en.oxforddictionaries.com/definition/intrapreneur

Unfortunately, the second version of this story is much more common. It is a tragic story but starts with many of the same plot elements: the fight for funding, the hiring of a large top-notch team, and of course the skunkworks under-the-radar work ethic. However, where this version of the story takes a wrong turn is that the product fails, customers hate it, and everyone blames the intrapreneur for syphoning off company resources on a dead-end project.

The story only gets worse from there. Many of the people from the intrapreneur's team, potentially some of the stronger and more entrepreneurial employees in the company, are now at risk of being laid off. After all, they have demonstrated that the rest of the established business can operate without them. If they do manage to find new roles within the company, they will forever be associated with the rogue project that failed and may find it hard to progress far in their careers without leaving to find a new employer. We have personally known far too many talented software engineers who were labeled "troublemakers" for their past involvement in disruptive innovation and then were repeatedly put on non-valuable special projects until they quit.

We have been saying that this was a failed project, which it ultimately and objectively was, but what was the root cause of that failure? Did the team have execution problems? Was it a lack of executive sponsorship? Did the market change? Could the team have focused or pivoted? Or was the idea simply bad from the very beginning?

Unfortunately, it is hard to ever know when a project is hiding and working in the shadows. Without the proper support system, once the "failure" is discovered, the project is shut down regardless if that is the proper course of action. Without an objective way of understanding what a reasonable expectation is for a project at this stage, it is too easy for an executive to see the project is not yet making money and simply assume it never will. As we see later in this chapter, this is a direct consequence of taking processes from an established business and applying them to a new business.

There are, of course, many variations of these stories. For example, often the team struggles to build out a complete product that fulfills their overly idealistic vision—every last bit of that vision they feel is absolutely necessary to meet their deadlines and revenue projections. At some point, someone higher up in the company catches on and figures out that all this time and money is being spent on a rogue project that they believe is going nowhere. The project is shut down and the product never even sees the light of day, regardless of any actual merits of the business.

In one of these stories, the intrapreneur built a great business, in the others, the business was a failure. Any guesses as to what the key difference is between the successful intrapreneur and the unsuccessful one in these stories? The successful intrapreneur got lucky.

Regardless of the endings, all these stories should be cautionary tales of how *not* to go about building a new successful business within an established organization. When done the wrong way, these are failures regardless of the outcomes of the individual new businesses. A mature, well executing company will be measuring the return on time and money they invest back in to the business. When you spend that time and money to pursue your new business idea, you distort those measurements of how the existing business is actually executing. If the funding for one of these projects was off-the-books and originally allocated to a different project, then almost by definition, some other business or product-line must have suffered. This can lead to potentially devastating consequences.

After all, at some point, the reporting from company's operations team would show that the original, planned, funding was being spent but the company was not seeing the business results they expected. With faulty information comes faulty decisions. What would happen next? Would the executive team decide to kill the sanctioned and apparently under-performing business? Would those, perhaps equally as talented, employees lose their jobs? Would the company's margin suffer and result in across the board cuts just to make the company's quarterly earnings projections?

With that lens, the morals of these stories may not be as clear as they initially might have seemed. In the successful version, the talented team in this story— our heroes—did grow a new and meaningful business when the odds were against them. But, on the other hand, they may have also diverted resources and distorted the performance of other parts of the business, inadvertently causing real and sustained harm. Put in that context, when acting independently in the shadows, perhaps these lone intrapreneurs are not the true heroes we originally thought they were.

Intrapreneurs should not have to go it alone, in secret, hoping they hit it big before someone catches on to them. They should not be putting the existing, established, line of business unintentionally at risk for the sake of innovation. Businesses of all shapes and sizes should celebrate intrapreneurship. These projects should succeed or fail based on their own merits, out in the open, and without fear of repercussions should their new business fail. In Chapter 1, we highlighted the need for established organizations to have a consistent, deliberate, approach to ensure new ideas, especially innovative ideas, have the best possible chance of success. That seems like an obvious answer, so why are these stories so common?

# Subverting Existing Processes

As discussed in Chapter I, large, established, businesses are naturally optimized for large sales volumes of mature products. This is not a flaw, it is a proper and necessary optimization when running multiple businesses at scale, but it unintentionally penalizes innovation and the creation of new businesses. A small product, with only $1 million per year in revenue, that is within a larger, established, company is simply not interesting or important to the larger business. It is a rounding error in the company's yearly financial report. Perhaps you are thinking that a $10 million business would be more meaningful.

The contradiction, of course, is that it is nearly impossible for a new business to make $10 million in revenue in their first year. This is true even in the fastest growing Internet companies. In Bessemer Venture Partners' *State of the Cloud Report 2017*[3], the successful venture capital firm analyzed public and private information to lay out a case for what they consider to be "good," "better," and "best" revenue growth. In their view, even the "best" and fastest growing cloud companies take two years to scale from $1 million to $10 million in annual recurring revenue. Even if you think you can compete with the best companies, those two years are not even counting the time it takes to build a successful product and get the first million in revenue. Of course, that all assumes you can build a successful business in the first place—roughly 40% of all new businesses will fail within those first three years[4].

Even if you have an amazing new business idea and the skills to execute on it, and even if you know something even the best venture capital firms do not, there is still the problem of mismatched processes. If you take a step back and think about it, it should appear quite obvious and expected that the existing processes tailored to established businesses are a poor fit for developing new, breakthrough, products that might take years to mature into something meaningful enough for the larger company. After all, measuring revenue on a non-revenue generating activity is always going to have the same result. How do intrapreneurs manage to survive in this process heavy environment that is tuned for something else entirely? More often than not, they will be forced to lie and cheat.

Imagine a budding intrapreneur who wants to secure internal funding to develop and bring a new product to market. The intrapreneur approaches the business unit operations team and asks them how to go about securing

---

[3]Anna Khan, "The State of the Cloud Report 2017," SlideShare, August 20, 2018, https://www.slideshare.net/AnnaKhan9/the-state-of-the-cloud-report-2017-bessemer-venture-partners

[4]Keith Speights, "What Percentage of Businesses Fail in Their First Year?," *The Motley Fool*, May 3, 2017, https://www.fool.com/careers/2017/05/03/what-percentage-of-businesses-fail-in-their-first.aspx

funding for their new project. "Easy!," the operations team enthusiastically replies, "You just need to fill out this 70-page presentation template that shows your three-year business plan. For those three years, make sure to provide a breakdown of all the budget and resources you will need, your complete go-to-market strategy, and how much revenue you will bring in, all summarized on a quarterly basis. Oh, and if you want to get funded, be sure to show a five-year internal rate of return significantly enough above the corporate hurdle rate to justify the investment risk."

Notice, in that semi-hypothetical dialogue, the focus on artifacts—the template. Instead of building a new business, the artifact has become the primary objective. Suddenly the job of the intrapreneur has shifted from innovation to presentation building and form filling. This is a direct consequence of this scaled process from an established business. There is no meaningful discussion of the merits of the new business idea, nor any inquiry into the research the intrapreneur may have already conducted to back up their assumptions. They are told to fill out the enormous template, because that is just how the process works—it does not matter if it is the right process or the right template for this business idea.

The intrapreneur responds the only way they know how, by filling in the template. Of course, they will need to be conservative. They will ask for extra resources to make sure they can hit the crazy hockey stick projections that are needed to show a high enough return-on-investment to make the business case worthwhile. In short, they have reverse engineered the business case based on what the template required for a project within an *established* business. It is not a plan based on what their *new* business actually needs to get started, nor more importantly, what is needed for it to actually be successful.

If the intrapreneur has convincing presentation skills, and on paper the project seems like a really good idea, it may get funded. Or perhaps the intrapreneur and the executives are friends and they simply trust that this project must be worth the money. It may seem obvious, but we have seen this often enough that it is worth putting into words: It is not a sound business strategy to have the company's investment decisions based on who you know.

Regardless, the focus of any evaluation was on the made-up information in the 70-page presentation without any validation if those assumptions were achievable or even remotely realistic. From these aspects, it appears to just be a waste of time if, after all this work, it does not even matter if the presentation and its assumptions were accurate.

Plus, as an added determent, because the process is typically very heavy weight—creating a 70-page presentation is not something you do in a day or even a week—there is a direct cost to these processes. Not only is this money wasted on useless process, but there is also a potential opportunity

cost to consider. Every dollar that is spent on one idea is a dollar not spent on another. Without a consistent framework to evaluate and compare these ideas, choosing one or another comes down to timing and how well the presentation template was filled out, instead of the one that will actually have a better chance of making the company money.

Either way, once the company makes a funding decision, they execute on the multi-year plan that contained the inflated budget. The company pours money into the new project in order to get it to market as fast as possible. In other words, they have made a bet, both figuratively and quite literally with their investment dollars, that this idea will make money. They have made this bet with no evidence other than made up numbers in a 70-page presentation. This is what we refer to as the committed bet model of innovation.

Regardless if it is made with a 70-page business case, or without any business case at all, in a committed bet, the company commits large amounts of money and resources to the project from the very beginning. The company assumes the investment will pay off without an appropriate amount of de-risking, typically citing excuses, such as "time to market," as the underlying reasons for jumping in head-first.

Often, this combination of putting a large investment into an idea with a general lack of upfront diligence results in the investment curve you see in Figure 2-1. In a committed bet, funding ramps up very quickly and remains at a very high level throughout the entire project. That is, right up until the point where someone figures out the idea will never work—then the whole thing goes up in smoke and the funding is pulled.

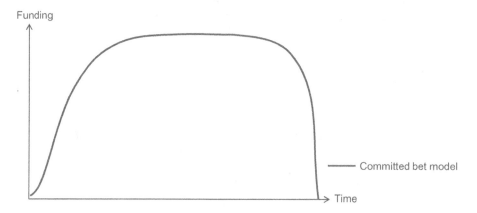

**Figure 2-1.** Committed bet model of innovation

While it may not always be clear at first glance, if you dig deeper, there are signs to look for to determine if a project is a committed bet. For example, it is not uncommon to see software projects with 20 software developers. A large number of employees on a project, in and of itself, is not a sign of a committed bet, but think of yourself in an investor's shoes. If you invested in a business that has 20 developers working as fast as they can, you would want to know that there is a clear market need for the product they are developing. Otherwise, you would never earn a return on your investment. If this is a brand-new project, without clear customer validation, then this project is a committed bet. The business is betting that, whatever is built, customers will love it. However, without any convincing evidence to show that customers will buy it, it is a gamble at best.

Not only do committed bets often have bad odds by their very nature, the irony is that a committed bet can itself jeopardize an idea's chances of success. George makes some great points about this in his blog post entitled "Four Signs Too Many Resources are Killing Your Innovation"[5]. In it, he points out that applying a large number of resources to creating the working product will siphon off an intrapreneur's energy and attention away from critical early stage activities—such as determining if the team is building the right thing in the first place. It can therefore drive focus toward an early solution hypothesis, lead to confirmation bias and, in some cases, drive emotional and resource commitment toward building the wrong thing—all with incredible speed and efficiency.

That said, not all committed bets are bad. A committed bet may actually be the right approach if this investment is a new feature or business line extension and you know everything there is to know about the market, the customer, their specific problems, and what solution they want to see. You may not need to further and more extensively test something in the market, because you have direct and current experience in that same market from your other products. In those cases, it may be prudent to accept the small risk of failure in exchange for that faster time to market.

Another common, and reasonable, committed bet is the "fast follower". In this model, you use the market validation of a direct competitor to quickly create a similar solution and follow them into the market. Your bet in this case is that you can sufficiently differentiate your product offering, and out market or outsell your competition to beat them in the marketplace. The key to a successful fast follow is not better innovation, it is better execution.

---

[5]George Watt, "Four Signs Too Many Resources are Killing Your Innovation," *Innovation, Technology, and Life in the Cloud* (blog), September 27, 2017, https://pragmaticcloud. wordpress.com/2017/09/27/four-signs-too-many-resources-are-killing-your-innovation/

However, understanding if a committed bet is the right approach is not always that clear and the lines can often seem blurry. The type of risk is one way to differentiate between extensions to established businesses and new businesses. In your established business, you already know the customers and what problems they need to solve. There is less risk that if you build it, they will buy it, because you have already spent years learning about your customers. If the remaining risks are primarily related to execution—Can you build it fast enough? can you sell it fast enough?—then most likely this is not an innovative new business as much as it is an extension of your existing business. In that case, a committed bet is less risky and might be appropriate.

It can sometimes make sense to follow heavyweight processes to make committed bets within your existing business, but new businesses are different. You probably have some good hunches of what you want to build and who it is for, but they are just that—hunches. Sure, there is risk that you may not be able to build and sell the product fast enough, but there are much larger risks and questions that need to be answered. Is the problem painful enough for a customer to actually pay for a solution? Is the market large enough to support a sustained business that is meaningful enough to your company? Is the product technically feasible to build and operate at a worthwhile profit margin? The answers to these questions can make the difference between an investment and a committed bet.

## A Committed Bet True Story

Just as you most likely have, we have come across examples of this pattern of committed bets many times throughout the years. One that always comes to mind is the true story of what was to be a new product in one of a large company's newer business units. This particular business unit had, and still has, incredible entrepreneurial spirit. They also had a wealth of really great business ideas.

One such, potentially great, idea for a new web-based software product stood out from the rest. To this day, we still feel their idea was extremely interesting and insightful. The employees who came up with the idea pitched it to their business unit management team with the promise of hitting significant revenue targets in the first year. With that pitch and promise alone, they secured enough funding to build a truly talented team that quickly grew to nearly 40 people.

If your company is in another business and you are not accustomed to building software teams, 40 people might be hard to put in perspective. We do not know the team members' actual salaries, but if we assume $135,000 per year for an average U.S.-based software engineer and their benefits[6], combined, a 40-person team would cost roughly $5.4 million per year—and that is not counting computers, software, office space, and many other miscellaneous expenses.

At a run rate of $5.4 million or more per year, there would have been a lot of pressure to make sure those talented software engineers were being used effectively. Indeed, the team did not waste any time getting to work building the product they thought was needed to hit their revenue goals. In a matter of weeks, the team began to show customers the parts of the product they had completed so far. Talking to customers early on is essential, but unfortunately, they were asking customers the wrong questions.

Instead of interviewing customers about the problems they had in order to figure out if they truly needed a product at all, they collected feedback specifically on how the product they had built already worked. This is a common trap inexperienced intrapreneurs can fall into. They know enough to understand that talking to customers is important, but not enough to ask the right questions of them. They walk away with the feeling that customers really *like* their product, but without knowing if those customers really *need* their product.

The team interviewed customers and collected feedback about what the customers liked about the product demo they saw. Of course, the customers were also happy to point out features they felt were missing from the product. The team members had always heard they should listen to customer feedback and wanted to satisfy these potential customers. To do that, they made sure to incorporate these feature suggestions into their product.

One of the suggestions was a user interface that could work on a smartphone. The team recognized that a second, entirely new, user interface would have been too much for their 40-person team to take on while they were still trying to get the initial release ready for sale to customers. The solution they came up with was to invest in developing a novel user interface software framework that would allow them to build both user interfaces—web and mobile—using a single set of programming code. They knew that developing this framework would temporarily slow them down, but it would allow them to ship the smartphone interface in their initial product release.

---

[6]The average software engineer's salary in the U.S. is $104,4463:
"Software Engineer Salaries," glassdoor, accessed August 20, 2018, https://www.glassdoor.com/Salaries/software-engineer-salary-SRCH_KOO,17.htm
Benefits in private industry average 30.4%:
U.S. Bureau of Labor Statistics, 2018, "Employer Costs for Employee Compensation," *March 2018*, https://www.bls.gov/news.release/ecec.nr0.htm

Creating a new user interface framework was an insightful technical breakthrough that allowed the team to deliver their mobile interface without sacrificing too many features. But what good are more features in a product that does not solve a problem? What good is a second user interface to a product that no one wants to use? The team was building what the customers asked for, but without understanding what the customers wanted to accomplish and therefore what they truly needed.

It is one thing to talk to customers, but it is quite another to get valuable information out of them. Unfortunately, it is extremely easy to trick yourself into thinking your customers have validated the problem and need for the product. The key is asking the right questions. If you ask a customer, "What do you think about this product?," they will tell you what they like or do not like about the product. When the customer answers with an example of a missing feature, it is too easy to infer from their answer that this product solves a problem for the customer and that once it has that missing feature, it will be worth purchasing a product to overcome. That is often not the case. If someone asks you what color sports car you like best, you might answer "red," but that does not mean your next car purchase will be a Ferrari.

Before they worried about features and function, the team should have first tried to determine if this was a problem their customers even wanted solved. If so, what was the most painful part of the problem? I suspect it was not a lack of a mobile phone support. Yet, 40 people were working as hard as they could on a very elegant solution.

Around this point in their story, executives higher up in the company started taking notice of all the resources being spent on this new, innovative, product. The team was asked to present on their progress. After all, the company had included this product's projected revenues in the following year's forecast and guidance to investors. Of course, at this point the team had no active users of product, not to mention any actual paying customers. They did not even have any customers who had raised their hands to say, "If you built it, I would buy it". Not only were they unsure when they would get their first customer, they did not yet even know how they would find their customers or how much they would charge for the product.

The executives were openly concerned and skeptical, and in turn, the team began to worry. Because the team knew the product did not yet have the value customers were willing to pay for, they released a free early version of the product. The hope was they could lure in early adopters and buy themselves time while they finished the salable product.

The few early adopters they found ended up using the product for a completely different set of use cases than the team had originally envisioned. The team reacted by scrambling to change their marketing messaging and website content, as well as pairing down the product's scope and features in an attempted partial pivot. Unfortunately, it was too late.

The executives could not see how this yet-to-be-finished product was going to help them achieve the following year's revenue numbers. Ultimately the project was shut down, but not before it lingered on as a zombie project for another six months while the business unit tried to figure out what to do with both the product and the talented team. Some members of the team remained at the company, but many others were either let go or became disillusioned enough to leave on their own. To add insult to injury, not only was the project a failure and the company lost good employees, they also lost upwards of $2.7 million just for the time it took to unwind everything.

In many cases, failing projects can continue on far too long, hoping the first customer is just one more feature away. Intrapreneurs and their teams are passionate, but when they are emotionally attached to the solution instead of the problem, they can blind themselves to reality. In addition to these unconscious biases, they may also consciously worry about their job and career if their business is not successful. Another reason projects linger is that it is not uncommon for teams to fall for the fallacy of sunk-costs. When making investment decisions it is often too easy to look at the investment you have already made and assume that is what the product is worth. After all, what is a few hundred thousand dollars more when you have spent ten times that much to get this far? In this case, the team had already spent millions of dollars, but how much is a product actually worth that no one wants to buy? Nothing.

Regardless if you are an employee in large enterprise, a small business owner, or an entrepreneur just starting out on your own, no one wants to build something that nobody wants. It is true you will not make money with a product that no one buys, but it goes beyond that. The goal of any product is to solve a customer's problem. If no one truly wants your product, it is because it did not solve someone's problem or add enough value to justify their cost.

Unfortunately, in this particular situation, we may never know for sure if this 40-person team was on to something or just wasting time on nothing. Given the proper guidance and support, and if everyone involved—from the individual contributor on the team all the way up to the executives—had approached building this new business slightly differently, it could have survived long enough to find out if their product idea was as good as everyone thought it was. What if they had talked to customers before building the product or even asking for funding? What if they pivoted to solve a different problem? What if they invested in a smaller, more targeted, feature set? What if they did not promise revenue in the first year? The list of potential things they could have done differently is nearly endless, but as you will read later in this chapter, there are a few simple changes that could have made a big difference.

# Frustration Leads to Competition

While that is an interesting story of a lost opportunity, most intrapreneurs would not get nearly this far in their company's existing processes. They either get rejected because the realistic business case does not show a return on investment in a short enough time period, or they get fed up with the heavyweight processes and never even attempt to put together a business case in the first place.

Even when employees do attempt to get internal funding for a new business idea, what they often hear back is one of a number of reasons why their request was rejected. In addition to the standard "Show us the ROI," other common rationale includes responses such as "This will never make enough money to make it meaningful to our bottom line." or "This is too far removed from what this company is known for." or "We have more important priorities for this money right now." and a personal favorite, "This will end up taking customers away from our existing businesses". Sometimes these are just excuses to get rid of you; other times they are based on sound reasoning and you simply did not yet have the data to prove them wrong. After all, that is why you needed the funding in the first place—to start working on your new idea.

But intrapreneurs are extremely passionate about their ideas. They will, often correctly, point out that if you do not invest in their idea, someone else will. Instead of giving up, they will talk to their friends and start a small project on the side—perhaps within the company but, just as likely, outside. If they do stay at the company, over time they may steal away more and more time and resources from their actual jobs. If they already control a budget, or if things sound promising enough to convince a manager who does, they will start building out teams of people working on their pet project without any formal approval or business case review. Although not kept as an actual secret, this under-the-radar approach is the only thing keeping the project alive.

The challenge is, of course, that the company rarely recognizes they have made this committed bet until it is far too late—the money has already been spent. The larger the company, the more numerous and larger the bets and the easier it is for them to go unnoticed, or worse, be intentionally hidden. Even when projects are explicitly funded, rarely is there the financial discipline to keep track of how much money is spent on each project at the level of detail required.

And then there are the second order hidden costs, as the team consumes time and attention from other supporting teams like sales, marketing, or human resources. The result is that these projects end up costing significantly more than anyone initially realizes. It is difficult enough to track the true costs of projects that are out in the open, but when hidden, it becomes impossible. Assuming the project is discovered, and once it becomes clear that the product will not make an immediate return on the investment, it will get rooted out and shut down.

Regardless if you follow the existing process and lie about your numbers or skip the process entirely and skim time from another project, the effect is the same. Your company's best and brightest are quickly demoralized and discouraged, and ultimately will stop bringing their ideas forward. Often their ideas will rot, and nothing will come of them; a huge untapped potential going to waste. But some of these employees will leave, either finding a job at a company that values their innovative thinking, or worse, they may decide to use their idea to create a new startup that competes directly against you.

# The Benefits of Transparency

Because an established business' existing processes force employees to either lie and inflate their business case, and subsequently fail when they cannot deliver on those expectations, or leave the company in order to bring their product idea to life, what is the solution? Being open and transparent. It may seem counterintuitive at first, especially if you are working on your idea on the side and syphoning off resources from another project. However, in our experience, being open about what you are working on and why is actually the key to avoiding corporate red tape.

Without the ability for projects to be transparent and open, the ones that do move forward often attempt to hide. It is a perfectly rational response to the system that has been inadvertently put in place and forced a halt to open innovation. Hidden projects are not only an accounting issue, but they also cause other unintended consequences. Some of these were highlighted previously in this chapter, such as employees losing their jobs. But there are less tangible, more indirect, consequences as well.

The strength of a company comes directly from its employees. Companies with a disengaged and disenfranchised workforce stumble and amble in the marketplace. A great way to demoralize your employees is to hamper their innovation. On the other hand, companies where employees are more engaged and productive thrive and often dominate their competition.

In his 2012 paper, Alex Edmans looked at the performance of companies listed in the "100 Best Companies to Work for in America". He showed, after controlling for other factors, that these companies financially outperformed their peers by up to 3.8% per year[7]. His analysis also showed that employee satisfaction was the cause of the company performance, rather than the effect. That is more than twice the financial return over the 27-year period that is linked directly to employee satisfaction and engagement. It would seem that even small and less tangible consequences can add up over time.

---

[7]Alex Edmans, "The Link Between Job Satisfaction and Firm Value, with Implications for Corporate Social Responsibility," Academy of Management Perspectives 26(4), 1-19, November 2012: 1-19, http://faculty.london.edu/aedmans/RoweAMP.pdf

While making it difficult to innovate can hurt an employee base, it is the indirect effects that can cause more lasting harm to morale. When we talk about projects "hiding," it is not as if there is some secret room in the basement where they sneak off to each day to do their work. They hide in plain sight, often with some level of visibility that simply goes unnoticed at higher levels of the company.

Imagine if you were an employee who knew your co-worker was working a project that seemed innovative and interesting, but you were not able to work on an innovative idea that you had. You would wonder, probably out loud to your colleagues, why that one group is so special and given the freedom to innovate while you slave away on more mundane projects. The rules do not seem to apply to them—that does not seem fair.

Or worse, imagine if you saw that someone else's project and thought that not only was it less innovative compared yours, but that it was doomed from the start. From the point of view of you and your teammates, their project was just wasting precious resources while your sanctioned, routine, project—which is needed to support actual revenue this quarter—was struggling and starved for the necessary funding. You would feel like you were supporting their salary to play around with a business going nowhere, while you actually made the company money. We can recall one particular instance where someone was angry enough at a project that he openly suggested to his manager that the project leader be fired. Talk about a morale killer.

On the other hand, there are projects that are innovative and where even the employees working on other teams recognize their importance. When these projects do get discovered and shut down for what is viewed as completely arbitrary reasons, the larger employee base looks at it as if the company does not understand or care about innovation. Perhaps they have a point.

The effects of these situations on morale and engagement can be debilitating. We have seen some employees in these situations put in a minimal effort and collect their paycheck while they look for their next job. In a few extreme cases, they simply stopped showing up to work in the meantime. How many of your company's employees feel this way? How many are just buying time with your company's money until they find something better? How many have great ideas they will take with them when they leave?

Transparency has clear benefits as well, the most obvious and tangible being better decision making. It is not hard to predict that teams hiding or blind to data that shows their business is not working will not take action on that data. Instead of crossing their fingers and hoping for the best, businesses should be listening to customers, and the overall market.

There are also less tangible benefits to transparency that are equally as important. Data and ideas that flow freely within a company are often worth more than the sum of their parts. This is because great ideas rarely come from a single person, isolated in a room, thinking to themselves. Much more often than not, great ideas are born from collaborations between people. In his book, *Where Good Ideas Come From*[8], Steven Johnson describes how "liquid networks"—fluid connections and communication between groups of people—are a key ingredient to innovation. (If you are not familiar with his work, his TED talk[9] is a great introduction.) When projects hide or are not honest with their data, this collaboration never has the chance to occur and you miss out on potential breakthroughs. These are the exact breakthroughs you need to keep achieving on a regular basis in order to continually beat your competitors in the marketplace.

# A Culture of Trust

In addition to the benefits of making good business decisions or sparking creativity and innovation through collaboration within your organization, transparency and openness builds a culture of trust. Perhaps in your latest quarterly review you have objectively shown the progress you have made and why you are deserving of more funding. Or, perhaps you have shown an objective lack of progress and have demonstrated that it is because the business is being built on what turned out to be a bad assumption. You make the hard decision to recommend the project be terminated. In either case, because you presented clear, objective, and transparent data, instead of being highly skeptical, the executives leave the room knowing you are the right person to figure this business out—one way or the other. You are a leader they can trust.

The thought of a leader coming forward and saying their project is no longer worth funding may seem like a foreign idea, but we have seen it more than once. It is a unique and refreshing experience, and it significantly raised our confidence level in the leader each time it happened.

A great example is one particular innovation project we funded a few years ago. The team had built the initial version of a product they knew at least some customers said they wanted. They managed to convince three early adopters to buy the product, but then struggled to find a fourth customer. The woman leading the project spent a lot of time talking to potential customers and users; she collected great data along the way. When she came into her monthly review

---

[8]Steven Johnson, *Where Good Ideas Come From: The Natural History of Innovation*, 1st Riverhead trade pbk. Ed, New York: Riverhead Books, 2011.
[9]"Where Good Ideas Come From," TED, July 2010, Video, 17:39, https://www.ted.com/talks/steven_johnson_where_good_ideas_come_from

meeting, she did not try to convince us that there must be something valuable there and we were just missing it. She did not try to convince us that just one more feature was needed and then the product would be a hit.

Instead, she outlined, very directly, a variety of different approaches she had already tried in order to make the business work but could not find a successful angle. She showed that, while customers had acknowledged that the problem the team was trying to solve was real, many customers just did not feel the pain of the problem enough to do anything about it. For the few who did, she demonstrated how the market was shifting, and customers were starting to use other vendors in adjacent markets that were solving the problem a different way, and more importantly, in a way we could not compete with.

Then, this leader told us point blank: Unless we had a suggestion that she had not already thought of and tried, even though she still had another month or two of funding left, there was no point continuing her project. She convinced us to shut it down. The project was immediately stopped, the three customers refunded their money, and the team was given a bonus for their great work coming to this conclusion efficiently. Each of these employees were then voluntarily redeployed on to other innovation projects.

And what happened to the leader of this failed project? A manager in an unrelated team was extremely impressed when he heard about what she had accomplished. He hired her onto his team and promoted her two levels.

# Measuring the Right Things

We have shown the pitfalls of opaqueness and how it can have several significant downsides. We have also shown how being transparent and sharing objective data can build trust and improve your chances of success. Sharing objective and concrete data about the state of your business is key, but there is no point in being transparent if the data you share does not matter. In the traditional processes within your established business, your finance or operations team would be looking for quarterly revenue. Recurring revenue, plus other metrics such as revenue churn and cost of acquisition, are exactly the right things to measure if you want to know if an existing and established business is still on track.

However, imagine you are building a business around a new and improved widget of some sort. You have just spent your first few months designing your new widget and you now have been asked to provide an update to the executive team. Just like in our story earlier in this chapter, you show up to the meeting with a graph of revenue that just shows a big, fat, zero. Clearly, that is not very compelling, and you will most certainly get many questions, perhaps every question in some form or another, asking why we are investing in this new widget in the first place. After all, from what you have shown the

executives, the business is clearly not working, and this is a wasted investment. You will of course attempt to explain how amazing your business idea still is and how you simply know that everyone will want to buy one of your widgets once they are available in the market. An executive in the room will then speak up and say, "Prove it!," which of course you cannot.

While right for an existing business, revenue, and related metrics such as churn and acquisition costs, are exactly the wrong things to measure for a new business that is just getting started. What good is measuring "zero" month after month before you even have a product and paying customers? Or alternatively, as we described in Chapter 1, going from one customer to two does not mean you have 100% growth and your product is a success. You need to measure something that will give you actionable information.

You need to measure what is most important to your new business right now, and what is most important will change over time as your business matures. In *Lean Analytics: Use Data to Build a Better Startup Faster*, Benjamin Yoskovitz and Alistair Croll call this the "One Metric That Matters"[10]. Certainly, revenue and churn will be important once you have customers but, until then, it is not an indication that your business is working or not. Building something new is inherently risky, with many unknowns, and you need the proper information to keep you away from the dreaded committed bet.

By measuring the wrong things, revenue in this case, you are blinding yourself to potentially larger problems. Do you know if customers really want this new widget? Perhaps they do but are only willing to pay a price that is too low to support a working business. Or perhaps customers really do need this widget but want a design that is slightly different than you originally envisioned.

These are the types of things you need to measure when you are just starting out with a new product idea so that you build something that matters to customers. Unfortunately, if you did not uncover these information nuggets up front, you have probably just designed and manufactured the wrong product.

Physicist Sir William Thomson, who is more commonly known as Lord Kelvin and for whom the Kelvin temperature scale was named, was very fond of measuring everything he could. He used to say in his lectures:

> "...when you can measure what you are speaking about, and express it in numbers, you know something about it; but when you cannot measure it, when you cannot express it in numbers, your knowledge is of a meagre and unsatisfactory kind..."[11]

—Lord Kelvin

---

[10]Alistair Croll and Benjamin Yoskovitz. 2013. *Lean Analytics: Use Data to Build a Better Startup Faster*. Sebastopol, CA: O'Reilly.

[11]Sir William Thomson, "Electrical Units of Measurement," *Popular Lectures and Addresses*, 1889, https://archive.org/stream/popularlecturesa01kelvuoft#page/73

This is certainly a statement we can agree with, but just because you *can* measure something does not mean you *should* measure it. Measuring the wrong things, the things that do not matter to your business at this very moment, will not only leave you without actionable information, they can also leave you with a false sense of reassurance. Knowing that customers *want* a feature in a product is not helpful if you do not know if they *need* the product in the first place. Optimizing that unneeded product's feature set is simply an exercise in futility and waste.

Another consequence of measuring the wrong parts of a new business is that it increases the likelihood that you will succumb to your own personal biases. As humans, we all have biases, and as business leaders or intrapreneurs, we all come with biases toward some set of assumptions when we begin the creation of a new business. Those assumptions are exactly what you should be testing and measuring early on. You assume your new product idea will solve a customer's problem. You assume your product will command a high enough price to eventually make the business profitable. Unless you measure and test these parts of your business early on, you are taking huge risks.

As you validate your initial assumptions, you will learn a tremendous amount about your customers and their problems. Their demographics, psychographics, purchasing habits or process, and most importantly, the problems they need solved. Unfortunately, you may also find that customers really do not want your new widget, but it is better to learn that as early as possible. You assumed they had a problem that this widget could solve, but once you really listened to what problems your customers needed to have solved, and once you measured customer engagement around your ideas, it may turn out you were wrong. It could turn out the problem really was not painful enough for customers to want to go out and buy new widgets. Or, it could turn out that customers do not have this problem at all. The only way you can know any of this information is if you were measuring the right things and were transparent—with others as well as with yourself—about the data you gathered.

## Tying It All Together

So far, we have covered the consequences of the subversion of existing processes, the lack of openness and transparency, and measuring things that do not currently matter to your business. When combined, these ultimately lead toward stifling innovation within your company.

A company fighting to stay on top in their industry needs to continually grow, but over the long-term, growing a business without internal, organic, innovation is extremely difficult. As a consequence, a company would need to acquire competitors or adjacent companies to provide the revenue growth missing due to their lack of internal innovation. But acquiring a company requires a lot

of capital, and capital applied to an acquisition can no longer be applied to the existing and more established part of your business. Without the resources and time needed to innovate, by definition, your employees will not be able to create the new businesses your company needs to grow. Of course, just like the other consequences we have discussed, this can also lead to marginalizing your passionate, innovative, employees and contribute to overall poor morale. That is the exact opposite of what your company is trying to accomplish.

That is not to say that acquisitions are automatically innovation killers or that all acquisitions are bad. On the contrary, the right acquisitions can and should be an important part of your company's long-term strategy. Targeted and well thought out acquisitions can also bring in new, innovative, employees that are full of great ideas to grow your business. But those new employees will need an outlet for their ideas, otherwise they too will feel marginalized and unwanted. Acquisitions must be done right and for the right reasons. If you use acquisitions as an alternative to organic innovation and new business growth, the ultimate consequence is that your company can end up in a downward spiral. The company's lack of organic growth will lead to poor acquisitions, which in turn will lead to even less organic growth.

However, if you can overcome the challenges that cause innovation to fail in established businesses, you can avoid these consequences and can be successful in building new businesses. Instead of a downward spiral, you can create a virtuous cycle without needing to leave and go it alone. You can build these businesses within the boundaries of your company that has existing established businesses, and alongside strategic, targeted, acquisitions. The key is to forget the existing businesses and processes and instead play by new rules.

## Completely Avoid Existing Processes

Instead of playing along and blindly following large-scale, mismatched, processes that were defined for a different use case and in turn being forced into lying about your future business, you need to change the game. Instead of trying to fight red tape, you need to sidestep it entirely, and create a holistic approach to building new businesses separate from the way you manage your established businesses.

Your goal as an intrapreneur, and your company's goal for that matter, is to build a business, or determine it is not viable, in the quickest and most efficient way possible. This efficiency is not just some cost cutting tactic, it is a fundamentally different way of approaching the problem compared to how the established business operates.

Rather than inventing a three-year financial forecast out of thin air to hit a made up financial target, actually acknowledging the uncertainty of your new business—being open and transparent—benefits both you and your larger company. The downside, of course, is that no one is going to give you tens of millions of dollars when you clearly articulate to them just how uncertain you really are.

## Acknowledge the Uncertainty

But that is the point. Acknowledge the uncertainty. If you are going to be successful building a new business, you cannot hide and ignore that uncertainty and just hope for the best. Asking for two orders of magnitude less money—three months of funding for a three-person team instead of three years and a 30-person team—is one way to acknowledge and mitigate the uncertainty.

Although often it may be unintentional, when starting a new business from the ground up, it is intellectually dishonest to pretend you know how much money you will need a year into the future, not to mention three years down the road. How much will your marketing campaigns cost three years from now? How many software developers will you need three years from now? Sure, there may be some general rules of thumb you could apply, but it is all just a guess, and pretending otherwise is simply a lie. It is even more dangerous if you do not even realize it is a lie.

But if instead you were asked how much money your business needed for your first three months so that your small team could lay the groundwork for your new business, you would not need a rule of thumb. You would have a solid plan. The ultimate outcome may still be uncertain, but how you would use that initial funding to accomplish an initial set of goals would be known upfront.

## Take Incremental and Transparent Steps

After asking for an order of magnitude less money, a second way to acknowledge the uncertainty is to report regularly on how the business is progressing. It is in everyone's best interest that you are open with how your business is doing from the very beginning. Traditionally, if you were given a large team and a large amount of money upfront, you would tell your executive team to check back with you in a year once the product is released. After all, growing revenue is the ultimate goal.

But as we described, when in the early stages of a new business, revenue will not tell you anything. In fact, it may tell you the wrong things, and a lot of things can go wrong in a year. Luckily, when you have a limited amount of time, regular reporting is a natural outcome. If you can demonstrate the business is on track in your first three months, you will be able to ask for more time, and an even larger team, to get the business one step further.

From your company's point of view, the allure of incremental funding and regular reporting is obvious. The company only has to spend a small amount of time and money for you to show that your business is a great idea. If it turns out your assumptions were wrong and the business does not work out, the company will have learned that this business idea is a dead end and not worth any further investment. It is a win-win from their perspective.

## Measure What Matters Most Right Now

In *Running Lean*[12], Ash Maurya does an excellent job explaining how, in a startup, the entrepreneur's job is to identify the riskiest parts of their business plan and then systematically de-risk that plan. When it comes to that advice, being an intrapreneur within your company, instead of an entrepreneur building an external startup, is no different.

At a high level, you want to know if your initial assumptions are still accurate, and if they are not, can you change your assumptions to align with reality and still come out with a working business. At the beginning stages, being transparent and measuring what matters means talking with potential customers, users, buyers—anyone and everyone related to your business idea—and analyzing the objective and subjective information you learn to confirm or invalidate the assumptions you made about your business.

When your new business begins to mature, and as one set of assumptions are at least partially de-risked, new assumptions will be formed. For example, instead of worrying if customers have a problem painful enough to solve, you will be more worried that the solution you have built actually solves their problem sufficiently. Instead of measuring customer engagement in conversations, you will be measuring customer engagement in actual product use. This cycle continues indefinitely, as you are always looking for opportunities to remove the current risks in your business.

## A Virtuous Cycle

Pulling these ideas together in your mind, and in Figure 2-2, you can begin to see a methodology forming. Using an incremental funding approach forces you to focus on what matters. By measuring what matters most to your business at its specific state of evolution, you can more objectively show that your business is making progress or no longer makes sense. Being open and transparent with this objective data about your business gives your larger company the confidence that you are spending their money wisely. Spending incremental funding wisely in order to build a new business is not a hard thing to sell to any competent executive.

---

[12]Ash Maurya, 2012, *Running Lean: Iterate from Plan A to a Plan That Works*, Sebastopol, CA: O'Reilly.

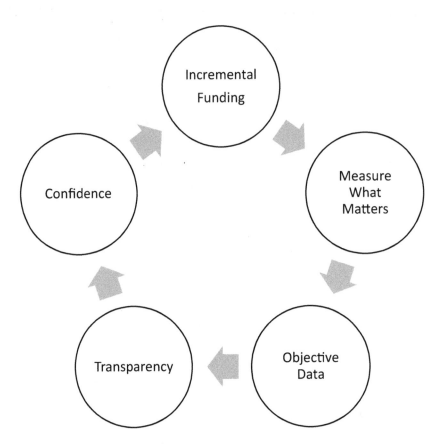

**Figure 2-2.** A better way to build new businesses

This is a virtuous cycle that should form the foundation of any new business, regardless if you are an intrapreneur or an entrepreneur. Even if you are building an external startup and you have raised a large sum of venture capital funding, you will want to hold yourself to only spending just enough time and money to learn and acquire the objective data you need to give you and your investors the confidence to move to the next phase of your business.

This iterative process of having incremental funding tied to specific, measurable, short-term objectives forms the basis of a repeatable framework for incubation—which also happens to be the subtitle of our next chapter.

# Lean Acceleration

## A Repeatable Framework for Incubation

*"Only through experience of trial and suffering can the soul be strengthened, ambition inspired, and success achieved."*

—Helen Keller, *Helen Keller's Journal: 1936-1937,*
*Doubleday, Doran & Company, Inc. 1938*

The goal of our Accelerator program is to drive innovation by nurturing ingenuity. If you are an intrapreneur or entrepreneur, the next two chapters will provide you with a structure you can use to give your idea the best opportunity to succeed in spite of the challenges we have covered thus far. You can evaluate your progress using these techniques and use these tools to decide whether you should pivot, persist, or pause your own idea. For those of you establishing a program of your own, we will also share our framework, structure, ceremonies, and tools.

Whether you are pursuing your own innovative idea or creating an incubation program, we believe a brief discussion of how we developed our program will greatly enhance your understanding of it. So let's begin there…

© CA 2019
G. Watt and H. Abrams, *Lean Entrepreneurship,*
https://doi.org/10.1007/978-1-4842-3942-1_3

# Our Journey

It was clear to us that the status quo was not a path to success. That was no surprise to most. There had been many ineffective attempts to improve innovation both within individual teams and companywide. We knew *something* had to change, but nobody had successfully figured out which specific changes would make a difference. Until now.

Through both our primary and secondary research we had a much more detailed understanding of why innovation fails in established businesses. We knew that in order to succeed we needed to establish an independently funded and governed program. That program needed to apply the appropriate level of rigor at each stage of each business idea's maturity to ensure each business focused on what mattered most at that stage. It also needed to ensure teams were not burdened by unnecessary and inappropriate process for process' sake; especially early on. We also knew we needed to provide innovators with access to the resources and skills required for successful execution of their current stage. So that was it. Simple, right? We wish it had been that straightforward.

While we had identified the key impediments to incubating new business ideas in an established organization, and some of the cultural impact and unhealthy behavior that resulted from them, we still had to figure out how to address those impediments. Of course, many of us had our own hypotheses regarding what would work. Some of us were happy to share those with anyone who wanted to listen—and also with those who did not. Frequently.

By the time we had concluded our research, a couple of new innovation programs had just commenced or were about to launch. Those programs showed promise, and they needed to be given a fair chance to succeed. About a year and a half later circumstances would generate an opportunity for some of us to put our research—and our careers—where our mouths had been. The timing could not have been better.

# A Perfect Storm

For entirely unrelated reasons, we (your authors) both joined the Office of the CTO in May 2015, along with a few other people who would become very active contributors to our Accelerator program. We were building a team in preparation for the arrival of our yet-to-be-named CTO. In June 2015, Otto Berkes officially became that CTO. Otto is no stranger to innovating in a large organization, having co-founded Xbox, and led the team that created HBO GO. He brought with him his own ideas and experience regarding what leads to successful innovation in established organizations—and what leads to failure.

That August we decided we would be deliberate about the creation of a new incubation engine for the company. We delivered a written commitment to our CEO, our C-level executive team, and our board that we would design, deploy, and launch a new organic innovation program; and have it fully operational by April 1, 2016. We pledged to move from having no proposal, to running a fully functional program in six months.

Timing was our benefactor in one other important way. In May 2015, CA Technologies announced the acquisition of Rally Software, a company that delivered software, consulting, and training to help organizations adopt Agile and Lean approaches to development. The creative team at Rally, led by their CTO, Ryan Martens, had also been working on a solution to the organic innovation puzzle.

In early September 2015, we gathered at the historic Hotel Boulderado to set ourselves on a path to keep that promise. We also invited members of four fairly new businesses teams that had been incubating their business ideas via different methodologies. Each business was at a different stage of maturity, and each had experienced a different level of success. Three had been operating within CA Technologies. One had been incubating in Rally prior to the acquisition.

In the midst of the charm of the century old hotel and the high-energy backdrop of the Boulder startup community, we vowed to create a program that would address the key impediments we had identified, both in our research and through our own experiences. At the beginning of the session we committed to create a new approach to ensuring these new, innovative ideas had the best possible chance to succeed that would:

1. Mitigate the reasons innovative people were not acting upon their ideas such as:

   - Risk of losing their job if the idea was not successful

   - Onerous business case requirements that made even suggesting an idea difficult, time-consuming, and stressful

   - Not knowing to whom to take their ideas

2. Address key reasons good ideas might fail, including:

   - Becoming crushed under the weight of heavy processes designed for mature businesses

   - Lack of executive attention span

- Unrealistic expectations of time requirements or revenue

- Unrelated operational pressures (e.g., companywide margin targets)

3. Reduce the risk of building things nobody wants through attention to things like:

   - Ensuring customers were engaged early enough

   - Ensuring businesses were perpetually customer focused

   - Helping businesses avoid the committed bet trap (described in Chapter 2)

4. Deliberately address key areas where breakthrough businesses differ from mainstream businesses, including that they:

   - Require exploration and experimentation

   - Require different metrics

   - Require different skills

   - Can be too far ahead of well understood customer needs

   - Often require new business model incubation

## Our Initial Hypothesis

By the end of the workshop, we developed a hybrid venture capital/angel investment scheme that leverages Lean, Lean startup, and Agile principles to ensure businesses make the appropriate investments and build things customers will pay for.

We developed an initial set of guiding principles and a basic structure. Figure 3-1 shows an unedited version of the structure hypotheses we developed during the workshop. Though we have since inspected and adapted them many times, the basic principles hold true to this day.

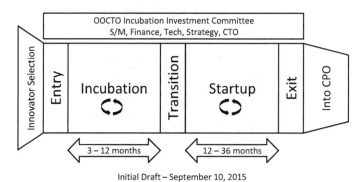

Figure 3-1. Initial draft of the incubator process outline, September 2015 (aka "The Rocket")

## Initial Program Hypothesis Highlights

A review of our workshop notes showed that our initial program hypothesis included items such as these, defined by each phase depicted earlier in this chapter:

Governance:

- Cross-organizational representation from organizations such as Marketing, Strategy, Sales, Finance, and CTO Office

- Regular updates to our C-level executive team

Entry:

- Confirm the business had a unique value proposition that addressed unmet customer needs that competitors could not address (i.e., hit the "high-value opportunity" shown in Figure 3-2)

- Articulated hypotheses, assumptions, and ideas regarding how those assumptions might be proven or refuted

- "Partial Lean Canvas"[1]
    - All Lean Canvas boxes completed
    - Little validation of initial hypotheses
    - Strong articulation of the problem, solution, customer, unique value proposition ("high-value opportunity"), and unfair advantage hypothesis
    - Less well explored hypotheses were anticipated for the other Lean Canvas boxes

Incubation Phase:

- "Lean Startup +"
- 1-3 rounds of investment
- Build small, initial team
- Building prototypes to validate hypothesis
    - Paper, wire frame, Wizard of Oz…
- "Completing" the Lean Canvas (i.e., de-risking the canvas and evolving it based on the outcome of experiments)
- Coaching, mentoring, and program management
- Access to resources and subject matter expertise
- Access to customers
- Execution at high velocity
    - Hiring, experimentation, iteration…
- Monthly, founder-led investment team reviews to determine whether the business should pivot, pause, or persist

---

[1]The Lean Canvas was created by Ash Maurya of Leanstack and provides a one-page business model format that is tailored for early stage ideas. https://leanstack.com/leancanvas/

Startup Phase:

- 1-3 funding rounds
- Growing the team through hiring, acquihiring, or using the "Accelerator Bench" (discussed further in Chapter 5)
- Building a minimum viable product (MVP)
  - A product that has as few features as possible while being functional enough to satisfy early customers and bring feedback to the product team to inform future direction
- Measurement via the "innovation metrics" (also known as the "pirate metrics" because their initials are "AARRR")
  - Acquisition
  - Activation
  - Retention
  - Referral
  - Revenue
- Business model validation
- Refined market positioning and go-to-market plan
- Named references and earlyvangelists[2]
- A path to revenue collection and technology to support it

Exit:

- Text book exit: The Chief Product Officer's organization acquires the business using the Company's standard criteria and process for external product acquisition
- An integration plan for movement of the business from the Accelerator to the mainstream product organization

---

[2]The term "earlyvangelist" was first used by Steve Blank in his book, *The Four Steps to the Epiphany,* K & S Ranch Press, 2005

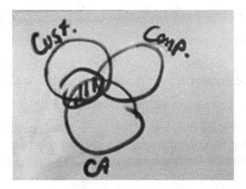

**Figure 3-2.** Flip chart image from September 2015 workshop illustrating the "high-value opportunity" at the intersection of unmet customer need, incubating business capability, and competition's inability to meet that customer need

This workshop was also the inaugural face-to-face meeting of the new office of the CTO team. As a result, we learned a lot about one another as we progressed through all four stages of Dr. Bruce Tuckman's stages of group development[3] in record time. All while developing this program hypothesis. We believe the team's values, and the high-performance culture that rapidly emerged, had an enormous amount of influence on our initial hypothesis, and ultimately on the program we eventually developed from it.

It was clear that the team was very customer-focused, both in the context of external customers of incubating businesses, and from the perspective of program consumers (the businesses themselves) and sponsors. Key values such as respect for people, transparency, speed, rapid iteration, and the assumption that all team members were working with good intentions and doing the best they could with what they had quickly became accepted, unbreakable norms. Two examples that might help you understand our team's personality came quickly to mind as we thought about the workshop.

## Words Matter

Throughout the early stages of the workshop we had been referring to decisions resulting from business review meetings as "pivot, persevere, or perish". A couple of times we noticed Ryan cringe when we said the word, "perish". Eventually he asked if we could stop using that word, and suggested, "pause" might be a more useful term. In hindsight, it is certainly less menacing. It was an early harbinger of our respect for people.

---

[3]Developmental sequence in small groups, Dr. Bruce Tuckman, *Psychological Bulletin,* 63(6), 384-39, 1965 http://psycnet.apa.org/record/1965-12187-001

Second, throughout the workshop the familiar phrase, "fail fast," was often heard. At one point, Otto asked if we could start using the phrase, "learn fast". His point was that an experiment that delivered results that were not as expected was not necessarily a failure. At least not if you paid attention to those results. We agreed. In fact, in our experience counter-intuitive results often lead to the most exciting discoveries or opportunities. Today in our Accelerator, "failure" is often referred to as "the 'F' word" and treated in much the same manner as its namesake, albeit lightheartedly so.

We shared those two examples as a simple illustration of the respect this team had for individuals and teams who would participate in our program. There were many others. As Peter Drucker's often paraphrased assertion dictates, culture can certainly eat strategy for breakfast. Fortunately, the corollary is also true. While *unhealthy* culture eats strategy for breakfast, *healthy* culture will fortify it with iron and nine essential vitamins.

What's more, use of these more positive terms sets a different tone for those in the program, and gives incubating teams explicit permission to learn fast and/or pause. In our Accelerator there is no shame in pivoting and pausing. We celebrate it. There should be no incentive to let an incubating business operate after it is obvious to the team that it is not viable.

The impact of a bias to transparency and celebrating good execution regardless of whether that led to pivot, persist, or pause might be greater than you think. During one pivot, pause, persist discussion where it became obvious the decision would likely be "pause," someone with venture capital experience exclaimed, "this is so great!" She went on to explain that she had seen cases in the VC world where investments persisted longer than they should have because it would have looked bad for the person who recommended the investment. This led to additional investment in businesses beyond the point where the lead investor knew they were not viable. She joyfully declared it was great to have the freedom to make the right decisions, and to be in a team where that is celebrated.

## Our First 3P Review

It was October 29, 2015. It's funny how some dates stick with you. Just over a month after we completed our Boulderado workshop an unrelated event brought almost the entire team to our Silicon Valley office. It turned out to be a very important week for us, though we did not know it then.

We thought we would take advantage of the fact we would all be together to advance our program. Though we had not planned to have our "Pivot, Pause, Persist" meetings so soon, we could not pass up this opportunity. We decided to run an experiment. We accepted that it might be a disaster or a waste of time, but we had to start somewhere. We all agreed to try something and to

simply adjust our approach, not to dwell on it, if it proved to be ineffective. Later we learned that this willingness to take small risks and run experiments on the program enabled us to develop and evolve our program with much higher than anticipated velocity. And much lower than anticipated stress.

We knew we wanted to operate the program based on Lean and Agile principles, so we created a very basic working agreement and definition of done, as well as a structure for the day. We also included suggestions for what should be included in each review. Before people arrived, we posted these on the wall for discussion and update prior to the commencement of the meeting (see Figure 3-3).

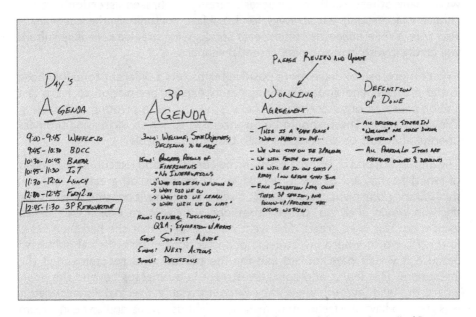

**Figure 3-3.** Draft agenda, working agreement, and definition of done on the wall of Room 1104 prior to the inaugural 3P reviews (Oct. 29, 2015)

You may have noticed that the individual 3P review times on the whiteboard wall added up to 46 minutes. We addressed that at the outset. "Inspect and Adapt" is the mantra of the Accelerator's program team. We believe that the only path to a successful program is to develop the program using the same Lean-Agile approach we are encouraging and coaching the incubating business teams to use. We do not suffer from the illusion of perfection. We know we will make mistakes, we know we will encounter new information and circumstances we had not anticipated, and we know that even in the unlikely event we were to achieve perfection—and that will not happen— that the world is ever-changing, and adjustments will be required over time. We believed that from the outset, and we began inspecting and adapting the program even before we started our first ceremony.

You may have also noticed that the day's agenda ended with a retrospective of the day's events. Retrospective inspection, and adaptation as a result, must be deliberate. We still perform 3P, and other, retrospective reviews. We regularly fine-tune the program as a result, and we often make substantial adjustments based on that feedback, discovery, and our experience.

So, that was it. We had run a successful 3P experiment, and we had performed a retrospective during which we discovered a number of ways to improve our effectiveness. We had actually unofficially launched our program five months ahead of a six-month schedule. We were able to achieve this due to our willingness to accept responsible risks, run experiments, and inspect and adapt the program. Though we still had a lot to do.

That week we also kept a promise. We unveiled our program to approximately 100 members of the company's senior leadership team. This was an important milestone, and it was the first time most of them heard of the program. We will discuss the importance of obtaining, and maintaining, executive buy-in Chapter 7. Though that meeting resulted in a request that drove us to one of the most important lessons we learned early on, and it resulted in one of our program's most innovative elements.

## It Takes a Village to Build an Accelerator

The Human Resources team had also taken advantage of the fact that many people were in the Silicon Valley office that week and, like us, they had scheduled their own team meeting. They had heard we were about to launch an innovation program and asked if we would provide an overview to their team. "Of course we will!"

It was a great opportunity to test our message, learn from them, and begin to socialize our program. Their feedback was great. They also asked how they could help, and this is where things went from great to outstanding. We shared a couple of the people-related challenges, which were covered in Chapter 1, and our *objectives* for the resolution of those puzzles. How could we create a program that would sufficiently reduce the risk of innovating such that budding intrapreneurs would be willing to jump in and pursue their passion?

In the weeks that followed, the Human Resources and Compensation teams contacted us and presented us with a proposal for a new company-sponsored program. This "incubation rotation" program would enable employees to move into the Accelerator full-time to pursue their ideas. Employees on this rotation would have access to their existing compensation package and benefits, and they would be able to return to their business unit if their idea did not work out. (We discuss incubation rotation further in Chapter 5.)

# The Phrase that Pays

The outcome was magical. We not only had a great new program, we had learned a very valuable lesson that would be of enormous benefit as we continued to build our program. The most important aspect of this experience, apart from the fact that we have an amazing Human Resources team, was that *we began by sharing our objectives. We did not prescribe* a method for addressing them. We simply shared the details of a puzzle we were trying to solve. We would love to claim that was intentional, though we are not sure it was. It likely was not. The significance—and the value—of this lesson are worth further explanation.

One of the key reasons innovation fails in established enterprises is that it is crushed under the weight of processes and procedures that were designed for mature, usually large, businesses. In order to create a program to address that challenge we would need to change many of our established processes. There are several ways in which we could have attempted to do that. We *could* have approached the team responsible for the process (e.g., Legal, Procurement, Marketing, Branding, Pricing, Human Resources, Talent Acquisition...) and told them that their process just wouldn't work for us—because we are "special"—and then explained exactly how their process must work. In so doing we would also be telling them just how bad they are at their job, either implicitly or explicitly, and how much better we could do it. You would be surprised at how often that is, more or less, explicitly stated. It's no surprise that this approach almost always results in a political tug-of-war as opposed to an innovative outcome.

Our experience with the Human Resources team led us down a different path. We learned that beginning these conversations with the phrase, "We need your help", explaining our challenges and objectives, and then letting the people who are experts in each of these fields do what they do best—design a solution based on their experience and expertise—leads to infinitely more interesting and productive outcomes.

When we empower and challenge our subject matter experts, as opposed to constraining their thinking, or even maligning them, we get better outcomes. Sometimes the new procedures they create for the Accelerator can even be made available to other groups in the company in order to make everyone more productive. Don't just leverage your partners, present them with puzzles and challenges. Give *them* the opportunity to innovate.

# Momentum and Opportunity

We held our second wave of 3P reviews in December 2015. While October's reviews included a lot of history and level-setting, December's were more structured and productive. Word of the program was beginning to spread, and we learned that people were interested in bringing their ideas to us. Our

plan was to receive the first such pitches in April 2016 following the program's official launch. We had some slack in the schedule, so we decided we could "run an experiment". That had paid off for us in the past, so why not!

We created a format for the event and accepted two pitch requests, which we hosted at the end of our 3P reviews. Both pitches were great. One pitch came from a seasoned engineer and someone who had been an engineer for only a few months. They had won a "canvas your hack" competition that had been added to a local hackathon. The other came from extremely experienced engineers who had worked in external startups. One of the ideas was accepted for entry into the Accelerator. Pitch ceremony hypothesis confirmed! Though we had a lot of work to do, we were fully operational three months ahead of schedule.

We believe the Accelerator team's willingness to run experiments with the explicit acknowledgement that a potential outcome of each is a spectacular failure, and without fear of reprisal, has been one of our most impactful "secret weapons". That is not to state that we just "try stuff" without thinking things through. Though when we have a solid hypothesis and a reasonable way to confirm or refute it, we go for it. Just like we would encourage our incubating businesses to do.

# Banana Loaf

We were making progress, and our program idea was getting traction. Though something was missing. When we spoke to people about it, they understood what we were trying to accomplish. At least it felt as if they did. But it was not sticking. Something was missing. We believed they understood the objective, but they did not fully understand how we planned to achieve it.

The timing for a puzzle of this nature probably could not have been better. It was February 2016 and we were in Tampa for an Office of the CTO strategy meeting. We were in the perfect frame of mind. We had extracted ourselves from operational details. We were solving puzzles and thinking deeply about tough problems and strategic opportunities. A few of us met for coffee early one morning in the café at the Hotel Meridien when inspiration hit. "Give me that pen!"

I (George) grabbed the wrapper that was formerly home to my banana loaf and feverishly scribbled an updated model (see Figure 3-4). As we discussed the model it became apparent that not only was this a clearer articulation of the program, it also was a useful platform for testing and developing new program ideas.

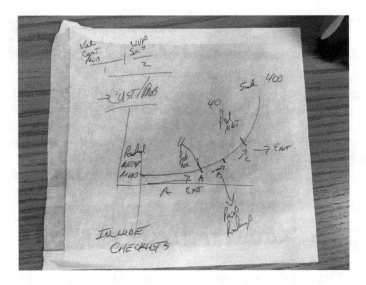

**Figure 3-4.** Banana loaf wrapper drawing of the CA Accelerator concept

The new model, which we describe next, resonated well with everyone. It helped incubating teams and aspiring intrapreneurs understand the focus of each stage. It also resonated with leaders and senior executives. We had traction.

## Executive Engagement—"Where Are the Lean Canvases?"

Later that month we presented the new Accelerator concept to our CEO and his C-Level executive team. We also presented each of them with a copy of Eric Ries' *The Lean Startup*. Even when you believe a discussion with senior executives was successful, you may be somewhat uncertain. We were, until Otto called and asked, "Where are the Lean Canvases?" Our CEO had walked into Otto's office and asked to review the Lean Canvases of all of the businesses incubating in the Accelerator. The program was beginning to get some traction. It was a moment of great excitement for the team.

Let's look at the Accelerator program that resulted from this journey.

## Our Program at a Glance

That journey brought us to the program we officially launched April 1, 2016. CA Accelerator is a hybrid angel/VC investment style model that executes leveraging Lean, Lean Startup, and Agile principles. This helps ensure teams

avoid building things nobody wants, or at least learn their businesses are not viable as quickly and efficiently as possible. Our operational principles include:

- Maniacal customer focus

- Small, incremental investments

- Rapid experimentation and iteration

- Learning and pivoting quickly

- Staged evaluation and disciplined governance following Lean principles to minimize cost, drive focus, and increase the probability of success

Figure 3-5 shows a conceptual diagram of the program.

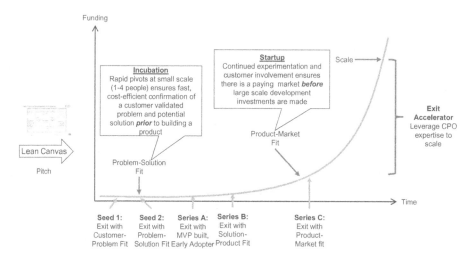

**Figure 3-5.** The CA Accelerator Program

We take you through the entire program at a high level in this section. In Chapter 4, we provide additional details about each phase of the program and share the artifacts and structure we use to support each program element.

## Innovator Selection

Without great ideas and great people there is no Accelerator. The primary objective of the Innovator Selection phase is to enable intrapreneurs to bring their ideas to us with a minimum of friction. This is the reason the only artifact they need to prepare is a one-page Lean Canvas. They should be able to complete the canvas in a few hours if they have truly thought through their idea. Once they complete the canvas they need only upload their idea. We

provide a single site to capture all types of ideas so intrapreneurs do not have to determine which organization their idea best aligns with. It is simple and almost frictionless.

You may have noticed that we call this phase, "innovator selection" as opposed to something like "idea selection" or "innovation triage". That is deliberate. The founding *team* is at least as important as their idea. Likely more important. A good team can pivot and turn a bad idea around, or at least determine quickly and efficiently that a business idea is not viable. A bad team is not likely to succeed even if their idea is great.

From beginning to end, this program is about people. It is about the people who conceive these breakthrough ideas and create businesses from them, and it is about those people maniacally focusing on the people whose problems they are solving (their customers).

## The Pitch Event

A prospective intrapreneur's first exposure to our program is during their pitch event. These ceremonies were designed to have maximum focus on the ideas, and to minimize the friction that discourages or prevents innovative people from proposing their ideas (as discussed in Chapter 1). For example, no fictitious "70-page" business cases are required. While people can bring any artifacts they believe will help them to make their case, the *only* required artifact is the one-page Lean Canvas.

We chose the Lean Canvas as our only required artifact because we have found it helps ensure that the team pitching has considered all aspects of their business. It helps them to build a stronger case, identify and address weaknesses in their initial hypothesis, and ensure they are customer and problem focused. In addition, teams that pitch successfully can use their canvas as a tool to help evolve their idea throughout their entire Accelerator journey. It's not process for the sake of process. It's a tool that helps teams bring their ideas to life.

Since we are a global company, pitch ceremonies are usually held via video conference. Teams are given 10 minutes, and only 10 minutes, to pitch their idea—*in their own style*. While the Lean Canvas is the only *required* artifact, each team can bring anything else they believe will help them successfully communicate their idea. Some bring slides, videos, or even prototypes. Some sandwich a brief overview of their Lean Canvas between those, some present only those other items, and some bring only the Lean Canvas. We have experienced successful pitches in each of these, and a few other, styles.

No interruptions or questions are permitted—by anyone—during the pitch. Following the pitch, the team deciding whether the idea will be brought into the Accelerator (we call them the "Angel Team") asks questions of the pitch

team to ensure the idea is well understood, and to ensure the Angel Team has sufficient information to make a good decision.

Among our Angel Team members is our CTO, who is a very active pitch event participant. Think about this for a moment. Anyone with a breakthrough idea can discuss it with our CTO for 20-30 minutes. We often receive very positive feedback from pitch teams as a result. We receive this positive feedback both from teams whose ideas are brought into the Accelerator and those who are not.

## Entry

As soon after the pitch event as possible, an Angel Team member informs each pitch team of the outcome of their pitch via voice or video conference. This is done whether or not the idea was selected for entry. We try to inform each team the day of their pitch event, or within 24 hours if it cannot be done the same day. That ensures that the details of the presentation are still top of mind for both the pitch team and the Angel Team.

Teams whose ideas are selected for Accelerator entry are given time to transition gracefully from their existing position into a full-time position with the Accelerator. Immediately upon selection, we send each founder a copy of Eric Ries' *The Lean Startup* and Ash Maurya's *Running Lean*. This helps prepare them for the Accelerator's Lean approaches, which may differ from the way in which their current mainstream business operates. It also presents them with some good tools and techniques that may help them throughout their journey.

The Accelerator team works with the founders' current mainstream business teams, leadership, and management to create a transition plan and schedule for the founders' Accelerator entry. This ensures a smooth transition at a reasonable pace that won't put the founders, or the businesses they currently support, at risk. Once the new business team is ready to join the Accelerator, each founder is placed into the Incubation Rotation program mentioned earlier in this chapter. Their entry also includes our "Accelerator Bootstrap" training, which prepares them for startup life.

You may have noticed an emphasis on training, especially early on. This is deliberate, though not only for the most obvious reason. Of course, we provide training to ensure that business teams have the best opportunity to succeed while they are incubating in the Accelerator program. In addition, we want to give them skills and create an environment for personal growth during their Accelerator tenure. Even with training and excellent execution, most of these businesses will not be viable. When businesses pause, the skills people develop in the Accelerator will make them more valuable whether they aspire to return to the mainstream business, pitch or join another Accelerator business, or decide to try something outside our company.

Thus far, most people have chosen to stay with the company when their business has paused. The result of this is that people who return to mainstream businesses bring their learning, their Lean approaches, and a startup mentality with them. This is also a deliberate aspect of the program, and another reason we focus on the development of our people constantly. We hope employees returning from the Accelerator will have a positive impact on the company's culture outside the Accelerator. It's still a bit early to tell whether that is the case, though early signs indicate this is happening. We discuss that further in Chapter 8.

## The Incubation Phase

Teams enter our Accelerator in what we refer to as the "Incubation" phase. The program aims to create an environment that is as close to an external startup environment as possible, albeit with a few advantages over stand-alone startups. Accelerator incubations are separately funded, autonomous, and compete on the merits of their business.

We try to emulate the external startup world as closely as possible. Incubating teams operate in what is often referred to as a "sandbox" environment. We refer to the people who form the initial core business team as "founders". As with an external startup, founders lead their businesses and are responsible for operations and decision-making.

Teams incubating in the Accelerator operate independently of mainstream businesses and are unencumbered by many of the mainstream businesses' constraints. For example, they have the freedom to explore their own value propositions, market positioning, messaging, and target customers. This gives them the flexibility to experiment via instruments such as:

- Off (mainstream) brand project and product names that authentically represent character and spirit of the business and its founders and better resonate with target customers

- Project-branded websites, merchandise, business cards...

- New routes to market

- New business models and payment models

- Pivots on any element of the business, including the items above

The Incubation phase consists of two rounds of investment. We refer to these as "Seed 1" and "Seed 2". While analogous to external investment rounds, they are not exactly the same. For example, the level of investment tends to be lower in our Accelerator because the ideas are often much less mature than something even an angel investor would invest in.

During this phase, which we believe should last four to six months but sometimes takes longer, teams are typically very small, usually between one and four people. Often teams that have been actively working on their idea prior to entry, or that have deep knowledge of their customer or market, are able to get through the Incubation phase very quickly. This is especially the case for Seed 1. For example, we have had teams satisfy their Seed 1 criteria in a matter of weeks and transition to Seed 2 during their first review.

---

**Note**   It is always important to be diligent to ensure that customer-problem and/or problem-solution interviews and experiments were not biased by the founders' experience. We have learned it is even more important to look for founder bias when a team moves through the Incubation phase quickly.

---

The primary Accelerator ceremony, the "3P Review" (short for "Pivot, Pause, or Persist Review"), begins at incubation Seed 1 and continues as long as a business is active in the Accelerator. During these founder-led reviews, business teams provide a progress update to the Angel Team. These reviews also provide the business teams with the opportunity to obtain assistance and guidance from the Angel Team. While the Angel Team is always evaluating the performance of the business teams (we cannot help ourselves), we encourage its members to present their comments in the spirit of coaching or mentoring. This was not always the case, and it created confusion and stress for the business teams.

There is one exception. When a business indicates they believe they are ready to move to the next phase of the program (e.g., they are ready to move from Seed 1 to Seed 2 and begin to work on problem-solution fit), they give notice that they are going to request that transition in their upcoming 3P review. We refer to this as a "transition request". During a transition request, the Angel Team focuses their questions on gathering the information required in order to decide whether they believe the business team has satisfied the criteria of the phase they are in, and whether they are ready to move to the next phase. They focus on judging whether the team is ready to make the transition, and whether additional—usually increased—investment in the business makes sense. They actively express much more judgment throughout the review.

Though we will dive more deeply into the Accelerator's ceremonies and criteria in the next chapter, we need to be clear about a few things now. The ceremonies serve the teams, and not vice versa. The Angel Team can decide to pause a business following any review, whether or not a transition request was made. The Angel Team can also recommend that a business is ready for transition, or even suggest a pivot at any time. Pivots almost always arise from the business team's evaluation of the data they have collected and the

experiments they have conducted. Each business team's board of advisors also can, should, and do assess the business' performance and make pivot and transition recommendations to the incubating teams outside the ceremonies.

Each 3P review is a step toward transition to the next investment round. The best performing incubating teams use them as a tool to help them evolve their business. The best performing Angel Team members (we sometimes refer to them individually as "Angels") use the reviews to help the businesses do the same. Everyone involved in the Accelerator program has a single, shared objective: A successful exit for each incubating business.

## Seed 1—Customer-Problem Fit

Our maniacal customer focus begins when teams enter Seed 1. The primary objective of this phase is to confirm that the problem stated in the founders' initial hypothesis actually exists, to identify and confirm the business' target customer segments and early adopters, and to confirm that enough potential customers would be willing to pay for a solution to the problem to make the business viable. That is, the objective is to achieve customer-problem fit.

This phase typically begins with a small team of 1-2 people, usually the people that pitched the idea. Founders will begin assessing their skills requirements and gaps during this phase. During this phase founders also begin building their minimum viable team and advisory board.

When the team believes they have satisfied the Seed 1 criteria and are ready to begin Seed 2, they request Seed 2 funding via a 3P transition request.

## Seed 2—Problem-Solution Fit

The primary objective of Seed 2 is to confirm problem-solution fit. Incubating teams will verify that their proposed solution, which has likely evolved since the pitch ceremony, will delight customers—specifically early adopters. In homage to the movie, "Field of Dreams,"[4] we often refer to this as the "if you build it, will they come" phase.

During Seed 2 teams also continue to build their minimum viable team and advisory board, define their minimum viable product, and develop a plan and budget for Series A.

Once teams believe they have satisfied the Seed 2 criteria, they request Series A funding during a 3P review.

---

[4]"Field of Dreams," Universal Pictures, 1989

# The Startup Phase

In the Startup phase teams begin building their minimum viable product. While teams are coached to maintain their customer focus throughout all program phases, emphasizing customer focus during the transition to the Startup phase is critical in order to avoid the committed bet trap discussed in Chapter 2. Team size and funding typically increase substantially throughout the Startup phase, and it can be easy for teams to lose sight of customers in the day-to-day chaos. The risk of a committed bet at this stage is especially high when the founders have little or no management or leadership experience. Management activity will likely draw an inordinate amount of the attention and time from founders with little management experience. That is why focusing on skill evaluation and addressing gaps is so important during the Incubation phase.

Regular 3P reviews continue throughout the Startup phase. In Series A, businesses continue the evolution of how they measure progress and success. This usually means that measurement schemes shift from things like validated learning to using measures such as the innovation metrics mentioned earlier in this chapter.

## Series A—Solution-Product Fit

In Series A, teams must prove their business can achieve traction with early adopters (solution-product fit). Team size usually increases as they create an MVP and deliver it to their early adopters. They measure traction and begin to evaluate the viability of the business in concrete terms. Teams are expected to attract and retain customers in this round. Furthermore, they are expected to develop references, and early adopters who are excited about the offering and, on their own, tell colleagues, friends, and family.

In further homage to the movie, "Field of Dreams," we often refer to this round as, "now you've built it, have they come?"

Teams that demonstrate sufficient evidence of business model traction request Series B funding.

## Series B—Product-Market Fit

The objective of Series B is to prove that the business model is viable and scalable. Teams continue to focus on traction and must show that market demand for their solution is accelerating. They must also build evidence not only that their solution can scale, but also that their business fundamentals will scale, focusing on things like their customer acquisition cost (CAC) and customer lifetime value (LTV). Customer focus remains paramount as teams confirm they are still building things that people actually want, and validate traction via measures such as growth rate and retention.

Teams begin looking for a "buyer" of their business in Series B, and eventually seek a letter of intent (LOI) to acquire from the mainstream product organization.

When the business is proven to be viable and an acquirer has been identified, it enters Series C.

## Series C—Exit

Series C is focused on preparing to move the business into the acquiring organization. We modeled our acquisition framework after the program our company uses for acquiring external businesses. It involves some due diligence and, usually, a number of specific criteria that the acquiring organization insists must be satisfied prior to the close of the acquisition. These criteria might include things like addressing technical debt, for example.

Though the procedures are modeled after our external acquisition process, Accelerator acquisitions should be much simpler. Acquiring businesses are able to watch Accelerator businesses evolve from their inception, and can participate in 3P reviews, etc., for businesses that interest them. This provides the mainstream organization with much deeper knowledge of the business, and the team, than might be the case for external acquisitions. In addition, Accelerator teams have access to all of the mainstream business' systems, tools, and processes. That enables incubating businesses to begin preparing for a smooth acquisition much earlier. Furthermore, since the incubating team members are already employees of the company, transition logistics should be much simpler.

## Expedited Exit

It should be noted that the product organization may signal intent to acquire a business at any time, during any round prior to Series C. There are a number of reasons this might happen. For example, it may be determined that the incubating solution would be a great feature or near adjacency, or that it might benefit from the scale, skills, or customers a mature business unit has access to sooner than would normally be the case. It could also be in response to a change in the market or competitive landscape, which creates a need to scale the business more rapidly. Response to requests of this nature can vary, though it usually involves an expedited trip through the remaining phases to ensure the business is ready to exit.

Care must be taken to ensure a business exiting early or quickly is not damaged by the acquiring organization, falling victim to one or more of the impediments discussed in Chapter 1. This may mean creating a sandbox-like environment for the business within the acquiring organization. Great leadership, both within the incubating business and the acquiring organization, is critical for the success of early exits.

# Defining Success

## Beyond Product Exits

During a panel discussion of corporate accelerators at the SXSW 2018 conference I (George) was asked how we define the success of this program. I believe the first part of my answer—successful exits of new businesses to the mainstream product organization—was not much of a surprise to the attendees. It is essentially how most programs of this nature gauge their impact. That is important to us, though we hope to achieve much more through our program. Thus, the remainder of my response appeared to generate more interest.

Successful outcomes of our Accelerator program include:

- Successful exits of business as new products, product lines, or business units

- Creation of product line extensions or near adjacencies (sometimes what initially looks like a breakthrough idea is actually one of these)

- Creation of technologies and shareable components that can be embedded in other products

- Creation and testing of new business models and delivery methods

- Efficiently pausing businesses that are not viable or that solve a problem nobody has

- Building organic innovation and leadership skills that people can bring to a new Accelerator venture or a mature line of business

- Driving Lean, Agile, and organic innovation culture companywide

- Visibly demonstrating our commitment to organic innovation, and our innovation capabilities, to current and prospective customers

Certainly, positioning our company for future growth via organic innovation is the reason we started this program. However, we believe that means more than just creating new products and services in our Accelerator alone. We believe that means driving a culture of innovation throughout the entire company, and ensuring other organizations are well equipped to take advantage of the innovative ideas that happen within. After all, the Accelerator team is tiny compared to the mainstream organization, and most of the innovative ideas will be born outside its constructs. Great ideas come from everywhere. We want everyone to be in a position to give those ideas the best opportunity to succeed.

We are deliberate about our focus on attracting, developing, and retaining our talented people. Helping our founders to grow not only increases their business' chance of success, it increases their chances to succeed personally no matter where their Accelerator journey ends. We consider their growth our duty.

## Lack of Commitment (and That's a Good Thing)

There are other, perhaps less than obvious, ways in which the Accelerator program drives success. We believe one of those requires discussion at this point.

In Chapter 2 we introduced the concept of the committed bet investment model, which is commonly encountered in established organizations. As was mentioned, committed bets often end in failure, usually due to insufficient customer focus and over-commitment to a solution early on. However, not all committed bets fail. In some cases, committed bet teams are able to make adjustments to address customer needs, and they deliver a successful product. In our experience, that often means an extended timeline and additional technical debt. Though even if we assume that both the committed bet and the Accelerator model deliver the same product, with the same product-market fit at the same time, the committed bet model is much less efficient. Figure 3-6 demonstrates the minimum amount of waste of a committed bet in both cases.

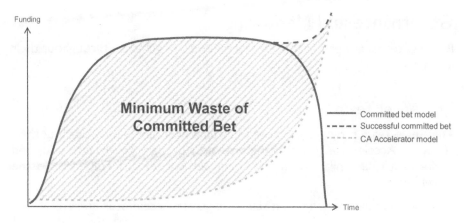

**Figure 3-6.** The CA Accelerator approach versus a committed bet

In the Accelerator, we take the funding that would be wasted (depicted in the shaded area in Figure 3-6) and we reinvest it in other innovative ideas. We would argue further that the timeline for a committed bet that is successful can sometimes be longer than illustrated. It can more closely resemble the timeline depicted in Figure 3-7, thus generating even more waste.

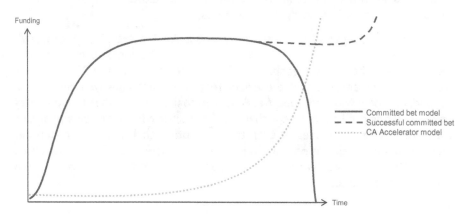

**Figure 3-7.** Successful committed bet with extended timeline

# Governance and Mentoring

Business teams are provided with several levels of guidance throughout their journey.

## The Angel Team

The Angel Team provides guidance to incubating businesses throughout their life in the Accelerator. It is also the program's primary governance body and performs a role similar to an investment advisory board. For example, the Angel Team:

- Evaluates pitches and selects ideas for Accelerator entry

- Conducts regular 3P reviews

- Approves budget, objectives, and timelines at each investment round

- Ensures teams remain customer-focused

The Angel Team is comprised of a diverse group of individuals with a broad range of experience in product development and delivery, strategy, venture capital, and entrepreneurial and/or intrapreneurial experience. Several were founders and/or early employees of startups.

Members of the Angel Team also represent a diverse set of the company's organizations and key stakeholders (e.g., lines of business; the Customer Success Team; the CTO organization; Corporate Strategy and Development; Marketing). This ensures that the Angel Team's decisions always benefit from a broad, companywide perspective. An additional benefit is that this diversity makes a strong public statement that the Accelerator is an inclusive program. It also reduces the chances of even the perception that a specific group has been excluded. A reputation that an innovation program is exclusive or elitist can be a fast path to its demise, so the importance of managing that perception cannot be overstated.

## The Investment Committee

Though they are informed of the state of all activity in the Accelerator, the Investment Committee becomes active when businesses reach Series B. In our case, the Investment Committee consists of the C-Level members of our executive team.

Increased engagement with the Investment Committee is necessary at Series B because the investments are large enough to warrant the attention and governance of a senior leadership team. In addition, the incubating business team will need assistance from the organizations these senior leaders represent.

For example, the product organization must prepare to receive/acquire the new offering, the Sales team must prepare to sell their product, the Marketing team must be ready to market it, and so on.

## Advisory Boards

Just like an external startup, the business leaders and their teams will benefit from advice and mentoring from people outside their team. As soon as a business enters the Accelerator, we help them to build their advisory boards. As with other boards of advisors, these boards are comprised of a diverse collection of individuals with a broad range of experience in the domain being addressed by the business, and elsewhere.

Though we often help identify candidates, we do not dictate whom teams select as members of their advisory boards. Even in this respect, teams act as independent startups. Though advisors are typically employees of our company—there are thousands of us to choose from—they are not limited to employees of our company. As you might expect, advisors help coach the founders and their teams on a broad range of topics ranging from data science, to architecture, to organizational behavior and development.

Like boards of external startups, each advisory board has a different "personality" and composition. That is the way it should be. These boards provide guidance to the incubating teams from entry to exit, and their composition can change throughout the journey.

## Bench Advisors

In the early stages of incubation, business teams will require the advice of subject matter experts for a wide range of topics such as marketing, procurement, talent acquisition, legal advice, and pricing. Teams that achieve product-market fit will eventually need full-time employees for some, or all, of these functions. However, early on their needs do not justify full-time employees with these skills, and their budgets likely cannot support them. For external startups obtaining this type of expertise can be difficult, expensive, or even cost prohibitive.

Fortunately, established enterprises usually have employees with all of these skills. Our Accelerator has created a matrix of advisors whom incubating teams can leverage on an as-needed basis, until such time as they can justify bringing in their own full-time employees. These advisors work in other areas of the company and provide ad hoc advice to the business teams as they require it.

Figure 3-8 provides an illustrative example of how it all fits together. Now, let us take a closer look at this, and all other aspects of the Accelerator program and its operation.

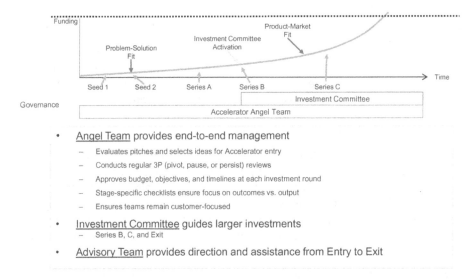

- Angel Team provides end-to-end management
  - Evaluates pitches and selects ideas for Accelerator entry
  - Conducts regular 3P (pivot, pause, or persist) reviews
  - Approves budget, objectives, and timelines at each investment round
  - Stage-specific checklists ensure focus on outcomes vs. output
  - Ensures teams remain customer-focused

- Investment Committee guides larger investments
  - Series B, C, and Exit

- Advisory Team provides direction and assistance from Entry to Exit

**Figure 3-8.** Mentoring and governance

# Inside the Accelerator

## How We Drive Innovation by Nurturing Ingenuity

---

*"I will not follow where the path may lead, but I will go where there is no path, and I will leave a trail."*

—Muriel Strode, *Wind-Wafted Wild Flowers* (1903)

## Proceed with Caution!

In order to illustrate the focus of each aspect of our program, and to help you better understand what incubating business teams prioritize in each stage, we share many of our artifacts and Kanbans in this chapter. We want to be clear that *these artifacts and Kanbans are meant to serve as guideposts, not as bludgeons*. We do not want the cure for innovation stall in established organizations to be worse than the disease. These tools, and the program itself, should be a resource for the incubating business teams and *not* a tax.

© CA 2019
G. Watt and H. Abrams, *Lean Entrepreneurship*,
https://doi.org/10.1007/978-1-4842-3942-1_4

---

■ **Note**　We want to be clear that these artifacts and Kanbans are meant to serve as guideposts, not as bludgeons.

---

# Process Hypnosis

We have seen many cases where incubating teams, both inside and outside our program, have become so mesmerized by tools that their objective became the tools themselves. They lost focus on their innovative idea. Both incubating business teams and leaders, and program teams and leaders, can fall victim to this. When it is the former, business teams can lose focus on their idea, sometimes even unconsciously pivoting away from their original concept. When it is the latter, the program team can create so much tax on the incubating teams that they create an environment that is not much different from the anti-patterns described in Chapter 1, where heavy and unnecessary processes crushed innovative ideas. Program teams can also lose sight of the fact that they, and their program, *only* exist to help give the businesses the best possible chance to succeed.

Whether the program team, the innovators, or others close to an incubation fall victim to this "process hypnosis" or "tool hypnosis," the result is the same. The impacted business' velocity is reduced, and their probability of success decreases. Teams must be careful to figure out when and where these tools are valuable, and where and when they are pageantry. Program teams must help them and keep an open mind. We tell teams that we want to always be available, but never in their way, and if we ever become a tax and not a resource they should tell us immediately.

# Bad Muscle Memory

We realize we are spending a lot of time on this, but it happens a lot and it can have a very negative impact on your program or incubation. In cases where Founders had been working in long-established businesses for a long time, it almost always happens. While preparing for events such as quarterly business reviews in the mature business—where it is often a legitimate requirement— they become so accustomed to having to complete every form, every slide, every box in every checklist, that they cannot break the habit.

For example, when we started our program, every artifact that might ever be used at any stage of a business' Accelerator journey was contained in a single electronic document we called, "the Accelerator Flipbook". Borrowing from the world of management consulting, we had named this the Flipbook because the intent was that teams could rapidly flip through the artifacts and choose only the ones most useful to them. We had even placed an icon at the top right of each page that shaded the phase in our Accelerator Rocket Ship (see Figure 3-1) where we thought the artifact would be most useful.

We recall some early 3P reviews where we learned that Founders—in Seed 1—had completed every page in the Flipbook. Ouch! They had completed dozens of artifacts because that is what would have been expected of them in the organization they came from. Many were very creative works of fiction, and the exercise took an enormous amount of time away from the important work of advancing their idea. We refer to that type of response as "bad muscle memory". It is bad only in the sense that it does not serve them well in this new context, and it is very hard to break these habits.

As soon as a business team enters our Accelerator we tell them that the intent of our artifacts is to help them achieve their objectives. *The objective is not completion of the artifact.* We explain that these are collections of resources that have helped others to achieve what they are trying to achieve. We also tell them that, if they know of other tools that will be more effective in achieving that objective (e.g., running their experiment, communicating their outcome or status…) they should use those. We add those new tools to our collection if they are effective. It's how we build these flipbooks.

Even though we explain this up front, it does not always stick. It requires diligent reinforcement, and a lot more of it than you might think. There are even cases where we think we have resolved this issue with a team and that team will backslide as a critical event approaches. We have seen fear-culture muscle memory so badly entrenched that someone actually had colored the x's on a checklist slide green instead of red—so we would not notice unsuccessful experiments or incomplete items. Think about that for a moment.

# Get the Big Picture

Addressing this requires constant reinforcement. As with driving a vehicle, a focus that is too narrow or short can result in disaster. We created the program overview shown in Figure 4-1 to help the teams see the bigger picture. This "one-pager" is not intended to show all of the program's details. It is intended to help people understand the spirit of the program. To help founders and business teams abstract themselves from the many detailed resources at their disposal and remember the objective they are trying to achieve at any given point. Some founders even use it very effectively during their 3P reviews to help set the Angel Team and other participants' expectations properly at the beginning of their review.

## Accelerator Program At a Glance

Incubation * Startup

| Seed 1 | Seed 2 | Series A | Series B | Series C |
|---|---|---|---|---|
| Early Adopter-Problem Fit | Problem-Solution Fit | Solution-Product Fit | Product-Market Fit | Exit |
| **Objective:** Validate that problem is worth solving for the identified target market, via early adopters. | **Objective:** Validate solution's likelihood to delight early adopters. | **Objective:** Prove ability to achieve traction with early adopters. | **Objective:** Prove business model is viable and scalable. | **Objectives:** Execute on business case. Align to acquirer requirements. |
| **Key Question to Answer:** Is this problem worth solving? | **Key Question to Answer:** If we build this, will early adopters come (with money?) | **Key Question to Answer:** Now that we've built it, did the early adopters come, & do we continue to attract new customers? | **Key Question to Answer:** Has our business scaled with the additional investment? | **Key Question to Answer:** Did we meet our acquisition commitments? |
| **Outcome:** Sufficient evidence of problem-early adopter pair. | **Outcomes:** Sufficient evidence that the problem-solution approach satisfies early adopters. Clearly defined and scoped MVP. Business model* baseline. | **Outcome:** Sufficient evidence of business model* traction. | **Outcomes:** Market demand for the solution is accelerating. Clear marketing & sales strategy. Confirmed intent to acquire. | **Outcomes:** Acquisition. Accelerator exit. |
| **Output:**<br>• Marketing: Segmentation / Early Adopter Analysis; Lean Persona(s); Rough Market Sizing.<br>• Traction: Animal You're Hunting.<br>• Seed 2 Plan. | **Output:**<br>• Marketing: Positioning Statement; Company Narrative/Pitch; Validated thinking on how you will reach early adopters; Competitive Landscape; Pricing Model.<br>• Traction: One-page traction model with assumptions outlined.<br>• Validated MVP Definition.<br>• Series A Plan.<br><br>*May include free/non-monetary models. | **Output:**<br>• Marketing: Website reveal; Go-to-Market Plan; Key Engine of Growth identified; Early/evangelist purchase of solution.<br>• MVP Released.<br>• Sean Ellis Test Baseline.<br>• Traction: Traction Model shows that you've met your first goal.<br>• Initial understanding of CAC, LTV, and COGs.<br>• Referenceable customers.<br>• Series B Plan.<br><br>*May include free/non-monetary models. | **Output:**<br>• Marketing: Evidence that GTM strategy is effective & will scale.<br>• Sean Ellis Test Passed.<br>• Traction: Target Weekly Growth Rate & Retention Achieved. Traction model shows you've met your goals and can scale usage. Firm understanding of CAC, LTV, and COGs.<br>• Acquisition: Pitch and Executive Summary completed; Input provided to Bus. Case & IC Deck. Contingent acquisition commitment.<br>• Series C Plan. | **Output:**<br>• Traction: Traction model shows you've achieved growth and scale targets defined in Series B.<br>• Acquisition: Technical Due Diligence completed. Input provided for Business Due Diligence.<br>• Documented final decision from BU for business to exit the Accelerator. |

**Figure 4-1.** Accelerator high-level objectives at a glance (Illustrative)

Though these examples have focused on business teams becoming hypnotized by the tools and artifacts, it can happen to anyone. Program teams, Angel Teams, and sponsors are not immune. So please take care not to create an artifact factory to the detriment of your incubator. Not all tools work in every scenario, and the tools must serve the businesses. In addition, these tools and program structures often require fine-tuning and adjustment to become well-suited to changes in culture differences in objectives.

---

■ **Note**   Take care not to create an artifact factory to the detriment of your incubator.

---

Your business or your program will need to take your own culture, industry, and business conditions into account. Like our program, yours will also need to evolve. Regardless of your program structure or culture, we believe you should *take warning if you find that an incubating business team:*

1. Uses every artifact in your flipbook, especially early in their life

2. Uses artifacts for a purpose they were not designed for

   - This can work, but care should be taken to ensure the artifacts are not misleading

3. Never comes up with their own way to present something

   - Even if they do present something incorrectly in their own style, at least they have not stopped thinking for themselves

These *could* be symptoms that the team has fallen victim to process hypnosis. As mentioned, others in your program such as program teams and Angel Team members are also susceptible to this kind of hypnosis. The impact of that can be even more damaging. If you notice an Accelerator Team member, angel, or sponsor speaks mostly about the artifacts or ceremonies when they describe your program, it may be a symptom they have become process or tool myopic.

We once attended a meeting where someone who was describing their incubation program concept uttered the phrase "Lean Canvas" so many times others began calling it "the Lean Canvas program". This person had become Lean Canvas myopic and had lost sight of their program's true objective. He had become hypnotized by the completion of that one artifact and had lost focus on nurturing teams and their new business ideas. Of course, completing the canvas was not their true objective, but that was how they were executing. His repeated use of the phrase was so distracting that those less familiar with his program, or Lean startup, were having trouble understanding what he was actually trying to accomplish.

# What About Cohorts?

Some successful Accelerators run their program in cohorts. They bring the maximum number of businesses the program can handle together for a pre-defined period of time and run them through the same program elements together. This approach can drive several advantages such as the efficiencies it can create around program administration and delivery of training. In this context, we are often asked whether we have adopted a cohort approach. While cohorts may work for you, we have decided not to adopt a cohort approach for the following reasons:

- Businesses enter our Accelerator at a much earlier stage than they typically would enter the Accelerators described above, and they typically stay for a longer time.

- All of the incubating businesses would require the same resources at the same time, which would create high peaks in demand for support resources and mentoring, resulting in a strain on our Accelerator Team and others who support incubating businesses (e.g., Legal Team, Marketing, Procurement...).

- It could create a periodically crushing workload for the Angel Team, since businesses would be at key inflection points at or near the same time (e.g., requesting transitions, requiring mentoring...).

- Spreading out new business entries enables newer businesses to learn from the more experienced teams that entered before them.

- Great ideas can happen at any time, and we want to bring them in when we find them—before founders lose their passion, are assigned to something else, or leave our company to pursue their creative passion elsewhere.

- Creating large cohorts can result in a budget crisis: Businesses require more funding as they mature (i.e., move through each funding round); they would all mature at the same time, which could create a condition where a potentially successful business would have to be shuttered or have its velocity intentionally reduced due to a funding crunch.

- Running cohorts increases the chances that two or more businesses may pause at around the same time, which can lengthen the employee placement queue and make finding a new role for employees of the paused businesses more challenging or stressful.

While we do not intentionally create cohorts, we do try to have a portfolio of businesses that are at different stages of maturity and that is distributed across all of the funding rounds. To date we have found this provides us with the ability to learn, delivers a balanced workload to the Accelerator Team that results in better service to the incubating businesses, and provides better financial balance.

With those caveats in mind, let's take a look at what happens behind the scenes in our Accelerator.

# Inside the Accelerator

Now that you have a basic understanding of the Accelerator framework and objectives it is time to explore the program in greater detail. To this point in the book we have discussed *why* we created the Accelerator, and *what* the Accelerator is. Throughout the remainder of this chapter we discuss *how* it works and provide you with the information you will need in order to create a similar program of your own.

We have found that the best way explain how the Accelerator works is to discuss its elements in the order an incubating business will encounter them. Thus, what follows is a detailed discussion of each phase of the Accelerator program following the flow of the Accelerator framework presented in Chapter 3 (see Figure 3-5).

*There is an important reason for this that goes beyond using a familiar framework as a guiding structure.* If you are creating an incubation program you may not have any incubating businesses and will need to begin by selecting them. If you do have incubating businesses they will most likely be in one of the earlier stages, possibly all in what we call Seed 1 or Seed 2. Therefore, you will need to have the elements we discuss earliest in this chapter—such as those related to Innovator Selection and Incubation Phase activities—functioning early in the life of the program. You probably will not require later incubation lifecycle elements such as those related to Series B or Series C until many months later, perhaps even a year or more later. Thus, there is no urgent need to have all of the finer details sorted out for those late stages early in your program's life.

We used this approach when we created our program. We defined the overall program at the outset, and focused on getting the details right for the earlier stages our businesses were in. As the program evolved we tried to stay one phase ahead of the incubating businesses to minimize the impact of program creation activities on them. This approach was very successful and enabled us to learn fast while making changes to an active program.

We begin our look under the covers of the Accelerator with a discussion of the idea submission process and some of the program ceremonies and structure required for their execution. We also discuss some of the pitfalls to avoid, and techniques for effective execution. We carry that through the Incubation and Startup phases, all the way to the successful exit, or pause, of a business. So let's begin by looking at how we capture ideas.

# Idea Submission

It is obvious that you will not be very successful with your Accelerator program if people with ideas cannot—or will not—bring those ideas to you. In the research we discussed in Chapter 1 we mentioned that one key impediment to the success of innovative ideas is the amount of effort required in order to simply propose them. We believe that this needs to be as near zero effort as possible. We decided that, even if the way in which ideas are initially articulated is less than perfect when we receive them, that is much better than not receiving them at all.

To propose an idea for our Accelerator, innovative employees from any location, in any job position, need only post their idea—in the form of a completed Lean Canvas—to our Accelerator site. Our internal resource site is named accelerator.ca.com, so it is easy to find.

## Nurturing Ingenuity

As you read the remainder of this chapter, you will notice the theme of personal development and individual growth is always present. That is deliberate. Though we created this program to help drive innovation and create new businesses that position our company for future growth, we believe that the personal development aspects of our Accelerator are at least as important as that primary objective. There are many reasons for this, and two are worth mentioning at this point.

First, many of the people proposing these ideas will not possess all of the skills that will be required in order for them to succeed as a founder. They may never have worked in a startup or a startup-like environment, and their new role may be quite different from their current role in the mainstream organization. Second, if we are honest in our expectations we will realize that more of these startups will pause than will exit, no matter how well they execute. When that happens, many people will move back into mainstream businesses. They will bring their training and Lean approaches and culture with them. We hope this will enrich the mainstream businesses and improve each Accelerator alumnus' own performance.

We begin supporting employee development even before people have pitched. We offer aspiring intrapreneurs a wide variety of resources to help them develop and communicate—and even execute on—their idea before they share it with us.

To make things as frictionless as possible, our Accelerator site has:

1. One-click idea submission

2. Resources to help people understand how to complete their material, including:

   a. Templates

   b. Step-by-step instructions

   c. Video tutorials

   d. Examples

3. Access to more detailed Lean startup material for those interested

4. A link to *all* of the material we provide to our incubating teams

*The only action that is required in order to bring an idea to our program is to click on the "Submit Your Idea" button and upload the idea (item 1).*

The previously-mentioned resource material is available to everyone in our company. We hope they can leverage it not only in the context of our program, but also within their own organizations. Making the material available and transparent has the added benefit that we receive feedback not only from people within our program, but from a much broader group of people with widely varied experience and missions. As mentioned earlier, a mantra of the Accelerator Team is "inspect and adapt". This broad feedback helps immensely.

There is one exception to our bias toward transparency. Ideas that are submitted to the Accelerator site are accessible only to the person who submitted the idea and the Accelerator Team. We have found that some innovators can be very protective of their ideas, and do not want to risk someone else taking credit for them or "stealing" them. In addition, sometimes our most creative people are not confident in the merit of their idea. Those people are often concerned others will think their idea is foolish, and therefore they must be a fool. Groundbreaking ideas often sound "crazy" when they are first introduced, and we want to receive those most of all. While making even the most early-stage ideas broadly available for comment and collaboration can be beneficial we have chosen to do that via other means. This approach ensures people of all personality types and skill levels will feel comfortable sharing their ideas with us.

The Accelerator application process is extremely simple:

1. Deposit a Lean Canvas on the Accelerator site

2. Pitch your idea in 10 minutes

3. Enter the Accelerator (if your pitch was successful, of course)

That's it.

There are already great resources to help you understand how to complete a Lean Canvas, such as Lean Canvas creator Ash Maurya's 20-minute YouTube video tutorial[1], and his book, *Running Lean,* so let's begin with Step 2.

# Innovator Selection

Without innovative people and their great ideas there is no Accelerator. Thus, the first phase of our program focuses on finding them. Though there is a lot of activity during this phase, we do our best to insulate aspiring intrapreneurs from all of it. In fact, much of this activity is related to ensuring intrapreneurs have a great, simple experience. It begins with intrapreneurs pitching their ideas to the Angel Team.

## Preparing for the Pitch

Though the pitch event is the first Accelerator ceremony participants will encounter, it is not their first encounter with the Accelerator Team. Once an idea has been posted to the Accelerator site, someone from the Accelerator Team will review it and contact the person or team that submitted it. Though the purpose of the initial contact is to schedule the pitch, the Accelerator Team member will also offer some informal coaching to help the innovator strengthen communication of their idea and, hopefully, increase the probability their idea will be accepted; or at least that it will be well understood by the Angel Team.

Though not always required, we also offer coaching on the pitch itself to those who are interested. That coaching is provided by Accelerator Team personnel with experience working in startup marketing and design and focuses on telling a compelling story. This, fairly new, offering is optional and, in the spirit of our discussion regarding it taking a village to build an accelerator, was proposed by the marketing and user experience people who volunteered to help our budding intrapreneurs.

---

[1]"Capture Your Business Model In 20 Minutes," Ash Maurya, https://youtu.be/ 7o8uYdUaFR4

When we first launched the Accelerator, the entire program was an experiment and one person was handling all of the outreach personally. When we received a new idea, he would call the person who submitted it and offer assistance with their canvases. He would explain to each aspiring intrapreneur that, if they were interested, we could offer them some suggestions regarding their canvas which—based on our experience with other pitches—might improve their chances of success. We cannot recall a single instance where someone did not want to have that conversation.

During this initial contact our comments were, and still are, focused on communication and capture of their idea. We do not attempt to change their solution. Though, following our conversations sometimes founders do change things on their own accord. We discovered that many, perhaps most, of the canvases we receive contain very similar errors.

## MOST COMMON LEAN CANVAS PROBLEMS

The most common Lean Canvas problems we see are:

1. The problem statement does not describe a problem.

2. The problem statement is "my solution does not exist" (or is not available…), which may or may not be a problem.

3. The problem statement is exactly the same as the solution statement, just worded differently.

4. Existing alternatives are not enumerated, including doing nothing, existing workarounds, and competition.

   - The Angel Team often finds competing solutions via a simple Internet search as we gather for a pitch. If a founder is not aware of those, the Angels may have some doubt regarding how well thought out the idea is. Expect questions on that following a pitch.

5. The customer referenced on the canvas does not actually have the problem presented in the problem section.

6. The customer is not well defined, is too broad, or lists all of the mature business' existing customer classifications or segments (often indicating a "cut-and-paste" approach to customers).

7. There is no early adopter hypothesis, or it is too broad.

8. The unique value proposition is not described in terms of the value the stated customer receives if the stated problem is solved using the proposed solution.

9. The stated unfair advantage can be easily bought or copied by others, so it is not an unfair advantage.

10. The stated unfair advantage is "we are <your company name here>".

- Just because an incubation program's parent company is large and established, perhaps even respected, does not mean an incubating business will have an unfair advantage over others in their space. While that pedigree could be an advantage, it might also be a liability.

---

**Honorable Mention**   Format changes including box sizes, extremely tiny font, adding pages…

---

**Note**   The "honorable mention" might not seem like a big deal, but it can have a more profound impact than you might imagine. Changing the format of the Lean Canvas can actually dramatically reduce its value. For example, the solution box is intentionally small because that is the aspect of the idea that most innovators have the best grasp. The size of that box forces innovators to focus on other aspects of the business they may have spent less time thinking about. In addition, while we might ignore a minor font change, there have been cases where teams have, essentially submitted a several page canvas through the use of "micro-fonts". As a result, the founders did not get to the heart of their idea, and it was not effectively communicated. Condensing an idea into a 10-minute pitch can require a lot of thought and effort, and it is well worth it. As Baltasar Gracián stated, "Lo bueno, si breve, dos veces Bueno"[2] (good things, when brief, are twice as good).

---

## It's Not Personal (But It Should Be)

Since, initially, this coaching was all delivered via audio or videoconference, the spirit and intent of the feedback was properly understood by the innovators. As a result, these were usually very positive and productive calls. Pitch teams responded very well to them, and the feedback we received from them was normally very favorable. The pitch teams reported that the feedback was helpful.

When we officially launched the program, we did not feel personal calls to every person submitting an idea would scale. We decided to move to email responses and to increase the number of people who would respond to submissions. That had the unintentional effect of making the contact much less personal. The initial context of an offer of assistance was often lost, and teams sometimes felt the program team was criticizing their idea. It was as if we were red-lining it like a professor grading a term paper. While this did not appear to have an

---

[2]Baltasar Gracián: Oráculo manual y arte de prudencia, Huesca 1647, #105

immediate impact on our pipeline, we were confident it eventually would. What's more, this did not accurately reflect the intended personality of our program.

While voice contact is always more personal, it may not always be possible due to time zone differences and request volumes. Furthermore, we do believe electronic communication can be effective, though it must be carefully worded. We have seen it work. This is your customer's first contact with your program. You want to ensure that they understand the program exists to help them move their idea forward. Most importantly, you do not want them to abandon their ideas.

Though the personality of your initial response will need to be compatible with your culture and norms, we believe a few key elements must always be present. Whether written or verbal, a good first response should:

1. Thank the innovator(s) for their submission, explain that you genuinely appreciate their bringing the idea to you and their effort, and explain why their idea and effort is important and valued (only if you mean it)

2. Explain the pitch event logistics

3. Provide the pitch date and time, tentative date and time, or options

4. Direct them to any resources that might help them to prepare for the pitch

5. Offer to provide the innovator(s) with feedback that might help ensure their idea is understood by those evaluating the pitch, and might increase their chances of success, but do not provide that feedback in the initial response if it is written

6. Convey a spirit of service to the innovator in its tone; be personal and sincere

7. Does not have the tone of a corporate process (or the word "process" in it—the word itself can either infuriate people or put them to sleep)

8. Be as brief as possible, likely much briefer than this description

---

**Note**  There are cases where you can break guideline number 5. These should be obvious, and are usually related to an incomplete submission. For example, if someone did not attach a Lean Canvas or did not complete one or more of the boxes you could let them know that right away.

---

## The Pitch Event

During a pitch event, one or more aspiring intrapreneurs shares their idea with the Angel Team. This is one of the most important aspects of the program. Pitch events are an intrapreneur's first exposure to the program, and to the Angel Team, so it is important that they are well run and create a good first impression.

### Ensuring a Quorum

Though every member of the Angel Team does our best to participate in all Accelerator ceremonies and events, we know there will be times when one or more of us is unable to join. In order to ensure we have sufficient diversity to make any required decisions we have established very simple quorum rules. For example, in addition to a minimum number of Angels we ensure that people with both technical and business backgrounds, people from inside and outside the CTO organization, a member of the product organization, and someone from the Accelerator program/operations are present.

Since we do not know the composition of your Angel Team, we cannot be prescriptive regarding what your quorum should be. Like we did, you simply need to discuss the composition of your team, the level and types of diversity you want to ensure is always present in these ceremonies, and whom in your team can represent each perspective. You should also think about whether it is okay for a single person to represent more than one of those groups when determining whether a quorum exists. We find that having a minimum number of Angels in our quorum rules usually takes care of that concern.

Our quorum rules apply primarily to pitch events and 3P reviews. Ensuring a quorum will be present is especially important for 3P transition requests, given the stakes.

To increase the probability that we will always have a quorum, we schedule pitch events twice monthly, up to a year in advance. We do this because scheduling the Angel Team on short notice can be extremely difficult, whereas scheduling their time far in advance is simple.

### Pitch Event Logistics

The remainder of the pitch event logistics are straightforward:

1. Pitch events are scheduled twice monthly, up to a year in advance.

2. Angels indicate whether they can participate by accepting, tentatively accepting, or declining each calendar invitation as the event approaches.

3. Angels update their calendar status if their plans change.

4. A week prior to the event a program team member verifies whether there are pitch teams who are ready to pitch, and whether a quorum will be present.

5. If there are pitches, and there will be a quorum, the program team updates the calendar entry for that event with a detailed agenda and schedules a follow-up conversation with each pitch team and an Angel as soon after their pitch as possible.

6. If no pitches are queued a week prior to the event, it is cancelled.

7. If there are pitches, but a quorum is not possible, the event is either rescheduled or the pitches are moved to the following pitch event.

8. If there is a large backlog of pitch requests, the program team may schedule additional events.

9. The program team facilitates each pitch event, ensures the agenda is sound, and ensures the smooth operation of the videoconference.

10. Individuals or teams who pitch are informed of the outcome of their pitch as soon after the pitch event as possible.

## A Quality Videoconference System Matters

Since both our Angel Team and our incubating businesses are in multiple locations, we have found it critical to have a high-quality videoconferencing system. This is imperative for high-stakes conversations such as those that occur during 3P reviews and pitch events, where body language and facial expression matter a lot. Pitch teams need to feel welcome, and voice-only is often not sufficient. Incubating teams need to know that—even when the Angel Team is asking tough questions—the Angels are doing so because they want them to succeed. And facilitators need to watch everyone, even those who are not speaking.

Both audio and video quality must be good. The system must be intuitive, easy to use, stable, and reliable.

In the early days of our Accelerator we used a telepresence system that delivered an amazing experience. It was almost as if everyone was in the same room. Body language was clearly visible, and facilitators could see everyone, all the time. During pitch events, it was as if the team pitching was in the CTO's office. The experience was fantastic, and the spirit of our program was properly experienced by participants in every interaction.

Unfortunately, that technology was not available to everyone as our program grew so we moved to a popular videoconference application. The system did not provide much control over how video from individuals or shared screens and applications were displayed. It showed only a few of the participants at one time, it gave little control over which of people were displayed (making facilitation challenging), and it displayed very small thumbnails of participants who were not the (one) active speaker. This dramatically changed the personality of the meetings. It made them colder and less personal, and it made facilitation more challenging and time-consuming. Furthermore, the system became unreliable over time. One or more participants always had difficulty connecting, experienced performance issues, or had their audio or video disconnected in the midst of a meeting. This was exceptionally disruptive when the facilitator or the presenter was impacted.

Fortunately, we found another system that addressed those issues. It is reliable, easy to connect to, has much better audio and video quality, enables much better control over the video display, and even automatically sorts video participants from audio-only participants. Meetings are much more personal, and facilitation is far simpler and less time consuming. Delivering a high-quality videoconferencing experience is a small detail that is worthy of a high priority.

## 10 Minute Pitches

As described in Chapter 3, the pitch event is simple. People are given 10 uninterrupted minutes to describe their idea to the Angel Team. The Angel Team then asks questions to ensure they understand the idea.

Starting the ceremony with uninterrupted time for the pitch keeps the Angel Team and other observers from taking the pitch off topic, enables teams to stay organized, and ensures they have sufficient time to make their key points. This is one of the main reasons 10 minutes is sufficient, and it enables us to stay on time. Having this guaranteed time segment also enables pitch teams to practice, polish, and refine their pitch.

*Active facilitation can be paramount to the success of these events,* and all other ceremonies. The facilitator should halt interruptions and keep pitch teams on time, though in most cases we find the pitch teams end exactly on, or slightly ahead of, time. If time runs out, we ask the pitch team to complete their final thought and we move to the question period.

We display an Agile timer in the host window of the videoconference (see Figure 4-2), since it is always visible there. We find a circular timer more effective than a digital timer, likely because people do not have to read the digits to understand how much time remains. Regardless of the presenter's level of experience, we have found that once the time wedge gets small, they instinctively wrap up.

**Figure 4-2.** We use a timer that provides simple visual cues and keeps teams focused

It is also important for the facilitator to guide the Angel Team question period. This is especially important when the Angel Team is new, or there are new Angel Team members. The facilitator should direct the Angel Team to ask questions that will help ensure they understand the idea that was pitched. This often means coaching the Angels away from long preambles to their questions or advocating for an idea they like (we refer to that as "cheerleading") during the question period. Though Angels should be coached in advance of the meeting, there are always opportunities for facilitators to put their skills into practice during these events.

## Pitch Event Agenda

A typical pitch event usually includes 1-4 pitches and ranges from 30-120 minutes in duration. Thirty minutes are allocated to each pitch. This includes 10 minutes for the pitch, and up to 20 for Angel Team questions and dialogue. We have included a sample agenda that is based on an 1:00 PM start time:

Sample Pitch Event Agenda (scheduled to begin at 1:00 PM)

- 1:05 – 1:35: Amazing First Pitch

- 1:40 – 2:10: Outstanding Second Pitch

- 2:10 – 3:00: Angel Team Deliberation

## Gathering Time

You may have noticed that, though the meeting is scheduled to begin at 1:00, we do not start the first pitch until 1:05. We schedule this gathering time to enable people to move from a previous meeting or to resolve any technical issues they may have connecting to the videoconference. This keeps us from falling behind before we even begin.

You will also notice five-minute gaps between each of the pitches to allow some time for the second team to get set up and settled in. We begin the second (or third…) session as soon as the pitch team is ready. We do not wait the full five minutes if they are ready sooner.

## Angel Team Deliberation

The pitch event ends with Angel Team discussion and deliberation regarding each of the pitches. Pitch teams are not present during the deliberation. Deliberation and decision making is also facilitated, and usually consists of 10 to 15 minutes of discussion for each pitch. The facilitator begins by reminding the Angel Team they are deliberating on a pitch to enter our Seed 1 round to ensure every Angel is deliberating in the proper context. There is usually slack in the deliberation portion of the agenda to allow some flexibility in discussion time, though it is almost never required.

If the deliberation ends ahead of the scheduled Angel Team deliberation time we usually end the meeting early. Though sometimes we take advantage of the fact the Angel Team is together and use that time to discuss other, unrelated issues that are important to them. Deliberation and discussions are always facilitated, and we never run past the scheduled meeting close time.

## Fist of Five Voting

When we are ready to decide whether an idea will be brought into the Accelerator, the facilitator will call for a fist of five vote (also referred to as "fist-to-five"). There are a few common variations of this style of voting, though they are all fairly similar. We explain ours.

When it is time to vote, the facilitator will ask each person to hold a fist so it is in view. Since we are usually working in videoconference the facilitator often asks them to hold their hands near their faces. When he calls for the vote each team member extends one or more of their fingers to indicate their vote. We interpret the vote as follows:

- One finger: This is a very bad idea; I am strongly against it.

- Two fingers: I do not think this is a good idea; I have serious concerns about some aspects of it, and I cannot support it.

- Three fingers: Neutral. I can live with, and support, either outcome.

- Four fingers: I believe this is a good idea and I support it, though I have some reservations.

- Five fingers: This is a fantastic idea! I strongly support it.

In rare cases someone in our group will flash a fist to indicate they feel it's an extremely bad idea. There are other styles for this type of voting, including using a fist as a sixth option, though we will not focus on those here.

Sometimes our first vote results in a strong signal in one direction or another. For example, if everyone flashes four or five fingers, we know there is unanimously strong support for the idea or proposal. In the context of a pitch event, that means we all believe the team should enter the Accelerator. Similarly, if everyone flashes one or two fingers, we have unanimous agreement that the idea should not be brought into the Accelerator.

Another key thing to note is that three fingers indicates someone can both live with—and support—a decision in either direction. So, in a case where most people flash four or five fingers, and someone flashes three fingers, the idea would be brought into the Accelerator, and the person who flashed three fingers will fully support it.

The fun begins when we have a split vote. For example, suppose seven people flashed four or five fingers, and one person flashed either one or two fingers. In these cases, the deliberation will continue, and we will ask the person who flashed one or two fingers to help us understand their concerns, and what—if anything—might move them from a two to a three or better. Once we have discussed their reasons and converged the team, we have another vote. Interestingly, sometimes the subsequent vote will be aligned with the one person who voted differently, because they shared information or a perspective that others were not aware of or had not considered.

It is important not to wait until the end of the deliberation time for a specific decision to call for the first vote, since each decision might require additional deliberation afterward. In addition, it is critical that whomever calls for a vote states a crystal clear, unambiguous question. Everyone present should understand they are empowered to request further explanation of the question if they did not understand it, or if they feel it is open to more than one interpretation. When we encounter this we usually have a brief discussion and then restate the question, so it is clearer and/or less ambiguous.

Regardless of whether a pitch was accepted for entry, the Angel Team agrees on, and explicitly captures, the final rationale for their decision. This is done to ensure the rationale is accurately communicated to the people who pitched. It is also an opportunity to confirm ownership of any follow-up activity that may have arisen from the discussion such as an Angel offering to mentor a team or to connect them with someone in the mature product organization.

## Why 10 Minutes?

As we were discussing options for our pitch format, we realized we had all been witness to 45- or 60-minute pitches that were, mostly, ineffective. There were cases where we had been very excited about an idea in the first five minutes of a pitch and were not certain we understood it 40 minutes later. With so much time, pitch teams often veered off course or went into too much unnecessary detail. As a result, the true value of their idea was lost.

We selected 10 minutes as the pitch duration so teams would be forced to focus on the heart of their idea and stick to the most important concepts. We have found it to be quite sufficient, especially since our facilitators ensure teams are not interrupted during their pitch. In addition, the question and answer session provides ample time for the Angels to ask clarifying questions if additional detail is required.

## Why Their Own Style?

In our early pitch event experiments we decided to allow people to pitch with their own material, in their own style, in order to lower entry friction and address some of the barriers to entry covered in Chapter 1. Early on we learned there were additional benefits.

When we give someone a mandatory slide template, not only are we potentially asking them to complete slides that may make no sense for their business, we are, in a sense, asking them to pitch their idea in our style. As if they were one of us. This can be very uncomfortable for many, perhaps enough to deter them from pitching. Permitting pitches in any style addresses this concern with the added benefit that we learn a bit more about the people pitching by watching them work in their own style.

## Informing Teams

An Angel Team member informs people whether or not their idea was selected for Accelerator entry as soon after the pitch event as possible. This is always done via voice or videoconference. During this call the Angel Team member will offer to further explain the rationale for the decision. To date, every team has wanted the additional information. Scheduling these conversations at the same time the pitch is scheduled (Step 5) ensures they are not forgotten, and that they happen as close to the pitch as possible.

## Nurturing Ideas That Do Not Enter the Accelerator

We want to be clear that, just because an idea is not selected for Accelerator entry does not mean it is a bad idea. In addition, "entry" or "no entry" are not the only possible outcomes. In one case we felt an idea was outstanding but, in order to succeed, it required a deep personal network in a specific domain that we did not possess. We knew we would not be able help nurture that idea. Bringing it into our program would not give it a better chance to succeed. We gave the person who pitched it permission to pursue it outside the company and offered to help connect them with an external accelerator that would be better suited to help them.

Sometimes we realize ideas would make great near-term product features or adjacent offerings for our mainstream business. In those cases we connect the pitch team with the appropriate product management group. In other cases the idea is already being explored somewhere, so we offer to connect the two groups. In addition, if we believe a team has found a good problem space but has not quite landed on a compelling case for a business, we offer one of the Angels as a mentor to help them further explore and/or articulate their idea.

We have some specific guidelines to help us determine which ideas are better suited for the Accelerator, and which are better developed within a mature line of business. The decision is fairly obvious most of the time, especially if you consider where the majority of the idea's risk lies. Figure 4-3 shows a conceptual illustration.

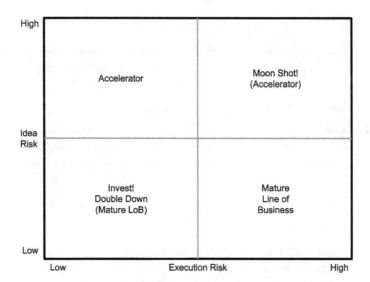

**Figure 4-3.** Evaluating where ideas are best served

At the highest level, if the majority of the risk is inherent in the idea itself, the idea is likely better suited for the Accelerator. If the majority of risk lies in execution of the idea, it is likely better served by a mature line of business. (Chapter 7 discusses this in additional detail, and Figure 7-2 shows some of the more detailed criteria we use.)

## "What If I Have an Idea But Don't Want to Lead an Incubation?"

There have been cases where people with a great idea were happy with their current career path, and they were not interested in actively incubating it themselves. No problem! We are still interested in the idea. If the pitch is successful we will help build a team to execute it, and place the person who brought us the idea on the advisory board. In fact, one idea of this nature has already been accepted into our Accelerator. The team that conceived that idea recruited a founder on their own and coached that founder to pitch their idea.

## Accelerator Entry

Our Entry Phase is a period of transition for the founders. During the Entry Phase, they:

- Receive a brief orientation from the Accelerator Team

- Work with their existing team to develop and execute a plan for a smooth transition from their current duties to working full-time in the Accelerator

- Register for the Incubation Rotation program mentioned earlier, with an effective date of their first full-time day in the Accelerator (discussed further in Chapter 7)

- Read *The Lean Startup* and *Running Lean*

- Are directed to all Accelerator resources, including a founder FAQ, bench advisor contact information, and material to help with execution of every stage of their incubation

- Receive access to the incubation team chat tools

- Participate in the Accelerator Bootstrap training

- Begin their Founder Fitness evaluation to help them identify areas for personal growth and skills they may need to bring into their team (discussed further in Chapter 6)

- Receive an invitation to observe the 3P reviews of every business in the Accelerator

- Begin working with the Accelerator Team to build their team and their initial staffing plan

Some of these activities may occur early in the Seed 1 round, depending on the timing of a team's Accelerator entry.

As soon as possible after a successful team has been informed of their selection for entry into the Accelerator, the program team schedules a brief orientation meeting. In this meeting the program team welcomes the new incubation team, explains the entry process, directs the team to Accelerator resources, explains the Accelerator Team's purpose, and helps them focus on the very few things that matter at this stage. At this time we also introduce the incubating team to online chat groups that members of all incubating teams use to ask one another questions, share information regarding how they were able to unblock a challenge, and share their experience with tools and approaches.

As teams enter the Accelerator we bring them to our Silicon Valley location for our two-to-three day "Bootstrap" training. The training is adjusted based on the unique combination of skills and experience each new team brings. That usually means adjusting the depth or emphasis of what is covered as opposed to dropping a topic completely. Even experienced teams can benefit from a refresher, and we find that even teams with experience in an area may want to retrain some of the bad muscle memory we referred to earlier.

The Bootstrap training provides an introduction to skills and resources required to execute a successful Lean startup and provides an opportunity for networking and teambuilding. Though content can vary, topics may include:

- Lean startup
- Running experiments/scientific method
- Agile coaching
- Design thinking
- Marketing
- Invention harvesting and patent capture
- Building a foundation (e.g., business systems, CI/CD pipeline...)
- Strategy and competitive intelligence
- Discussion of "Accelerator life" with other founders
- Creating a team working agreement
- Development of a Seed 1 plan and budget

This training is a balance of specific in-depth discussion and brief introduction designed to give the teams skills they require in order to get started. It also provides an introduction to other skills they will need to develop or acquire later in their journey. In addition, it gives the incubating team an opportunity to network with the Accelerator Team and other founders, and to build a network with some of the other people who will support them in their endeavor. Incubating teams and individuals are continuously learning, and they usually blend training and coaching supplied by the Accelerator program's team with training from other Lean startup coaches and Accelerators.

One of the first artifacts we give teams as they enter the Accelerator is the high-level overview we shared earlier in this chapter (see Figure 4-1). We do this to help teams understand that—though we will give them a lot of tools, techniques, and resources that they *may* use to help them achieve the objectives of each round—they should not lose sight of the reason they came into the Accelerator to bring their idea to life. Furthermore, we try not to be too prescriptive in our guidance. (This is tough, because we all like to solve problems.) Ultimately it is up to the incubating team to make decisions regarding *how* they will achieve each objective. We also give this one-page overview to our Angel Team to help keep their guidance relevant and focused.

We provide teams with an online Kanban at the beginning of each round of incubation to help them keep track of each round's major activities. These are instantiated from a template into each team's individual copy. In addition to helping ensure we all focus on what is most important at each stage, using an online Kanban tool gives us the added benefit that we have an historical record of when each team executed each stage, the duration of each activity, and which version of the Kanban and criteria they were using (because we regularly update them as we learn).

---

**Note**   Our Kanbans are not intended to be used as a prescriptive step-by-step guide to round completion. They are intended to provide illustrative examples.

---

Understanding the intent and purpose of these checklist-like Kanbans is critical. While they contain activities that most businesses typically complete during a specific phase, they are not intended to be used as a prescriptive step-by-step guide to round completion. They are intended to help teams remember the types of activities they should be focused on at each stage of their business' maturity by providing illustrative examples. The live versions of the Kanbans do have additional detail not shown here.

Figure 4-4 shows an example of the Entry Kanban. We will use this list form in our illustrations, as opposed to Kanban form, since we believe it is better suited to the book's format.

| RANK ^ | ID | NAME | SCHEDULE STATE |
|---|---|---|---|
| 1 | US199409 | Accelerator Ops Welcome and Entry Review (Ops) | N |
| 2 | US119172 | Read Eric Ries 'The Lean Startup' (Team) | N |
| 3 | US119176 | Read Ash Maurya's 'Running Lean' (Team) | N |
| 4 | US119175 | Read Sam Altman's 'Startup Playbook' article (Team) | N |
| 5 | US266993 | Read Point Nine's "5 Ways to Build a $100 Million Business" (Team) | N |
| 6 | US431193 | Notify Founders' managers of Pitch acceptance (Program Office) | N |
| 7 | US431190 | Founder Fitness Program (HR) | N |
| 8 | US431189 | Minimum Viable Team Assessment (Angel Team) | N |
| 9 | US119181 | Establish Business Roles and Reporting Structure (Founding Team) | N |
| 10 | US119294 | Establish Business Location and Collocation Reqs (Bus Lead) | N |
| 11 ▶ | US119183 | Seed 1 Plan Established (Bus Lead) | N |
| 12 | US119217 | Solicit for Lean Startup Mentor and Advisors (Bus Lead) | N |
| 13 | US183882 | Business Name Review (Bus Lead) | N |
| 14 | US119291 | Watch Patent eLearning Courses - 3 @ 15 min each (Team) | N |
| 15 | US119292 | Conduct an Invention Harvesting Session (Team) | N |
| 16 ▶ | US119198 | Program Logistics (Accelerator Ops) | N |

**Figure 4-4.** Entry stage Kanban

You may have noticed that this Kanban contains items for the incubating team and for other groups such as the Accelerator program and operations teams. In some stages, such as entry, the Accelerator Team does a lot of work "behind the scenes" so the incubating team can focus on bringing their idea to life. Clicking on any of these items will provide additional detail and resources. You may have also noticed that some items, such as number 16, have a small triangle next to their Rank number. Clicking on those triangles will expand the line item so additional detailed tasks are displayed. Figure 4-5 provides an example of an expanded list and will give you some insight into some of the work the Accelerator Team does on behalf of the incubating teams. (The Rank has no meaning. We only use this number to sort the items.)

**Figure 4-5.** Accelerator Operations Team Entry stage tasks

Teams move the item status, for example, from "New," to "In Progress," to "Complete" as they execute. This not only helps them keep track of what they are working on, it also provides everyone interested in the business with up-to-date view of their activity without the need to interrupt the team's flow. Incubating teams can also add anything they wish to their Kanban, or they can create a separate Kanban to help move their work. Most choose to do the latter.

## "Why Would a Mainstream Business Let Their Smart People Go?"

We are often asked whether an existing business ever blocks someone from entering the Accelerator. Fortunately, that has not been a problem so far. Though it may seem counter-intuitive, senior leaders from our mature lines of business have been very supportive. We are also frequently asked why they would let smart, creative people go? We can think of several reasons:

- If the idea is successful they get to take it. Any time they want to.

- The Accelerator takes all of the exploration risk, and they get to reap the reward whenever they are ready.

- It costs them nothing. Our Accelerator pays all salaries and other costs for the people who move into the program full-time to incubate an idea.

- Business leaders are aware of the challenges of incubating a breakthrough idea in an established organization (as discussed in chapters one and two). They feel an idea has a better chance to thrive outside a mainstream organization.

- They get their smart, creative people back at the end of an incubation, whether the business was successful or not.

- People returning from the Accelerator will bring new skills and experience to help their organization to innovate.

- They know that some of their best people need a creative outlet now and again. They are also aware that, if those innovators cannot find that outlet in their current organization, they will go elsewhere to get it—potentially leaving the company altogether.

## Incubation Phase

The Incubation Phase consists of two rounds of investment: Seed 1 and Seed 2. It focuses on discovering whether incubating teams have discovered a problem worth solving, and figuring out how to solve it in a compelling way before they make a large investment building a solution. The primary objective of this phase is to bring the idea to problem-solution fit and put incubating teams in a position to build a compelling MVP.

Teams in the Incubation Phase are usually small, typically consisting of one to two people as Seed 1 commences and growing to three to five people near the end of Seed 2. Having stated that, there are no program-imposed limits on team size. The nature of a business may dictate hiring more people earlier for technical de-risking and prototyping, for example. Founders are free to build the team as justified by the nature of their business and its requirements. They can hire from within the business, externally, bring in contractors, or even contract-to-hire.

Some teams begin very small and grow quickly in the Startup Phase, and others stay fairly modest throughout their life. Though teams control their own budget and team composition, they must be capable of explaining the rationale behind their hiring plan. The Angels and advisors help coach teams regarding how to grow, and when they might need to bring people in. What may surprise you is that the Angel Team often recommends founders acquire a little *more* budget than they originally requested so, for example, they might hire someone with skills they had not realized they needed in their current stage.

## Ceremonies

Most of the ceremonies in the Accelerator program operate following the same basic structure. The most frequent ceremonies are the pitch event described earlier and 3P reviews. The basic structure and personality of a ceremony may seem inconsequential. Our experience is that this could not be further from the truth. We have witnessed attempts at creating programs and ceremonies similar to these where failure to get these things right was a major cause of their demise. We share these key points in the next section.

### 3P Reviews

The primary ceremony for both the Incubation and Startup Phases is the 3P review (Pivot, Pause, or Persist Review). The majority of 3P reviews consist of updates from the incubating teams that include results of experiments, adjustments or pivots that resulted, data on the progress of the business, requests for assistance, and coaching and mentoring from the Angel Team. When a team is ready to move to a new funding round, they inform the program team they would like to use the "transition request" format during their review. Transition requests follow the same format as other 3P reviews, with an added block of time for the Angel Team to deliberate. The transition request format is also used for other exceptional situations, such as when a team wants to request a significant amount of additional funding in their current round.

To keep logistics as simple as possible we group 3P reviews together and schedule them twice monthly. The 3P reviews use the same Agile style as the pitch events discussed earlier in this chapter. We use the same technique to ensure there is a quorum, and voting on transitions or key questions is done via fist-to-five.

At a minimum, each 3P review is attended by the incubating businesses' founders and the Angel Team. Other members of the incubating business and their advisory teams are almost always in attendance. We also invite founders of other incubating businesses who are scheduled to present on the same day to observe all of the day's reviews, so business teams can learn from one another.

Each 3P review begins with an uninterrupted presentation from the founding team and is followed by open dialogue with the Angel Team. Prior to the meeting the founders declare how much uninterrupted time they need, and the program team schedules sufficient open dialogue time based on that. Typical 3P reviews consist of 10-15 minutes of uninterrupted presentation followed by 15-20 minutes of dialogue. Founders sometimes request additional time if they have reached an inflection point and have a lot of data to present, have a difficult puzzle to solve, or have achieved a milestone and want to provide a product demonstration. Reviews rarely exceed 30 minutes of uninterrupted presentation time.

### 3P Review Logistics

The Accelerator Program Team is responsible for logistics for every review. They follow the following procedure to ensure every event is valuable and runs as efficiently as possible:

1. To increase the probability of a quorum, 3P reviews are scheduled for a full afternoon twice monthly, up to a year in advance.

2. Angels indicate whether they can participate by accepting, tentatively accepting, or declining each calendar invitation as the event approaches.

3. Angels update their calendar status if their plans change.

4. One to two weeks prior to the event, each founder indicates how much time they will require, and whether they need to use the transition request format.

5. One week prior to each scheduled review session, the program team verifies whether all founders have confirmed their time requirements and whether a quorum will be present.

6. One week prior to the review, the program team updates the calendar entry for the upcoming 3P review session with a detailed agenda and reduces the duration of the calendar entry to match the total time required for all 3P reviews and the subsequent Angel Team meeting.

7. If a quorum is not possible, the event is rescheduled.

8. If a quorum is possible, but not for the full time required for all reviews, the program team may move one or more of the reviews to another day and leave the remainder scheduled for the original date.

9. The program team facilitates each pitch event, ensures the agenda is sound, and ensures the smooth operation of the videoconference.

10. Founders are responsible for capturing and owning all follow-up actions resulting from their review.

### Establishing a Heartbeat

Scheduling a meeting of this nature can be extremely challenging, especially on short notice. We have found that scheduling these far in advance dramatically reduces the probability they will have to be rescheduled. We have also learned that extending these meetings can be a challenge, so we reserve a conservatively large block of time (an entire afternoon). Establishing this regular heartbeat of events has enabled the team to operate with far fewer last-minute logistical challenges. Since review schedules are predictable, we are almost always aware of any quorum conflicts far in advance, which makes adjusting for them much simpler.

You may have also noticed that we return any time not required for the reviews a week in advance. Many of our Angels have very tight schedules. We have learned that returning the time one week in advance of the reviews is both close enough to the review that founding teams will be confident they have requested the proper review duration, and far enough away that the Angel Team can effectively repurpose any time that is returned to them.

### 3P Agenda

The agenda for a single 3P review is very simple, consisting of a block of time for uninterrupted presentation by the business team, followed by a block of time for open dialogue. Since we usually hold several reviews consecutively, our agenda typically looks something like this:

Sample 3P Agenda (review scheduled to begin at 1:00 PM)

- 1:05 – 1:35: Amazing Business, Founder Name (15/15)

- 1:40 – 2:10pm: Another Business, Another Founder (15/15)

- 2:15 – 2:45: Breakthrough Business, Amazing Founder (10/20)

- 2:45 – 3:15: Break (30 mins)
- 3:20 – 4:20 Incubating Business, Founder Name (30/30)
- 4:25 – 4:55: Final Business, Founder Name (10/20)
- 4:55 – 5:30: Angel Team Meeting

---

**Note**   The numbers at the end of each agenda item indicate the number of minutes of uninterrupted time and the number of minutes that will be made available for open discussion (review/discussion).

---

As we do for the pitch event, we provide five minutes of gathering time at the beginning of every meeting to enable people to connect and resolve any equipment and logistical problems they may have. If everyone is ready early, we begin early. We also provide five minutes between reviews for teams to switch over, and to provide a little slack in the schedule in case there are problems in the midst of a review (e.g., someone becomes disconnected). These "phantom 5s" enable us to stay on time all the time.

While the structure of each 3P review remains the same throughout the Incubation and Startup Phases, the content will vary in each round. We cover the focus of each round later in this chapter. At the end of each review the founder recaps each of the actions that were captured, and the Angels and Accelerator Team comments on anything they missed. Founders tend to capture actions in a document that they display for all to see during the open discussion, so they rarely miss an action.

To make the most efficient use of the Angel Team's time we also schedule a brief Angel Team meeting at the end of each 3P review. This provides the Angel Team with an opportunity to address anything they need to discuss without the need to schedule another block of time. If there are no topics at the time the Angel Team meeting is scheduled to begin, we conclude the session and return the time to the participants. We use Instant Agenda (instantagenda.com), a tool created by one of our incubating businesses, to manage our meetings.

Roman Voting

When we need to vote on something and there are only two alternatives (e.g., "yes" or "no"; "add more time" or "do not add more time"), we use a simple Roman vote as opposed to a fist-to-five. To vote in this style participants hold a fist where it is visible and when the vote is called they extend a thumb either upward, downward, or horizontally. The vote is assessed as follows:

- Thumb upward: I support the proposal

- Thumb downward: I do not support the proposal

- Thumb horizontal: I can live with and support either outcome

The outcome of Roman votes is typically determined by a simple majority.

### Avoiding Bias in Fist-to-Five and Roman Votes

Introducing bias into a vote is extremely easy, and it is often done unintentionally. Having people show a closed fist in preparation for a Roman or fist-to-five vote, then having everyone flash they vote simultaneously helps ensure each person voting is not influenced by the others. The facilitator can also introduce their own bias as they call the vote. For example, if the facilitator calls for a Roman vote and points their thumb upward as they say, "let's have a Roman vote," they can influence people to vote thumbs-up. Holding a number of fingers up as a fist-to-five vote is called can also influence people to increase or decrease their support.

Introduction of bias in this way can be very subtle and, when done intentionally, is an extremely dirty trick. Though this is often somewhat subliminal, the impact can be striking depending on whom is calling the vote, and their influence, position, and rank.

### 3P Agenda with Transition Requests

Transition requests follow the same format as regular 3P reviews, with a few exceptions. They are always scheduled for 30 minutes of uninterrupted review followed by 30 minutes of open dialogue. Though using the entire time is not mandatory, we find scheduling 30 minutes is optimal.

Sample 3P Agenda (review scheduled to begin at 1:00 PM Eastern Time)

- 1:05 – 2:05: A Business, Founder Name (30/30, Transition Request)

- 2:05 – 2:35: Angel Team Deliberation

- 2:35 – 2:45: Transition Decision and Guidance

- 2:45 – 3:15: Break (30 mins)

- 3:20 – 3:50 Incubating Business, Founder Name (15/15)

- 3:55 – 4:25: Final Business, Founder Name (10/20)

- 4:25 – 5:30: Angel Team Meeting

Whether the transition review is first, last, or in the middle of the agenda does not matter. The order of the agenda items is determined by the program team based on founder and Angel Team schedules, quorum rules, and their assessment of what would create the best flow for the meeting. We try to schedule breaks of at least 10 minutes every 90 minutes, and never have a block of time longer than two hours without a break. We typically take a longer break sometime between 2:30 and 3:30 Eastern, since that aligns with the lunch break in our Silicon Valley office. (We don't want "hangry" Angels.)

Following the open dialogue period of each transition request the Angel Team will move into a private videoconference workspace to discuss the review. We begin with an open discussion where Angels bring forward the facts they believe are most important to consider when making the decision. Once all of the Angels have weighed in, we call for a fist-to-five vote, as discussed earlier in the chapter. Once the Angel Team has converged on a decision, they return to the main videoconference session to deliver their decision, along with the rationale that led to it.

### Working Agreement and Definition of Done

In keeping with our Agile mindset, we collaboratively developed a working agreement and definition of done for our 3P reviews. These evolve over time, though they tend not to change frequently.

## Sample Working Agreement

- Each business leader owns their 3P session, including the follow-up and/or redirect items that are identified within

- The 3P meeting is a "safe place" (i.e., what happens in the 3P meeting stays in the 3P meeting)

- We will stick to the agenda

- We will finish on time

- We will be in our seats and be ready to begin at least one minute before start times

- We will mute microphones when not speaking

- We will associate our actual name with our videoconference or audio connection (helps with context, makes follow-up easier)

- Each founder will upload a draft of their materials to the event library two business days prior to the event so participants can prepare for the meeting, three days in advance for transition requests

- Founders may update their material at any time prior to the commencement of their review, but should highlight any substantial changes during the review

- Angel Team members will review the uploaded material prior to the 3P meeting

- Reviews will be cancelled if materials are not posted within 24 hours prior to the event

- For significant pivots and transition requests, the session will be cancelled if materials are not posted by three business days prior to the event

- We will not interrupt business teams during the "uninterrupted review" portion of the ceremony

- Only Angel Team and incubating team members will ask questions during the Q&A portion unless they, or the business team, invite others to do so

## Sample Definition of Done

- The business Leader has reviewed or made available in their material, for example:

    - An update regarding actions taken from the previous 3P review

    - The business' progress since the last 3P meeting

    - A review of experiments since and what was learned as a result

    - Planned experiments and next steps, and what the business believes they will learn as a result

    - Relevant metrics (e.g., validated learning, innovation metrics…)

    - The stage-appropriate Kanban, updated to show their progress

    - An updated Lean Canvas, traction model, and customer model

- All decisions requested by the business team have been addressed

- All action items are assigned owners and deadlines as they are identified

Angel Team: Coaching versus Judging

Our Angels tend to be seasoned and senior executives. As such, their default state is often "judging". While that is the perfect state for them to be in during a transition request, it may not be the best state for them to be in during a routine 3P review, where a team may require mentoring or coaching. An objective of those routine reviews is to help ensure business teams are on course to successfully achieve their next transition, whatever that may be. While we do not want our Angels to shut down their judging senses completely, we find that having our facilitator periodically remind them of the coaching objective helps them to remember to provide guidance and assistance as opposed to only being judgmental. We will often keep this reminder lighthearted and offer a tongue-in-cheek comment as simple as "remember this is a coachy review versus a judgy review". We do this when a facilitator senses the Angel Team has adopted the wrong bias, and not at every review. (This also makes the Angels a little less intimidating.)

Seagull Management

We had to directly address this bias toward judging head-on in the early days of our program when we were experiencing what is often referred to as "seagull management". One or more Angels who had not been in contact with a team in a while would (during a 3P review for example) swoop in, criticize everything the team had done, and the fly away without further explanation. This was often mostly a context-switching issue. The Angels would arrive without important context, and then attempt to help the teams; but it was not perceived as helpful. Furthermore, in response to this kind of direction, incubating teams would often spend a lot of time and effort working on something that had no real benefit to their business.

Chasing Shiny Objects

At times a founder will include something in their review that is not truly germane to the review. For some reason, these items often capture the attention or imagination of one of the Angels, like a crow might be attracted to a shiny object. When that happens the Angel and the founder can consume all of a review's dialogue time discussing that, irrelevant topic. What's worse, if the Angel and the founder disagree on the topic, or if the founder is not adequately prepared to discuss it, the entire review can be negatively impacted. The impact of this can be especially bad when nobody realizes the item is irrelevant while the review is in progress. The Angel Team may simply leave with the impression the founder was not prepared or not knowledgeable in general.

Facilitators must be diligently on the lookout for these shiny objects and facilitate the discussion away from them when necessary. When facilitating our Angel Team, we often remind them that we love to "chase shiny objects" to keep this top of mind.

This should also serve as a cautionary tale for founders, or anyone who will lead or speak in a review of this nature. Keep unnecessary items out of the material and discussion or they could become the review's "most important" items. Everything included in the review can—and usually will—become the focus of discussion, so make sure you only include the things that you believe are worthwhile discussing. You can always put other information you wish to include, but not discuss, in an appendix. Even outside the context of a review of this nature we have seen irrelevant items become the focus of a discussion with senior executives and result in extremely negative outcomes for the teams or individuals involved.

### Being Too Prescriptive or Being Perceived as Being Prescriptive

It should be no surprise that, like any board, diversity—of all types—creates a stronger and more effective Angel Team. Our Angels have varied experience and opinions. We love to solve problems, and we love to think aloud.

From time to time this has resulted in confusion for our incubating teams, especially those with less experienced founders. They were unsure whether the Angels were sharing their ideas, stating their opinions, or giving the intrapreneurs direction. The Angels were usually brainstorming and sharing ideas and hypotheses, though when those ideas were shared during a ceremony such as a 3P review they were often interpreted as directives. This often resulted in less experienced teams chasing all of the ideas that were discussed, while lowering the priority on the data-based experiments they should have been running. What's worse, different Angels often had different ideas, and teams would squander time and resources on all of them, metaphorically chasing their own tail.

When we realized this was happening we coached the founders regarding how to deal with it (e.g., by asking clarifying questions). We also coached the Angel Team to be explicit about when they were brainstorming or sharing an idea, when they were voicing an opinion, and when they were making an explicit request. We've been working on Angel Fitness too so, fortunately, we have not experienced that issue very often lately; but our facilitators still listen for it.

Drifting Out of Funding Round Context

Drifting out of funding round context can be one of the most disruptive behaviors an Angel can manifest. This is exhibited when, for example, an Angel asks a question that is appropriate for a business that is in Series A to a founder who is in Seed 1. During a 3P review, this can be very distracting and confusing to the founders, and even to other Angels. However, the impact can be far worse during a transition request. If, for example, an Angel who is evaluating a business requesting transition from Seed 1 to Seed 2 takes into account even one Series A exit criterion, a transition may be blocked. This can become especially confusing if more than one Angel is in the wrong context.

When the Angel Team is not aligned on context, at best transition deliberations can become confusing, clumsy, and exhausting. At worst they might approve a transition for a business that is not ready, or hold back a business that *is* ready for transition.

To help Angels set the proper context for transition requests, we created a high-level overview. Similar to the program-level overview shown in Figure 4-1, the artifact is intentionally vague. It is intended to get the Angel Team thinking about the right types of things without being an inflexible set of criteria or becoming a distraction. This is useful for level-setting the team during transition requests and keeping the dialogue relevant. It is also useful in non-transition 3Ps, helping Angels remember what types of things business teams may be working on and/or may need help with.

In keeping with our bias to transparency, we have made this overview available to all of the business teams in our Accelerator. Making this available to the businesses did introduce a risk teams would become too focused on it, perhaps even to the point where they treated it as an immutable list of graduation criteria. Thus, explaining the spirit and context of the artifact to the business teams was paramount.

Since releasing this document the Angel Team has been much better aligned during reviews and while making decisions. While we still debate, we are debating the right things. The decisions we have made since we published the document appear to have been stronger. Though, in fairness, we have recently held a lot of deep retrospectives, and we have made a number of other changes that we also hoped would improve our performance.

The Angel Team overview consists of a set of cascading questions that enables the reader to begin at a high level and drill into further examples if they need further illustration. *All questions in the document are illustrative in nature.* The intent of the document is to communicate the spirit of each round and help Angels to set themselves in the proper context. *These are NOT exit criteria checklists.*

Figure 4-6 shows the aide-memoire with all questions collapsed (the program-level overview at the bottom can also be seen in Figure 4-1), Figure 4-7 shows the Incubation Phase expanded to a second level of detail, and Figure 4-8 shows the Startup Phase expanded to the second level.

Drill-down questions are intended to be illustrative of the top-level, key questions. To expand or collapse a section, click the small triangle to the left of the question.

# CA Accelerator: Key Questions by Phase

Intro: This list is intended to enable the Angel Team to stay aligned, and to use consistent criteria for making transition decisions.

Seed 1 Key Exit Question: Is this problem worth solving?

Seed 2 Key Exit Question: If you build this, will early adopters come (with money)?

Series A Key Exit Question: Now that you've built it, did the early adopters come, and do you continue to attract new customers?

Series B Key Exit Question: Has your business scaled with the additional investment?

Series C Key Exit Question: Did you meet your acquisition commitments?

Innovation ▪ Startup

| Seed 1 | Seed 2 | Series A | Series B | Series C |
|---|---|---|---|---|
| Early Adopter-Problem Fit | Problem-Solution Fit | Solution-Product Fit | Product-Market Fit | Exit |
| **Objective:** Validate that problem is worth solving for the identified target market, via early adopters | **Objective:** Validate solution's likelihood to delight early adopters | **Objective:** Prove ability to achieve traction with early adopters. | **Objective:** Prove business model is viable and scalable. | **Objectives:** Execute on business case. Align to acquirer requirements. |
| **Outcome:** Sufficient evidence of problem-early adopter pair. | **Outcomes:** Sufficient evidence that the problem-solution approach satisfies early adopters. Clearly defined and scoped MVP. Business model* baseline. | **Outcome:** Sufficient evidence of business model* traction | **Outcomes:** Market demand for the solution is accelerating. Clear marketing & sales strategy. Confirmed intent to acquire | **Outcome:** Acquisition. Accelerator exit. |
| **Key Question to Answer:** Is this problem worth solving? | **Key Question to Answer:** If we build this, will early adopters come (with money)? | **Key Question to Answer:** Now that you've built it, did the early adopters come, and do you continue to attract new customers? | **Key Question to Answer:** Has your business scaled with the additional investment? | **Key Question to Answer:** Did you meet your acquisition commitments? |
| **Output:**<br>• Marketing: Segmentation / Early Adopter Analysis, Lean Persona(s), Rough Market Sizing<br>• Traction: Animal You're Hunting<br>• Seed 2 Plan | **Output:**<br>• Marketing: Positioning Statement, Company Narrative/Pitch, Validated thinking on how you will reach early adopters; Competitive Landscape, Pricing Model.<br>• Traction: One-page traction model with assumptions outlined<br>• Validated MVP Definition<br>• Series A Plan.<br>*May include free/non-monetary models. | **Output:**<br>• Marketing: Website reveal, Go-to-Market Plan; Key Engine of Growth identified.<br>Earlyvangelist purchase of solution.<br>• MVP Released.<br>• Sean Ellis Test Baseline.<br>• Traction: Traction Model shows that you've met your first goal.<br>• Initial understanding of CAC, LTV, and COGs<br>• Referenceable customers.<br>• Series B Plan.<br>*May include free/non-monetary models. | **Output:**<br>• Marketing: Evidence that GTM strategy is effective & will scale.<br>• Sean Ellis Test Passed.<br>• Traction: Target Weekly Growth Rate & Retention Achieved. Traction model shows you've met your goals & can scale usage<br>• Firm understanding of CAC, LTV, and COGs.<br>• Acquisition: Pitch and Executive Summary completed, Input provided to Bus. Case & IC Deck<br>• Contingent acquisition commitm<br>• Series C | **Output:**<br>• Traction: Traction model shows you've achieved growth and scale targets defined in Series B<br>• Acquisition: Technical Due Diligence completed. Input provided for Business Due Diligence.<br>• Documented final decision from BU for business to exit the Accelerator |

**Figure 4-6.** Angel Team aide-memoire of illustrative questions—top level

**Seed 1 Key Exit Question:** Is this problem worth solving?

1. Who is your early adopter?
2. Does your early adopter have enough pain to change what they're doing/using in order to solve the problem?
3. What animal are you hunting?
4. Who are your competitors and why will you beat them?
5. What is your Seed 2 plan?

**Seed 2 Key Exit Question:** If you build this, will early adopters come (with money)?

1. Who is your first Series A early adopter? (Provide names.)
2. Does your positioning resonate with your early adopters?
3. How will you reach your early adopters?
4. Why are these the key features needed to solve your early adopters' problem(s) and improve their lives?
5. What differentiates your product from competitors'?
6. What is your pricing model?
7. What is your MSC?
8. What is your Series A plan?

**Figure 4-7.** Incubation Phase illustrative questions expanded one level

**Series A Key Exit Question:** Now that you've built it, did the early adopters come, and do you continue to attract new customers?

1. Have you met your first traction goal?
2. How do your early adopters articulate your UVP (unique value proposition)?
3. Who are your referenceable customers and what are they saying/doing for you?
4. What evidence do you have of ROI for increased Marketing spend in Series B?
5. What is your Series B plan?

**Series B Key Exit Question:** Has your business scaled with the additional investment?

1. Have you achieved product-market fit?
2. Have you met your Series B traction goals?
3. Have you completed your acquisition-related requirements?
4. What is your Series C plan?

**Series C Key Exit Question:** Did you meet your acquisition commitments?

1. (If the business has not met commitments and is therefore not being acquired) What do you plan to do?

**Figure 4-8.** Startup Phase illustrative questions expanded one level

## Administrative Burden of a 3P Review

Sometimes, early in the life of an incubation we receive comments regarding the large amount of preparation required for their 3P review. We hear that some teams have spent days, or even a week or more, getting ready. That makes sense early on. They begin preparation for their first 3P review having nothing. They have no presentation material apart from the templates we give them, they haven't prepared for a 3P review in the past so they need to learn how it works, they have to figure out the timing and the level of commentary that is appropriate, and they are sorting through the logistics—everything is new. It takes time to learn anything new.

However, we sometimes receive similar comments later in the life of a business. In some cases the additional effort was required because teams wanted to achieve a milestone ahead of their review, and they had doubled their effort to do so. In those cases, the effort actually advanced the business' progress but had been associated with the 3P event. That is not a bad thing; it is a conscious choice made by the team.

There have also been cases where the extended effort of a more mature team was actually directed solely toward preparation for a 3P review. When that happens, we take notice and perform a retrospective to see whether the program is generating unnecessary overhead. Though this can also be a sign that the business may be exercising some of the bad muscle memory we discussed earlier, or that they may have adopted an inefficient approach to 3P preparation.

Most of the material teams use in a 3P review should be material they have to prepare to run their business in any case. Material they would have to create even if there were no 3P reviews. Our reviews typically include things like results from experiments and surveys, traction model and pirate metric analysis, and a discussion of hypotheses and experiments. These are things the teams are, or should be, doing as a matter of course. If teams simply drop that material into their review during their workday (e.g., when changes are made to the business model hypothesis, at the end of an experiment...), preparation for the 3P review should consist largely of fine-tuning or updating those artifacts and preparing a narrative. More experienced founders have the ability to instantly recall most of this important information at any time. So, a high 3P workload can also be a sign the incubating team is distracted or disorganized. In addition, it can indicate that their minimum viable team does not have business development skills. Both are worthy of exploration.

## Collaboration and Learning from Others

As was mentioned earlier, personal growth is a deliberate goal of our Accelerator. In addition to some of the learning opportunities we mentioned earlier, we encourage our founders to collaborate, to work with one another, and to learn from one another. Though we encourage them to do this on their own, our program also creates some of the conditions that enable them to do so. For example, we encourage founders to attend 3P reviews of other teams on the day they have their own review so they can listen dispassionately to how the business and the Angel Team interact and learn from it. We encourage them to:

- Pay attention to how teams that have been in the program longer leverage the Angel Team, and the requests they make of the Angels.

- Listen to the questions from the Angels, since the Angels will likely ask similar questions during their own reviews.

- Observe the responses of the other founders to the Angels' questions, and see how those responses are received by the Angels.

- Observe the body language of both the incubating team and the Angels.

- Look for patterns: Which styles resonated, which artifacts and charts were effective, what got the Angel Team excited, and so on.

- Look for anti-patterns: Which unproductive behaviors made the meeting less effective than it could have been (e.g., being defensive, not listening).

# Seed 1

We believe it is worthwhile to begin this section with a reminder that, *while analogous to external seed and series investment rounds, our program's rounds are different.* Though the basic constructs are the same, businesses in our program are often less mature and the investments tend to be lower than their namesake. We have found these labels are easily understood by our intrapreneurs and executives, have resonated well with participants and stakeholders, and communicate the spirit of the program well.

The objective of Seed 1 is to validate that a team has identified a problem that it is sufficiently painful that people would be willing to take action to solve it (customer-problem fit). Emphasis is placed on customer sensing and identification of the business' target customers and early adopters. Business teams in Seed 1 typically focus on activities such as:

- Identification of Target Market Segments and Early Adopters

- Estimating market size to determine the potential of the business

- Interviewing potential early adopters and conducting experiments to validate the problem is painful enough for them to take action to solve it

- Investigating how potential early adopters are dealing with the problem today, and how satisfied they are with their current state

- Qualifying the type and size of customers the business will likely work with

- Developing Lean personas (with help from design and marketing subject matter experts)

- Opportunistically de-risking other aspects of the business

- Forming the business' advisory board

- Developing a Seed 2 plan

| RANK ▲ ID | | NAME | SCHEDULE STATE |
|---|---|---|---|
| 1 | US224742 | Incubation Boot Camp (Incubation SMEs, Founders, Ops) | N |
| 2 | US258664 | Identify Your Target Market and Early Adopter Segment (LC Box 2) | N |
| 3 | US393152 | Rough Market Sizing | N |
| 4 | US123157 | Form Advisory Team and Begin Regular Collaboration With Them (Bus Lead) | N |
| 5 | US131639 | Obtain Initial Proof That the Problem is Painful, Significant & Needs to be Solved By Your Target Market (Especially Early Adopters) [ie: Validate Upper Lean C... | N |
| 6 | US131640 | Provide Evidence That You Understand How Your Early Adopters Are Working Around the Problem Today & Their Level of Satisfaction With the Workaround(s... | N |
| 7 | US119184 | Identify your Seed 1 Assumptions & Hypotheses and Run your Seed 1 Experiments (Bus Lead) | N |
| 8 | US299188 | Perform High-Level Survey of Competitive Landscape (Bus Lead) | N |
| 9 | US131683 | Market Type is Understood (Team) | N |
| 10 | US175456 | Initial Assessment of Traction Goals (What Animal Are You Hunting?) (Bus Lead) | N |
| 11 | US326023 | Lean Persona | N |
| 12 | US123207 | Establish Seed 2 Plan (Bus Lead) | N |
| 13 | US123163 | Conduct Invention Harvesting Session (Team) | N |

**Figure 4-9.** Seed 1 Kanban

Though we provide interview guides and templates to help teams analyze the results, founders can conduct and analyze customer interviews using any of the many other effective techniques and guides that are available.

We also provide references to other useful resources and external sources of education. Among our favorites are:

- "How to Interview Your Users and Get Useful Feedback," Garrett Moon (https://blog.leanstack.com/how-to-interview-your-users-and-get-useful-feed-back-8f5550618ad2)

- "Market Type and Revenue. 2 Minutes to Find Out Why," Steve Blank (https://steveblank.com/category/market-types/)

- "5 Ways to Build a $100 Million Business," "What Animals are you Hunting," Point 9, (http://labs.openview-partners.com/wp-content/uploads/2016/11/5-Ways-to-Build-a-100-Million-Business.png)

## Early Intrapreneurs Will Face Every Obstacle: Set Their Expectations Properly

Those who enter your program early—your intrapreneur-pioneers—are blazing a trail for the intrapreneurs who will follow them. They will encounter virtually every obstacle that exists. These obstacles will include both mainstream business processes that are not well suited to incubating businesses *and* elements of your program that do not drive the result you thought they would. At times they will likely face several obstacles at once.

You may be able to anticipate many of these roadblocks and begin working on them proactively to minimize their impact. Though, even when you do, it may take longer than you expect to address them. And there will be plenty of surprises. It is important to prepare the trailblazers for this journey.

We try to insulate the incubating businesses from these frustrations. We tell them that if they become frustrated with something of this nature and spend longer than three minutes trying to resolve it, they should stop and give the problem to the Accelerator team. Though even when we take the work of addressing those issues away from the incubating teams, time delays, uncertainty, and reduction in velocity can still occur and create stress and frustration for intrapreneurs.

It is important to be transparent with those who enter your program early, prepare them for what they may face, and let them know your team is there to help and make it as painless as possible. It is also important to help them to understand the value of addressing these obstacles beyond the scope of their own businesses. Incubating teams that enter your Accelerator after them will not have to deal with the stress and frustration they faced and will execute with greater ease and velocity. Furthermore, their friends and colleagues in the mainstream organization may also benefit from their trailblazing.

## Seed 2

In Seed 2 teams focus on validating that their solution to the problem explored during Seed 1 is likely to delight early adopters (problem-solution fit). During this phase, teams remain maniacally customer-focused, continuously sensing as they develop and test their solution hypotheses. Teams are not usually developing an MVP during Seed 2. They are typically creating prototypes of various types, which may include wire frames, manually operated applications ("Wizard of Oz"), functioning prototypes, or even crude, but functioning, code.

Typical Seed 2 activities include:

- Early adopter experiments to validate that the solution solves their problem in a compelling way

- Identification of at least one viable business model

- Continuous business model viability assessment and refinement

- Traction model creation

- Development of an early adopter go to market plan

- Positioning statement development and refinement

- Pricing model development

- Visual communication of the idea

- Development and delivery of the company narrative/pitch

- Development of initial evidence that the market opportunity is large enough to sustain a business

- Definition of the MVP via customer experimentation and interview

- Technology de-risking via early development and POC building

- Creation of a high-level solution architecture (we refer to this as a "blockitecture"), with validation by experienced architects from our bench of advisors

- Creation of an architecture-level backlog

- Research of the relevant startup landscape with help from our Corporate Development Team

- Creation of a Series A plan

| RANK ^ | ID | NAME | SCHEDULE STATE |
|---|---|---|---|
| 1 | US201961 | Read Ash Maurya 'Scaling Lean' (Team) | N |
| 2 | US393149 | Company Narrative/Pitch | N |
| 3 | US299178 | Visually Communicate Your Idea (Business Owner) | N |
| 4 | US131632 | Initial proof that your solution solves your early adopters' problem(s) (Team) | N |
| 5 | US131634 | At Least One Viable Business Model Identified (Bus Lead) | N |
| 6 | US393047 | Positioning Statement | N |
| 7 | US123262 | Initial proof that the market opportunity is big enough, based on your early adopters' perceived value of a solution. (Team) | N |
| 8 | US393150 | Pricing Model | N |
| 9 | US393151 | How Will You Reach Your Early adopters? | N |
| 10 | US123300 | Validated Definition of MVP (Team) | N |
| 11 | US192490 | Blockitecture (Bus Lead) | N |
| 12 | US268267 | Architecture-Level Backlog (Bus Lead) | N |
| 13 | US123308 | Conduct an Invention Harvesting Session (Team) | N |
| 14 | US176122 | Conduct Startup Exploration with Corporate Development | N |
| 15 | US123305 | Series A Plan Established (Bus Lead) | N |
| 16 | US197515 | Program Logistics (Accelerator Ops) | N |

**Figure 4-10.** Seed 2 Kanban

As with Seed 1, we provide interview guides and templates to help analyze the results, and teams can conduct and analyze customer interviews based any of the many other effective techniques and guides that are available. We also provide references to other useful resources and sources of education.

## Startup Phase

Once teams have satisfied the Seed 2 criteria and achieve problem-solution fit, they request a transition to Series A. This also marks their transition from the Incubation Phase to the Startup Phase.

We believe the Seed-2-to-Series-A transition decision may be the most important and risky decision the Angel Team makes. Once a team transitions to the Startup Phase investment in the business will increase, usually substantially. The most common reason for this cost increase is that businesses will add engineers to build their product, increasing their size from two to four people to 10 or more. Team size does vary widely. Some teams never reach 10 people. Others continue to grow past that as their business scales.

By the end of Seed 2, the Angel Team will have witnessed the incubating team operating for several months, and they should have a decent idea of the team's abilities and faults. However, damaging behavior such as founder bias can be tough to spot. Furthermore, even if the team has managed to retrain their bad muscle memory, those behaviors have a way of creeping back in during Series A once founders have a larger team to run and operational pressures begin to present themselves. When a founder or team has a bias, they can structure their experiments so the results are guaranteed to support their hypotheses. This is tough to spot, and even the founders may be unaware they are doing it.

As a common saying suggests, the most challenging aspect of unconscious bias is that it is unconscious.

As teams enter Series A, their measures typically shift from validated learning toward more emphasis on the "innovation metrics" (activation, acquisition, retention, referral, and revenue), eventually moving to measures that more closely represent full business models as you might see in a mature business.

## Series A

In Series A teams begin creating, adapting, and selling their minimum viable product. They focus on proving they can find traction with early adopters, and therefore must remain maniacally customer-focused as they build their team, and their offering. Reaching Series A is far from a guarantee of viability. In fact, we believe more businesses will pause than will make it to Series B. To date that has been the case. Customer traction is the key metric that matters, and there is nowhere to hide.

Key activities in Series A include:

- Hiring and training a sufficiently-large engineering team
- Building and shipping a minimum viable product
- Continuous adaptation based on customer feedback
- Validation of the business' unique value proposition, activation flow, and pricing model
- Creation and refinement of a Go To Market plan
- Sales of the offering
- Creation and update of a marketing-focused website
- Creating a baseline Sean Ellis test[3]
- Obtaining an understanding of the business' fundamentals including customer acquisition cost, lifetime customer value, and cost of goods sold
- Identification of the business' key engine of growth
- Building earlyvangelist relationships
- Building referenceable customers
- Achievement of Series A traction and monetization goals
- Creation of a Series B Plan

---

[3]For additional information regarding the Sean Ellis test, visit `http://steenkamp.tumblr.com/post/15766708874/the-sean-ellis-test`

| RANK ^ | ID | NAME | SCHEDULE STATE |
|---|---|---|---|
| 1 | US224740 | Read Croll and Yoskovitz 'Lean Analytics' (Team) | N |
| 2 | US124054 | Engineering Team is Hired (Bus Lead) | N |
| 3 | US124139 | Team Trained (Team) | N |
| 4 | US298587 | Prior to MVP launch, your Positioning and Messaging, Activation Flow, and Business Model are Validated | N |
| 5 | US298480 | Marketing Website Is Built and Reviewed with Angel Team | N |
| 6 | US411442 | You have a Go-to-Market Plan | N |
| 7 | US124138 | MVP is Released | N |
| 8 | US301582 | Conduct Sean Ellis Test to Establish Baseline | N |
| 9 | US124133 | Cost of Acquiring Customers (CAC) is Understood | N |
| 10 | US131628 | Initial Understanding of the Lifetime Value of a Customer (LTV) | N |
| 11 | US323676 | Initial Understanding of COGS (for software or SaaS) | N |
| 12 | US298591 | Key Engine of Growth is Identified With Assumptions Outlined | N |
| 13 | US125153 | An earlyvangelist has purchased your product (Bus Lead) | N |
| 14 | US124134 | Solution is On Target With Traction and Monetization Goals (Bus Lead) | N |
| 15 | US411441 | You have referenceable customers | N |
| 16 | US131574 | Sticker on CEO's Laptop :) | N |
| 17 | US124135 | Conduct an Invention Harvesting Session (Team) | N |
| 18 | US124136 | Series B Plan Established (Bus Lead) | N |
| 19 | US197523 | Program Logistics (Accelerator Ops) | N |

**Figure 4-11.** Series A Kanban

## A Sticky Situation

Item 16 in Figure 4-11, "Sticker on CEO's Laptop," is a bit different than our other criteria. We thought it might catch your attention, so we thought we had better address it first. Having our Global CEO put a business' sticker on their laptop is *not* a blocking criterion. However, the presence of this item might give you some insight into the camaraderie that develops among different incubating teams.

Fairly early in the Accelerator's life, we received a photo of our CEO in which one of our business' stickers was clearly displayed on his laptop. Everyone associated with the Accelerator was thrilled. It is a great example of the engagement and support our program has received from our most senior executives. We are sure you can imagine the banter between the incubating teams that resulted. Following that good-spirited banter, other founders made it their mission to achieve that feat.

In addition to the morale boost that results, satisfying this criterion is nice source of promotion for the teams who achieve it. We have even seen one of the teams' stickers on the iPad of a member of our corporate Board of Directors. The addition of this criterion was intended to be lighthearted, though there is a strong sense of pride and accomplishment for those teams that decide to pursue it and succeed.

## A Few Caveats

At this stage teams can often become even more excited about their product than they were initially, with good reason. This renewed passion can cause them to drift away from their maniacal customer focus and their discipline of experimentation, inspection, and adaptation. While you might believe a change like this would be easy to detect, that is not always the case.

---

Focus had insidiously morphed from customer sensing, to selling their solution. This led them down a path where they began developing a solution that was not exactly the product their customers needed or wanted.

---

For example, we have discovered cases where business teams were spending a lot of time with customers in what appeared to be a continuance of their maniacal customer focus. However, their focus had insidiously morphed from customer sensing, to solely selling their solution. While there is nothing wrong with selling, this team's drift away from sensing led them down a path where they began developing a solution that was not exactly the product their customers needed or wanted. So let's take a look at a few of the most common traps teams must be diligent to avoid as their ideas mature.

### Too Much of a Good Thing: Increasing Team Size Too Rapidly

In Series A teams begin hiring in earnest as they prepare to build and sell their offering. This is an exciting time, as the incubation begins to feel more and more like a "real business". Thoughtful planning of the rate and order of hiring is paramount in order to avoid problems similar to those discussed in Chapter 2. If teams bring too many people in at once, they risk becoming overwhelmed with the effort required to onboard, train, manage, and lead them. When this happens, the leadership team can end up spending all of their time on overhead and operational issues, and not spend much—or any—time advancing their business, running experiments, or de-risking. If they do not bring the right people in early, the business can stall or veer off in the wrong direction.

These errors, and others like them, can consume runway (funding and time) at an amazing pace. Falling victim to them can mean the difference between having enough time and funding to successfully experiment, pivot, and gain traction; and never truly knowing whether an idea was viable. We have even seen businesses that became so distracted managing their company they lost sight of their original value proposition until it was too late for them to adjust. Their run rate was too high, their progress was too slow, and their investors lost interest as a result.

Less Is More: Remember the "M" in MVP

As teams begin building their first MVP, we have found they can lose sight of the fact that "M" stands for "minimum". As a result, scope creep can occur resulting in delayed time to market and delayed customer feedback. In addition, teams can unconsciously stop experimenting as they build their MVP and, thus, not receive valuable customer feedback that would enable them to adjust their MVP *before* they ship it.

There is already a lot of great material on minimum viable products, so we won't expand on that further here. Though we believe this is an area where the Angel Team, Advisory Boards, and other resource people can make a real difference by coaching teams to keep experimenting, continue sensing, and remember the "M". When he is coaching teams regarding how to bring an MVP to its true minimum, Howard Abrams, one of this book's authors, often cites the following quote attributed to Coco Chanel, *"Before you leave the house, look in the mirror and take one thing off."*

Insidious Committed Bets

We find teams can be especially susceptible to insidious committed bets early in our Series A, as they begin to build their product in earnest. The insidious committed bet often begins when a founder or team receives a signal from one or more potential customers that they are on track to achieve problem-solution and/or product-market fit. The signal can be something as simple as the receipt of a few favorable comments regarding a prototype or specification. As they are about to breathe life into their first shippable MVP, they can unconsciously commit to building only the specific product they envision at that point in time. That unconscious commitment can often be sustained well beyond the delivery of their first MVP. As a result, they can perpetually execute toward the vision they developed prior to creating their first shippable product without ever adjusting, or even questioning it.

This unconscious commitment to a larger vision can be difficult to detect because the teams may still have a great deal of interaction with customers. That interaction may give the intrapreneurs—and everyone else—the impression that they are still sensing. It may even appear to outsiders that the team is testing hypotheses, obtaining customer feedback, and adjusting their course based on that data when, in fact, they are only selling their current vision to those customers.

It can also be the case that intrapreneurs are running experiments, but not making adjustments based on when they learn. Thus, they stop learning. We have seen cases where founders were being presented with staggeringly obvious evidence that customers would not use their product—as it was currently defined and being built—and ignored it. They had become so myopic they could not see their harbinger of doom. We have also seen experiments crafted in such a way that they could only confirm a founders' hypotheses.

The unconscious nature of this trap, or its foundation in founder bias, can make it very difficult to detect, especially early on, and its impact can be very damaging. In the worst case it could even cause teams to run out of runway before they get a chance to truly prove whether their business may have been viable. To help you better understand what to look for, let's explore a few of the ways this can manifest itself.

### Insidious Committed Bet: Premature Scaling

One way in which an insidious committed bet can negatively impact a business is very similar to the classic committed bet discussed in Chapter 2. As teams become passionate about their idea, and confident they have identified the right solution, they can increase their team size too rapidly (see Figure 4-12). This hiring ramp is usually not as large as in a classic committed bet, because the incubating teams tend to be smaller as are their budgets, but the impact can be at least as severe, if not more so.

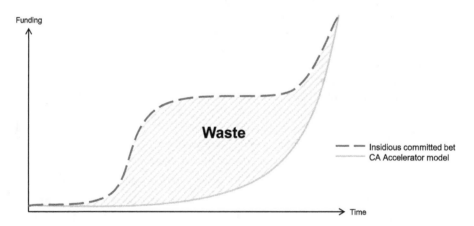

**Figure 4-12.** Insidious committed bet resulting in premature scaling

As mentioned in Chapter 2, in addition to the potential budget pressure that can result, hiring too early can put too much of a strain on the management team, distracting them and impeding them from achieving their primary objective of obtaining product-market fit. In addition, if the founders increase their team size too early, they can wind up with an annual run rate (the projected amount they will spend on personnel and other expenses over the next 12 months) that is out of sync with their progress. That can cause investors to lose confidence in the management team or simply make the investment unattractive.

*Insidious Committed Bet: Reduced Velocity*

Another type of insidious committed bet occurs when a team prematurely commits to a solution (stops experimenting), but does not increase the size of their team (see Figure 4-13). In essence, they are building the wrong solution at the right pace and cost. Though the team's run rate is not out of sync, this type of misstep can still put the business in jeopardy as they lose time pursuing the wrong solution. Assuming the team is eventually able to pivot to a viable solution (and that is a big assumption), it will cost them more to achieve product-market fit. Though that waste may not be the worst impact of this trap.

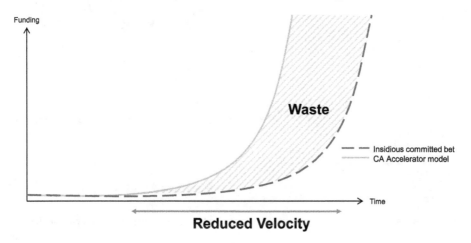

**Figure 4-13.** Insidious committed bet resulting in reduced velocity

At best, pursuing the wrong solution will result in a later time to market. This can erode any first mover advantage—or even deliver first mover advantage as a gift to someone else who encounters the incubating business and realizes they are missing the real opportunity. In the worst cases they can be blocked from the space they pioneered if, for example, the second (or third…) mover is able to gain strategic control via patents or establishment of thought leadership or a viable community. Furthermore, even if the incubating team is able to find the right solution they may find themselves facing an enormous amount of technical debt, turning their first mover advantage into a first mover disadvantage.

*Insidious Committed Bet: Premature Scaling and Reduced Velocity*

When these insidious committed bets evolve, they often result in both premature scaling and reduced velocity. Figure 4-14 illustrates a case where a team scales too early, eventually realizes they are headed in the wrong direction, and then has to extend their timeline to pursue a more viable solution. When this happens, teams can be subject to any or all of the negative impacts discussed earlier in this section.

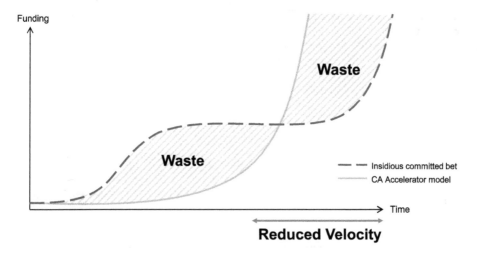

**Figure 4-14.** Insidious committed bet resulting in premature scaling and reduced velocity

---

Thus far our experience is that insidious committed bets are most likely to manifest themselves a few months into our Series A.

---

Falling victim to insidious committed bets, no matter how small, steals funding from other potential incubations at best, and may even destroy a business' chances of survival. Thus far our experience is that insidious committed bets are most likely to manifest themselves a few months into our Series A. This may be because, as teams begin to build shippable products and their work becomes a bit more like their work in the mature line of business, some of the bad muscle memory we discussed earlier starts to exercise itself. Therefore, founders, Angels, and program and operations team members must be deliberately and diligently on the lookout for insidious committed bets. They can be a business—and a program—killer.

# Series B

The objective of Series B is to achieve product-market fit and bring the business to a point where the mature product organization is willing to acquire it. As was mentioned earlier, the product organization can acquire an incubating business before it achieves product-market fit. They would typically do so if the incubation has sufficiently demonstrated its viability and they believe the mature organization can accelerate its achievement of product-market fit. Businesses that receive Series B funding are significantly more likely to exit successfully than businesses in earlier rounds.

Key activities in Series B include:

- Providing evidence that the business has achieved product-market fit and delivered on its unique value proposition

- Providing evidence of growth and ability to scale

- Developing a clear sales and partnership strategy

- Completing Series B-specific acquisition-related requirements

- Achievement of a contingent acquisition commitment from a line of business (often referred to as a "letter of intent")

- Developing a Series C plan

In Series B teams begin preparing to exit. We use the same procedures for acquisition of Accelerator businesses that we use for external acquisitions, with very little modification. We believe that, though acquisitions from our Accelerator should be simpler, they should be held to the same standard as external acquisitions. Since employees of incubating businesses already work for the company, many of the procedures are much less costly, less error-prone, and can be executed much more rapidly. Figure 4-15 shows our Series B Kanban.

| RANK ∧ | ID | NAME | SCHEDULE STATE |
|---|---|---|---|
| 1 | US125139 | Product-Market Fit: Pass the Sean Ellis Test (Team) | N |
| 2 | US324502 | Product Market Fit: Achieve Targeted Monthly Retention Rate | N |
| 3 | US125163 | Evidence of Growth and Ability to Scale: CAC, LTV, COGS (Bus Lead) | N |
| 4 | US125473 | Evidence of Growth and Ability to Scale: Traction Model Validated with Target Weekly Growth Rate Achieved (Bus Lead) | N |
| 5 | US125160 | Evidence that Go-to-Market Strategy Is Effective and will Scale | N |
| 6 | US125156 | Clear Sales & Partner Strategy (Bus Lead and Sales Ops) | N |
| 7 | US350898 | Acquisition Related Requirements: Investor Pitch | N |
| 8 | US351844 | Acquisition Related Requirements: Executive Summary | N |
| 9 | US351851 | Acquisition Related Requirements: Input to Business Case and Investment Committee Deck | N |
| 10 | US351855 | Acquisition Related Requirements: Documented, Contingent Acquisition Committment | N |
| 11 | US125140 | Series C Plan Established (Bus Lead) | N |
| 12 | US125499 | Conduct an Invention Harvesting Session (Team) | N |
| 13 | US197524 | Program Logistics (Accelerator Ops) | N |

**Figure 4-15.** Series B Kanban

## Series C and Exit

Series C focuses on scaling the business and successfully exiting to the mature product organization.

Key activities in Series C include:

- Demonstration of the business' viability through continued growth and increased scale

- Completion of the acquisition-related requirements (usually outlined in the "letter of intent" contingency agreement)

- Completion of acquisition due diligence

- Exit from the Accelerator to the mature organization

As was mentioned previously, incubating businesses follow virtually the same acquisition process as external acquisitions. This includes the same due diligence process as an external acquisition. While execution of the process should be simpler, it is no less rigorous. Figure 4-16 shows our Series C Kanban.

| RANK ∧ | ID | NAME | SCHEDULE STATE |
|---|---|---|---|
| 1 | US125738 | Evidence of Continued Growth and Scale (Team) | N |
| 2 | US350906 | Technical Due Diligence Completed (Team) | N |
| 3 | US350907 | Business Due Diligence Completed (Corp. Business Dev) | N |
| 4 | US350909 | Final Decision to Acquire (BU) | N |
| 5 | US125744 | Conducted Invention Harvesting Session (Team) | N |
| 6 | ▶ US239159 | Program Logistics (Accelerator Ops) | N |
| 7 | US387844 | Consider transition of Source and IP to standard CA repositories for BU governance alignment (Contact ... | N |

**Figure 4-16.** Series C Kanban

## Pauses

To date, most of the teams that have paused in our program have made the decision to pause on their own.

As is the case in the world of external startups, it is more likely that a business incubating in our Accelerator will pause than exit as a viable business. Sometimes the pause occurs when the Angel Team decides that a business is not viable or not headed in a productive direction and decides not to fund it any longer. However, often a business team will make that decision on their own and declare to the Angel Team that they believe their business should pause. To date, most of the teams that have paused in our program have made the decision to pause on their own. We believe our commitment to Lean startup discipline, our Agile mindset, our bias to transparency, and the absence of fear due to our "learn fast" versus "fail fast" culture are all major contributors to this.

Key activities that take place during a pause include:

- Winding down business activities
- Capturing and repurposing IP
- Ensuring a smooth transition for customers
- Ensuring incubating team members have a smooth transition to their next role
- Celebrating

Figure 4-17 shows our Pause Kanban.

## Celebrating "Learning Fast"

Just as we celebrate exits, we celebrate pauses. In fact, you will notice item seven in our Pause Kanban (see Figure 4-17) specifically reminds us to spend time thinking about recognition and rewards as a business pauses. In Chapter 2 we highlighted a great example of that in the story of the woman who called a pause on her own business and was rewarded with a bonus for one of the most effective executions of an incubation we had witnessed, and eventually a double promotion. We celebrate and reward successful, effective risk-taking.

| RANK ^ | ID | NAME | SCHEDULE STATE |
|---|---|---|---|
| 1 | US217413 | Communicate Pause Decision | N |
| 2 | US217380 | Disposition IP as appropriate | N |
| 3 | US429123 | Turn over ownership of any active research projects | N |
| 4 | US217382 | Assess Code Reuse | N |
| 5 | US217383 | Assess New Business Opportunities that leverage IP | N |
| 6 | US217384 | Back Rotate Incubation Rotation team members | N |
| 7 | US217399 | Recognition Awards? | N |
| 8 | US217408 | Cancel Services / Reassign Ownership | N |
| 9 | US460600 | Provide Product Marketing with your businesses contact database | N |
| 10 | US429190 | Remove product mentions from internal systems | N |
| 11 | US217410 | Return Equipment | N |
| 12 | US211803 | Prepare and Schedule your Business "Respin" (if applicable) | N |
| 13 | US431065 | Handle the Turnover and Funding Allocation for Any Active Research Projects (if applicable) | N |

**Figure 4-17.** Pause Kanban

Rewards and recognition are a key aspect of our culture. We believe in rewarding good performance and excellent execution, even if it leads to a discovery that a business is not viable. Whether a business exits successfully or pauses, we reward the team and throw them a party. Another advantage of operating the Accelerator in an established organization is that we have access to all of the reward programs the mainstream business provides. For us these include, for example, the ability to give a cash award to any employee who deserves it, any time we believe it is justified.

### Benefiting from "Successful Failure"

You may have also noticed the Pause Kanban reminds us to reuse and repurpose any technology that may have been developed, and to appropriately capture any IP that was developed through activities such as invention harvesting. We look for other teams and projects that might benefit from any research done by the incubating team or any technology they may have developed. We leverage our InnerSource[4] system to capture that technology and share it companywide.

### Winding Down

Other activities during the Pause Phase are largely related to gently winding down the business. People who entered the Accelerator on Incubation Rotation return to their business units once the business has paused, or once they are no longer needed to help with pause activities. Others move to "The Bench," which is discussed in detail later. We also work to ensure early adopters of the business have a smooth transition.

# Conclusion

We provided a lot of information in this chapter in order to enable you to create a successful, mature, fully-functioning program of your own. However, do not let the amount of information here overwhelm you. Though this material represents the current state of our program, it did not look like this when we started. You may recall that we built our program incrementally. We encourage you to do the same. We recommend that you:

- Do not attempt to apply all of the material in this chapter at once; we didn't

---

[4]InnerSource takes the lessons learned from developing open source software and applies them to the way companies develop software internally. For more information, visit InnerSource Commons at https://paypal.github.io/InnerSourceCommons/

- Begin by creating only the artifacts and ceremonies that are absolutely necessary for the current state of your program (your MVP)

  - e.g., If you have no incubating businesses, you need only create the submission mechanism, you do not even need to have the pitch event structure ready until you have a backlog of pitches

- Think lean: Make the smallest possible additions or changes to your program and release them as experiments

- Don't be upset when something does not work; celebrate because you've just learned something

- Inspect and adapt as you execute
- Remember you need only stay one phase ahead of the most advanced team in your program

  - If you can exceed that, great, but don't sacrifice the quality of the program or your quality of life to do so

You should also keep in mind that you, and the teams incubating in your program, have a huge advantage over startups not operating inside an established organization. You have access to a vast support structure. Our next chapter explores how to take advantage of that.

# Innovation Support Structure

## An Established Business' Unfair Advantage

*"Innovation is not the product of logical thought, although the result is tied to logical structure."*

—Albert Einstein

Unfortunately, it is not enough to put a formal incubation program in place and simply walk away. As we pointed out in Chapter 4, there needs to be a team to take ownership of keeping the incubation program, and its spirit, on track. There have been times when we have attempted to turn over even small portions of the program to other teams and things started to get off track quickly. It is not simply a matter of skill, although that is important; it is a matter of context and having the right resources and support. People need to truly understand the intent of the program and be properly trained on the elements they will be responsible for. Otherwise, they can become blindly artifact-focused—much like the 70-page template example from Chapter 2.

© CA 2019
G. Watt and H. Abrams, *Lean Entrepreneurship,*
https://doi.org/10.1007/978-1-4842-3942-1_5

The same requirements apply to your intrapreneurs. They need to have the proper skills, resources, context, and passion for the problem, to be successful. To do that and take advantage of everything the larger corporation has to offer, your intrapreneurs will need a support system. The individual pieces of this support system will take many forms—some as formal programs, others as informal business relationships—but all critical to the program's success. As we pointed out in Chapter 2, the odds of success of any given new business are slim and this is even more true of the types of very early stage businesses that we accept into our incubation program—where they start with nothing more than an idea. Your incubations will need every bit of your company's expertise that they can get in order to gain a leg up and have the best possible chance to succeed.

Today, your company already has expertise in a variety of domains. Some of this proficiency is simply in the day-to-day running of an established business. For example, your company's resources and experience related to legal, finance, and human resources took time to perfect, but a brand-new startup would need to build those capabilities from scratch. Building those competencies takes time and is often very expensive—it can be hard to find the right people and even harder to turn them into the right team. Without this capability in-house, a startup may need to contract or outsource these functions, which can be more expensive and may not have the quality or results they require.

That said, while those business functions are very important, unless your business is in innovating in those back-office functions, they do not provide differentiating value to your customers. Over time a startup will eventually build experience and catch up in those areas. Instead, it is the expertise in your company's specific business domain areas that gives you a sustainable advantage over your external startup competitors. By leveraging inherent capabilities within your company, especially your domain expertise in the markets you already serve, you can extend your competitive edge into new businesses and in ways your smaller rivals cannot. Together, all this additional help forms an innovation support structure that gives your company a substantial advantage compared to building an external business from scratch.

# Leverage Your Company's Experts

There are pros and cons to building a new business as a virtual entity within a larger organization versus creating a truly separate external company. The benefits of creating an internal incubation can easily outweigh the downsides, but only if you effectively use the full scope of the established company's resources. When you are successful at using those resources, building a new business internally can give you a significant head start, and sustained advantage, compared to building a new external startup from the ground up.

There are the obvious benefits of building internally and leveraging the existing infrastructure of the established business. For example, there is no need to waste time and money finding the right office space to lease because you can use the company's existing facilities. There is no need to shop your company around to multiple venture capital firms and hire lawyers to review term sheets each time your business needs more funding because you can follow a set incubation process and approved funds can be allocated quickly and easily.

There are also some less obvious advantages of leveraging the established company's infrastructure, such as utilizing the existing employee on-boarding, accounting, payroll, and benefits administration. When these advantages are all used effectively, it means that on day one, your intrapreneurs and their teams can immediately focus on what matters: determining if there is a customer and market for their potential business idea. Your incubation teams are not wasting their time on tasks unless they can yield business learning.

## Business Functions

If you are within a large, established, business, think for a moment about the breadth and depth of the resources available to you. Finance experts to help you manage an incubation's budget, a legal team to write and review contracts, a group of human resources professionals to help attract, develop, and retain the best talent, an IT team to keep the network running and replace computer hardware when it fails—this list goes on and on. When Founders can effectively take advantage of these horizontal capabilities, it means they can focus on their potential business and not get bogged down in the minutia and busywork that comes with running a standalone company. While back-office work must be done, it does not provide any direct and differentiating value to your customers. Every minute and dollar spent on those nondifferentiated tasks is a minute and dollar not spent on de-risking the new business.

While you certainly could leave it to each Founder to figure out how to best leverage these corporate resources on their own, a more effective approach is to build a network of support that each incubation team can draw upon from day one. To be effective, you must build a virtual team made up of representatives from each and every part of the business that a Founder could possibly need. This way, when an incubation team does have an issue and needs help, they instantly know who within the company they can call. Remember, what these incubation teams are doing is much different than what the rest of the company does day-to-day, so it is very important that the person they call has the context needed to help them. Otherwise, the Founder will feel like they are caught up in red tape and will need to justify every move they make, without making any forward progress.

## You Want to Do What?!

When we first started our program and put this virtual team in place, there were gaps. We had talked to many teams and people, but we missed collaborating with some others. The teams we overlooked were therefore missing the context of what we were trying to achieve and how we were trying to achieve it. A great example was the first time we tried to create a separate web presence for one of our new incubations. There was an upcoming company tradeshow and, since this business was brand new, the incubation team was asked via email what they wanted the sign above their demo station to say. They replied to the marketing team with their recently chosen name, "offbrand.com".[1]

Alarm bells instantly went off within the brand marketing team: "You want to call it what?!" and "But that product name does not have 'CA' in it!" and "Who approved that name?!" and "You cannot do that in our company!". These responses were completely understandable. After all, the branding team works hard to maintain consistency in how their company is represented in the marketplace and is known to customers. That is what an established business does, but that is not what a new business actually *needs*. We had included marketing in our initial virtual team, but "marketing" is a fairly broad term with many sub-disciplines. We had neglected to coordinate with the Brand Marketing team and hence their confusion and concern.

After nearly a dozen phone calls across multiple levels of the company—from C-level on down—and a lot of background and context, we were able to not only get the Brand Marketing team's agreement but, with the proper context, they, as well as the overall Marketing team, became one of our biggest champions. We accomplished this by explaining what we were trying to achieve with our new incubation program. We explained why this off-brand marketing was important to the incubation team—how they needed to stand out among startups with clever and unusual names. Perhaps more importantly, we also explained how it was also very important to keep these incubations separate from CA Technologies' overall brand.

What resonated most was their realization that most of these businesses would not be viable, and "some could leave a spectacular crater" when they failed. When we explained that when a business did fail, they probably would not want it to take the CA Technologies brand with it, they got it. Together we came to an agreement that we would use a "CA Accelerator incubation" tagline for each business. This would ensure that we were being transparent about this business being part of CA Technologies, but at the same time helping customers of the incubations understand exactly how immature they are. We highlight the more strategic benefits of this brand separation in the next chapter.

---

[1]This was not their actual name, but it might as well have been.

Without this brand separation between the core business and the businesses we are incubating, customers may make assumptions about the business' maturity. For example, customers might expect the same level of support from their incubation products as they get from their enterprise-grade products. Conversely, incubations might be forced into catering to larger business customers even if that is not the right fit for the current state of their business. If you recall, treating your new businesses the same way your treat your established businesses is one of the core problems we identified in Chapter 2.

Fast-forwarding to today, there is near-zero friction when it comes to our interactions with the corporate marketing and branding teams. Corporate marketing supports the brand and go-to-market freedom as it demonstrates a healthy focus on innovation by the larger company. We have policies in place on what our incubation teams can and cannot do, as well as a simple process the team can follow to get a new product name checked for trademark clearance, get branding approval, and have domain names purchased. Not only is our process easy and lightweight, when compared to a startup, it is also faster and more thorough. Most incubation teams have an off-brand website up and running within days—no lawyer to retain, no IT professional to call.

Our branding process is lightweight and tailored for the needs of the incubation program, but it is just one example of many. We get tailored support for our incubation program from many different teams within the larger company. The teams not only do this willingly, they often volunteer. What is in it for them? In addition to wanting to see the program be successful and play a part in that success, they know which parts of their processes for the established business are important and which can be skipped when it comes to the incubations. They would much rather have teams follow a lighter-weight process than skip it entirely and cause problems for the entire company. For example, keeping incubation teams to the same high standards the rest of the company follows when it comes to trademark and legal compliance.

## Domain Expertise

Still, the resources available to you go beyond horizontal business functions. Your secret weapon in this fight against your smaller startup competition is your ability to take advantage of your company's domain expertise. You have experts in variety of related domains. Experts in Marketing and Sales in your core business markets can help your incubations understand and reach their customers with messaging that resonates and differentiates their new offering. Experts in strategy and pricing can help your incubations understand the competition's strength and weaknesses and price your new offering strategically. They can also give you an understanding of what you need to be thinking about for the future as you scale and move beyond early adopters.

## Incubation Advisory Board

As we mentioned in Chapter 4, each incubation should recruit its own independent advisory board. This group of people should be made up of experts, sourced internally or externally, that the Incubation Founder can draw from to advise their team on anything and everything—from help introducing them to new customers, to software architecture advice. The key is that the Founder needs to be proactive and take advantage of the advisory team's expertise—and they may need to be reminded of that periodically. Because an incubation's needs will change over time, the Founder should periodically change the makeup of this group based on their current needs.

Not only does this interaction between advisors and Founders help these new potential businesses, it is helpful to these domain experts as well. For an hour or two each week, they get to step out of their day job, which is often primarily about execution, and think strategically about the bigger picture and the potential whitespace in the market—the market they are in today, the market the incubating team is working to capture a piece of, or perhaps something in between. It is very easy to get stuck in an operational groove. Advising a team gets them out of that groove and gets them back to open-ended creative thinking.

Opening up how and what they think about is not only a morale booster, but it can be a big benefit to the overall company. The things they are exposed to in their role as an advisor—market information, emerging competitors, new technologies—might also be helpful to the advisor in the context of their day job. Letting these employees take time from working on the established business to think outside the box—outside their existing business unit strategy—and imagine "what if?" is invaluable. After all, that is what innovation is all about.

## Ad Hoc Angel Team Advisors

In addition to leveraging this existing expertise directly on a particular incubation advisory board, it can also be leveraged across teams. Regardless of an individual's specific domain of expertise, there are multiple ways you can leverage these internal specialists. These experts already have full-time jobs, so exactly how you leverage them will vary depending on the amount of time they and their management chain can commit to.

There are the subject matter experts whose opinions are highly regarded but who are exceptionally busy and cannot commit to helping on any regular interval nor for any fixed amount of time. For these types of people, you might only leverage their expertise time-to-time and on an ad hoc basis to review an incubating business. This can be a huge help in a situation where the Angel Team feels they lack sufficient expertise to make an investment decision independently. For example, asking a technical domain expert to review the feasibility of building a new product, or a business domain expert to validate there will be a large enough market for a new product to make an investment worthwhile.

## Dedicated Cross-Team Resources

On the other end of the commitment spectrum, there are subject matter experts who work for teams outside the incubation program but who *can* be dedicated to helping your incubations full-time. For example, the marketing team might be able and willing to commit the time of a product marketing generalist. This person's full-time responsibilities would involve spending a few hours a week with each incubation team to make sure they understand how to craft their messaging to convey the value of their solutions. Exactly which expertise is used in this full-time manner depends not only on commitment but also need. For our program, a large percentage of Founders come from a technical background. Therefore, if we can pair Founders with a marketing expert at the start of their project, the team can move faster and execute better while they search for a dedicated marketing lead for their incubation.

## Standing Advisor Relationships

Between these two extremes is the most common interaction. Experts who can dedicate a small number of hours each week to help advise or review these incubating businesses. Some of these experts may join incubation advisory boards, but others may be appropriate for the Angel Team to round out the team's domain knowledge. Some may engage with the team on a nearly daily basis, while others are only utilized on an as-needed basis. The choices you make will all depend on the expertise you have in-house and the flexibility of those individuals.

For expertise you do not have in house, you will need to look externally. Remember, by definition, these incubations are not simple adjacencies to the established business. There will be some instances where their markets may extend well outside the bounds of the current company's expertise. While we have not often needed to look externally, there are occasions when external advisors can be extremely helpful to the incubation. It is important to work with your legal team ahead of this becoming an issue so that you can understand what type of contract is needed in these situations.

In Figure 5-1, we present an overview of the various categories of experts that should be leveraged in your program. The figure includes examples roles they each play, but this is just illustrative. The specifics will depend on your organization and the types of businesses you are building.

**Incubation Advisory Board**

Individuals chosen based on the needs of each incubation team at its current state

**Dedicated Cross-Team Resources**

Program Management, Marketing, User Experience, Technology De-risking

**Business Functions**

Sales Operations, Legal, Finance, Information Technology, Procurement, Human Resources

**Standing Advisor Relationships**

Strategic Research, Corporate Strategy, User Experience, Pricing, Communities, Marketing, Sales

**Angel Team**

CTO, SVP Incubation, Business Unit Representatives, Mergers and Acquisitions, Strategy, Marketing, Finance, HR, Engineering

**Figure 5-1.** Illustrative example of advisor categories

For our company and the type of businesses we are building within our program, it makes sense to have a mixture of approaches. For example, for the functions that we want involved early in the incubation process, such as Product Marketing and User Experience, we have a limited number of full-time resources that are dedicated to the incubation program. For teams that are in the earlier stages—Seed 1 and Seed 2—these horizontal resources are working directly with Founders as part-time members of their team. Once an incubation reaches the later stages of the program, they hire their own full-time resources and our cross-team experts move into an advisory role. Some of these resources work directly for the Accelerator program; others work for centrally managed teams in the larger company but are dedicated to the Accelerator program. We never turn down help from the right person simply because of organizational structure.

Using your company's resources effectively is a key tool at your disposal that can help you beat your competitors and give your incubations the best chance of success. Once you have built a successful new business within your incubation program, the hard work does not end there. You also need to give these businesses the best chance of success within your larger company and over the long term.

# Handling Success

Roughly half of all new businesses will fail within the first five years.[2] It is a blunt message, but important to periodically remind yourself and to say out loud to your intrapreneurs. However, you do not want those failures to be due to forced execution errors that could otherwise be foreseen and avoided. Innovation and new business creation are hard, but when a team does find the magic combination of the right people, the right product, and the right market, you want to position the team for continued success and avoid putting unnecessary roadblocks in their way.

Imagine what it would be like to create a successful, but still very small, new business within your organization. Unfortunately, your intrapreneur has just been incubating their new business as a standalone virtual company for the last few years. They operated with a different set of processes and a different sense of urgency than the business unit they are about to move into. Since they have not yet reached sufficient scale they also have been losing money. While that is common for early stage companies, there will be a limited amount of patience for losses in the business unit. How long can they continue to run at a loss without getting shut down? Will they get the proper and necessary investment to successfully scale their business and burn down their technical debt? What will happen to their existing brand and online presence? How long will they be allowed to operate independently and continue to ignore the corporate processes that are necessary for a scaled and established business?

Luckily, your company already knows how to handle these problems, because they are the exact same set of problems you already have with any small external acquisition. The answer is therefore simple: Treat these internal successes as you would an external acquisition into your business unit. This approach not only provides you a known roadmap to follow within your company, but it also gives you permission to not artificially constrain the incubations. It allows these new businesses to do things differently while outside the core business units. When someone protests, "But that is not how our process works! If your incubation is successful we will have to do all this work to fit them into our business.", your reply is simple: "This is no different than a startup we want to acquire. We would never think about forcing every other startup in the world to follow our processes, and we should not try to force this one." Point made.

Of course, while unshackling your incubations will help them execute better and faster, it also means that they could be operating in significantly different ways than your core business operates. It means these new businesses will

---

therefore need more time and money to integrate into a business unit if they are successful. When an external startup gets acquired, they must do the same, but the benefit of acquiring an internal business is that the Founders know what to expect ahead of time.

When going through acquisition due diligence, an external startup's leadership would need to answer literally hundreds of questions ranging from legal and finance issues through technology and product development practices. Not only are some of these questions irrelevant for an internal business, the remaining questions that are relevant are known in advance. An incubation team can weigh the costs and benefits of aligning themselves with an existing business and the tradeoffs they would need to make in their business execution. In some cases, they may want to conform to a particular business unit's practices to make it easier to get acquired down the road. In other cases, they may opt for less friction and higher speed knowing they will pay for that at a later date once they are acquired.

There are pros and cons to trying to align an incubation with an existing business unit. While making it easier to get acquired, it is quite possible that alignment is the exact opposite of what a team needs to fully explore the possibilities of a new business. It is also quite possible that the end result of a truly successful incubation is the creation of an entirely new business unit. Even when entering an existing business unit, an incubation may bring new and better approaches and processes with it and the business unit might be the one who needs to conform and adapt. The incubation team must keep their potential acquirers in mind, but at the same time, be careful not to prematurely optimize for that business unit.

That does not mean the incubation should completely ignore the established business' potential requirements or their due diligence questions. The business unit still needs to do its homework and feel comfortable that this new business is going to be scalable and meet their tactical and strategic needs. That means, just as with an external acquisition, they need a business case that both the business unit and the acquired business can commit to. That business case needs to include not only justifiable financial projections—costs, revenue, and additional investment—but also lay out how it fits into business unit's long-term strategy.

The General Manager of the business unit and the Incubation Founder must both feel comfortable agreeing to this plan. Once that agreement is in place, it forms what in the outside world would be called a "letter of intent" to acquire the business. With that formal agreement, the incubation program team and the business unit operations and finance teams can work together to orchestrate a smooth transition and begin the hard work of integration and scaling the newly acquired business.

As the transition begins, the business case forms the basic high-level blue-print for how the integration should progress. For example, how it will fit into the business unit's marketing messaging and branding or what additional resources will be required to begin scaling sales. Because there is no capital expense—no stock to buy—as there would be with an external startup, all the financial discussions come down to operational expenses in the business case. However, there is no need for further haggling. The additional operating expense the business unit needs to run this additional business and any profits and losses are already taken into account and agreed upon in the business case.

Without this clear business case to follow, established companies can easily fall into a common trap that often kills the new business. When the incuba-tion first enters the business unit, everything is wonderful. However, because it is now operating within an established business that has committed financial metrics to maintain, if or when that business unit hits a downturn and rev-enues fall, there will be a need to save operating expenses to maintain margin. There are other scenarios that may also lead to the same outcome, such as a change in leadership or a new internal competing project. Regardless of the cause of this friction and rethinking of the investment, without a written and committed business case and rationale, there will be the tendency to see this new business that does not yet have meaningful revenue—because it is still trying to scale—and make the short-sighted decision to kill the product and eliminate the team to save on operating expenses. Depending on the depth of the downturn or impact of leadership change, a business case cannot com-pletely prevent that situation, but it does mean there will be an objective and data-driven conversation to consider and weigh all the options.

If you get this entire sequence right, you end up with a process that moves a successful business into a business unit. A process that moves the new busi-ness as a self-contained unit—a business that is ready to be scaled—into the established business and not projects that will ultimately be cannibalized for people or cost savings. Because intrapreneurs know all the steps of the pro-cess ahead of time and know all the questions they will need to have answers to, they can prepare well in advance. They can make intelligent and informed decisions on what company processes to follow and which to ignore.

The incubation team does not need to wait until their final negotiations to determine how this new business will fit in with the rest of the company. The Founders can and should be planning this as they incubate their business—for example, talking with general managers or socializing their success stories with the sales team. Anything and everything they feel will help them learn what the larger business needs and help the larger business understand the value they can bring. They know they need to build a repeatable, scalable, and meaningful business if they want to claim success. They also know they need a business case that can clearly articulate why this business is a good use of the company's money and deserves continued or increased investment. Sure, there are still many of the same challenges as there are when integrating an external business, but because the nature of the work is known up-front, it can be planned for. If done right, there will be significantly less work and risk than acquiring an external startup—just one more advantage your internal business has.

The success of a business ultimately comes down to people. Once an incubation moves into a business unit, how do you retain your talented and successful intrapreneurs? How do you keep this critical talent engaged and dissuade them from immediately leaving the company and building a new external startup? After all, when it finally comes down to it, they are going to ask themselves, "what's in it for me?"

# What's in It for Me?

We are often asked to talk to many of our company's customers about our incubation program. In our presentations, we explain at a high level why we built the program, how it works, as well as the success and failures we have had, and the lessons have learned along the way. At the end of the presentation, we will often get questions on how we handle when something is not successful, or just as important, when something is successful. Out of all these sessions, one of the most frequent questions we are asked is, "Do these employees have a stake in the business?"

Initially, our answer was an emphatic "no". We thought this through when we initially put the program in place and deliberately decided we wanted to attract employees who were passionate about solving their customers' problems and seeing their vision come to life. We did not want to attract employees who were just in it for the money and saw the program as a way to gamble and land a big windfall. We decided that we already had our standard corporate tools to bonus and retain our most talented employees, and those tools would be just as effective in our situation as they are in the rest of the company. Interestingly enough, with only one or two exceptions, our Incubation Founders and employees never asked us what was in it for them. They were ecstatic to have this opportunity and were content with their risks and rewards as they stood. Two years into our program we changed our minds, but not because Founders started asking for it.

Hiring talented employees is always tough, especially when looking for entrepreneurial oriented people in markets like San Francisco or New York City. Our allure, and what we considered our unfair advantage, was that we offered the best of both worlds: As an employee on one of our incubation teams, you get the lower risks and higher rewards of working in a large, established, business combined with the fast-paced and rewarding work of building a new business in a startup-like fashion. This message resonates when we are talking to job candidates, especially since we can offer a more competitive package as compared to many startups. However, periodically a prospective new employee would be negotiating their salary and press for more money, claiming that if they went to a startup they would get stock in that startup and could therefore make a lot more money than they would with their corporate salary and bonus.

We did not immediately buy this argument. We had assumed that as a typical employee in a typical startup, the amount of stock you would get combined with the chances of a successful exit would mean our compensation packages would be very competitive. But when we began to hear this argument come up on a recurring basis, we decided we needed some ammunition: we needed to do the math.

We pulled our internal compensation market data for the San Francisco Bay area and compared it against data we pulled from websites such as AngelList.[3] In many respects, AngelList is like any other job site on the Internet, except that it caters specifically to startups. Because of that targeting, and unlike most jobs sites, the positions list equity ranges in addition to salary ranges. What is more, from what we saw and when it comes to technology and the type of work, we were able to find job descriptions that seemed very comparable to the positions and work within our incubation teams.

Table 5-1 gives an example of some of the data we synthesized in our analysis. In addition to using the information from AngelList and our internal market data, we also made some assumptions on dilution, valuation, time scales, and other factors we distilled from articles we found on *80,000 Hours*[4] and *Entrepreneur*.[5]

In the table, the third column lists how much we would pay for an equivalent position compared to the startup, including the additional equity stake. In the end, the takeaway was that the average, non-founding, employee is better off monetarily working in our Accelerator program than joining a startup—even without taking into account additional corporate bonuses and benefits.

[3] AngelList, https://angel.co
[4] Ben West, "Startup Employees Don't Earn More," *80000 Hours*, October 7th, 2015, https://80000hours.org/2015/10/startup-salaries-and-equity-compensation
[5] Scott Shane, "What Slow Exits Mean to Startup Investors," *Entrepreneur*, December 3, 2015, https://www.entrepreneur.com/article/253459

**Table 5-1.** Comparison of Expected Annualized Earnings for Employees Working for a Startup vs. Working for an Established Business. Compiled from Internal and External Data in 2016.

| Startup Role | Startup Equity | Corporate vs. Startup Salary + Bonus |
|---|---|---|
| Full Stack Engineer | 0.50% | 107.6% |
| Tech Lead | 0.08% | 133.1% |
| Sr. Full Stack Engineer | 0.75% | 128.9% |
| Engineer | 0.48% | 125.9% |
| Engineer | 1.50% | 93.9% |
| Sr. Full Stack Engineer | 0.08% | 136.3% |
| Sr. Full Stack Engineer | 0.43% | 122.8% |
| Sr. Full Stack Engineer | 0.20% | 144.9% |

It may seem easy to discard those additional benefits as inconsequential, but they are not. Established business know they must complete for talent against the latest shiny new startups and their extensive benefits are one way they do that. Those corporate benefits include monetary rewards such as bonuses for filing patents, 401K matching and profit sharing, and restricted stock awards used to retain top talent. There are also benefits designed to help employees maintain a balanced life such as matching charitable donations, tuition reimbursement, or pet benefits. For example, CA Technologies allows employees to take time off for bonding with new pets or to grieve the loss of a beloved pet. Last, but certainly not least, you get all these benefits upfront, without needing to wait years for a potential exit. Sure, this analysis only looks at the average case and there will be some cases where an employee would be better off at a startup. You can always get lucky and be an early employee of the next Facebook or Google, but you may not want to bet on that.

Where this favorability started to break down is when we compared our internal founders with their external counterparts. As you can see in the previous table, it is more profitable to work in an established business in every case except one. When an employee owns a significant percentage of the company's equity—typically only the very earliest employees in the least dilutive companies—over the long term and on average they could be better off financially in a startup than creating a new business within our incubation program.

A founder in a successful venture capital backed startup could, on average, own as much as 15 percent or more[6] of their company when it is eventually sold or has a public offering. Sure, the odds still mean that the average windfall will be reduced, and as founders they will most likely not be able or want to liquidate their entire stake, but if they can build and sell a business for $100 million, compared to the corporate intrapreneur, they are still way ahead.

This meant, while we were correct in assuming most employees are better off financially working for an established business and getting standard benefits and compensation, our analysis showed that the founders and early key employees may not be. These are the exact people who most deserve to be rewarded and are most needed to be retained. Another point to back this up is that our existing rewards compensated incubation teams for doing their job, but there was nothing substantial in it for them if they built a $10 million business verses a $100 million business. We would treat both as great successes, but there is an order of magnitude difference in the results. We want teams to build the biggest businesses they can, and when they do, we want to make sure they are compensated fairly.

We considered many options to correct this imbalance. For example, one option was we could pay every member of a successful team a bonus based on the value of the business they created. While technically possible, practically speaking that option posed so many potential problems to the point where it was nearly intractable. Who would determine the valuation? What methodology would be used? Would it bias us to create only certain types of business? How would we handle team members who are more valuable than others or have put in different amounts of time and effort? Where would the money come from to pay this bonus? Would the group paying the bonus have too much incentive to short-change the team?

We wanted a program that could address all those questions and concerns and that could be transparent—as transparency is a core value of our team and program. The answer we eventually came up with did not cover every corner case, but it did cover our primary use cases and achieved our goals of being fair and objective, and at the same time easy to explain and administer.

Our solution was to create a new bonus plan that pays a percentage of revenue from the incubation business for the first two years after it successfully moves into a business unit. While, as a public company, we could not create a separate equity structure and give out stock shares of the incubation like a startup could, the team founder is authorized to distribute portions of this bonus to members of their team in any way they deem appropriate and at

---

[6]Sammy Adbullah, "The Median Level of Founder Ownership at Exit," *Blossom Street Ventures* (blog), November 3, 2016, https://blossomstreetventures.com/blog_details.php?bcat_id=106

any time up until the point of their exit. The business unit will always have the budget available to pay the bonus because the plan only pays a percentage of revenue actually brought in and this amount was already accounted for in the business case used to acquire this business.

Take a hypothetical example of a founder who creates a successful business that is projected to earn revenue of $10 million next year and $20 million the year after. In this example, the bonus plan pays 10% of revenue, so if the team hits those milestones they split $1 million after the first year, and $2 million after the second year—$3 million in total payments. It is up to the founder to decide prior to exit how this bonus is divided among the team. Perhaps in this case the founder gave each of their top five people 15 percent and kept the remaining 25 percent for themselves. That means the founder would earn a bonus of $250,000 the first year and $500,000 the second year. Each of the five key employees would earn $150,000 the first year and $300,000 the second year.

However, if in this example the team was not able to scale the business and was only able to hit 10 percent of their projected revenue targets—$1 million first year and $2 million the second year. In our plan, the team would still earn a bonus, but substantially less—only a total of $300,000 instead of $3 million. Even though the business was not scaled successfully, the money to pay this bonus is still available because it comes out of the revenue as part of the overall business case. If, instead of paying on actual revenue, we tried to value the business based on its future potential—the way a startup might be valued in an acquisition—the business unit could be in trouble. In this scenario, they might only pull in $3 million in revenue and be required to pay that all to the founding team. This is a situation we did not want to put the established business in and is why we built our bonus program in a way to avoid it.

With this bonus plan, in addition to the standard corporate tools we already had to attract the best talent, we now had a new tool in our belt. While this can be an effective tool for recruiting employees who otherwise would have gone to a startup, we believe this bonus plan is particularly important for retaining founders and key employees *after* a successful incubation. This transition time is at a critical juncture, right as a founder is considering what to do next, and is a key use case to plan for.

Just like we explained in the previous section, moving an incubation into a business unit is really no different than any other acquisition. Typically, in an acquisition of an external company, in addition to a large payday from selling the stock they own, key employees will be given retention bonuses. Sometimes these are paid based on corporate goals, but often they are simply based on time. If the employee sticks it out a year they will get a large bonus. If they stay a second year, they will get another large bonus. While expensive, these bonuses are an important tool to keep the critical knowledge about the newly acquired business in the company long enough for it to be assimilated into the larger company. Otherwise, the key talent would leave as soon as they got paid for their stock and the acquiring company would be left with an empty shell instead of a working business. The same is true with this internal acquisition, so using a similar tool would make sense.

Imagine you are an intrapreneur who has just spent your last three or four years building a successful business. You stuck it out through good times and bad and have finally made it to a successful exit into a business unit. It seems like the end, but for the business unit and your employer, it is just the beginning. Now comes more hard work to take your repeatable business and scale it up into something meaningful to the larger company. If the new business is going to be successful, they are going to need your help for years to come. They will need you and your key employees to stick it out through more good and bad times to get this business to be a true financial success. Why would you want to do that? What is in it for you? You have enjoyed the autonomy of running your own mini company, and while you may want to see your dream continue to thrive, chances are you will find dealing with the bureaucracy of a large established business utterly painful. With this new bonus plan, you are now financially incented to stay. In addition, because this bonus plan is aligned with revenue, these key employees are not incented to just buy time while they wait to get paid. The more they help scale the business and make it successful, the more money they stand to make.

The business case that was used to decide when an incubation is ready to be scaled is a critical piece to get right. Often, as the market landscape changes, a business unit will discover they have a gap in their portfolio and there is a susceptibility to want to move a matching incubation into the business unit right away to plug that hole.

For example, perhaps a competitor has created new product category and the business unit now needs a new product in that category to stay competitive. This bonus plan creates an additional incentive to move the team into the business unit as soon as possible, because it will save the business unit money. However, without this new bonus plan, the intrapreneur and the accelerator program overall *also* had an incentive to move an incubation teams into a business unit as soon as possible, as it showed a tangible measure of success. Without an opposing force, that could create a situation where incubations were moved into business units before they had proven they were ready to be scaled.

However, with this plan, the intrapreneur now has an incentive to stay as long as possible within the incubation program so they can grow their revenues ahead of the payout period. This creates a beneficial tension: The business unit wants to acquire this new business before it gets too big, and the intrapreneur wants to wait until its bigger. The arbiter of this tension is the business case. If, and only if, the financial numbers show that this business is ready to be scaled, only then should it be moved.

This bonus plan is an insurance policy; it will cost you money, but it is aligned to business success and will never leave you in the negative. Also, like an insurance policy, you will not need it often—as we keep repeating, most incubations will not be successful.

# All Good Things Must Come to an End

Outside of true tragedy, one of the most stressful things that can happen to someone is losing their job. This fact is backed up by decades of research, most notably with the work of Thomas Holmes and Richard Rahe in 1967. On their *Social Readjustment Rating Scale*[7], losing a job ranked as the eighth most stressful life event, only behind traumatic events such as death, divorce, and imprisonment. Additionally, more recent research has shown that the looming threat of a job loss can have an even more adverse effect on your health than actually losing your job[8]. Regardless if the threats are real or imagined, we have seen this stress often paralyze an employee and prevent them for performing well. Obviously, the words "often paralyze" are not how you want to describe the innovation within your company.

## A Safe Place to Innovate

Employees are often well aware of this stress when making job decisions and they are also well aware that building a new business is risky. As we mentioned in Chapter 2, high levels of risk without higher levels of reward making finding top people extremely difficult. A talented and valued employee will feel secure in their current role and may not want to risk their career and paycheck to work on a project that is likely to fail. "Pitch us your ideas and there is a 10 percent chance we will let you keep your job" is not a great recruiting slogan. Even without this stress, for an even slightly self-conscious person, it can be hard enough to bring your ideas forward. To overcome this inertia that your employees feel in their current jobs and find really great ideas and people that might otherwise be too risk obverse, you need a safety net. Intrapreneurs need something they can count on, so they do not feel as exposed. After all, many of these intrapreneurs are still in your established company and not at startups for precisely the reason that they want to innovate without taking on excessive risk.

---

[7]Thomas H. Holmes and Richard H. Rahe, "The Social Readjustment Rating Scale," *Journal of Psychosomatic Research* 11, no. 2 (1967): 213-218.
[8]Sarah A. Burgard, Jennie E. Brand, and James S. House, "Perceived Job Insecurity and Worker Health in the United States," *Social Science and Medicine* 69, no. 5 (2009): 777-785.

In addition to creating the exciting work environment required to attract employees to an incubation program, you also need a plan to limit the disruption caused when these businesses do not progress, and an incubation must be shut down. Deciding to stop funding a business can be a difficult and intense decision, but once that decision is made, you want to able to execute on the shutdown and keep your company's innovation alive by bringing in a new incubation in the old one's place. If you have a team of 10 people who are suddenly out of work, or worse, due to inopportune timing you have multiple teams all pausing simultaneously, helping the effected employees all find new positions will be difficult if not impossible. Losing top talent this way, even when it is not by choice, can be enough to sour the appetite for the program across the company. No one wants to be known for being great at letting good people go.

Once employees are in the program, you need to make them feel safe enough to innovate effectively but yet still feel a great sense of urgency and not become complacent; it is a tough balance. You also want to make sure your incubation teams are as unbiased as possible. They need to be making decisions based on the data they are seeing instead of ignoring it, even unconsciously. They need to be focused on how to create a meaningful new business, not how to keep their jobs.

## A Safe Place to Make Decisions

The same is true for the Angel Team making investment decisions. If they are taking into consideration the careers of the incubation employees, they are not being objective about deciding if the business is worth continued investment. Without this objectivity by both the incubation and the Angel Teams, your incubation program will become a series of small committed bets that only succeed or fail based on luck and blind intuition.

By separating out both the incubation and Angel Teams' concerns for their employees from pragmatic decisions that need to be made—e.g., is "this business working?"—we can be objective, but we can also be more kind. In our incubation program, we pride ourselves with the fact that we treat everyone in the program with thoughtfulness and in a way that external venture capital firms cannot. This can give our established business, and yours, an unfair advantage over external startups because it allows us to attract and retain the top people without sacrificing objectivity. There is much less incentive for a Founder to hide or obscure the facts, and much less incentive for the Angel Team to give a team "a pass" because they are good employees or nice people.

Like everything we describe about the incubation program you build, you will need to tailor your program to your company's own processes and culture. This is just as true, if not more so, for these safety nets. How they are set up primarily depends on factors such as your workforce plans, office locations, fiscal processes, budget, internal employee mobility, and employee attrition. With that in mind, below we describe the programs we have put in place for our accelerator to mitigate these problems. While it is quite likely your programs will ultimately be set up differently than ours, the important takeaway is that you need to put at least some safety nets in place that will allow your program to continue, even as the individual incubations do not.

# Incubation Rotation

In an idealized world, a team member from an incubation that was shutting down would simply go back to the job they held prior to joining the incubation team. However, in reality it can be difficult to make that commitment when an incubation could go on for years before it eventually ends unsuccessfully. Depending on the fungibility of skills and the size of the overall employee base, the larger business may not be able to absorb these returning employees. This is especially true if a large number of employees return all at once or too large of a time period has passed. After all, to keep the company functioning well, the established business will need to backfill the positions of the people who leave to join an incubation team.

Striving for those ideals while simultaneously addressing the real-world challenges was the balance we tried to strike with our Incubation Rotation program. It allows employees to move from the core business onto an incubation team with the promise of returning to their original job or business unit if we determine that their incubation business is not viable within their first 12 months on the team.

There are of course unforeseen circumstances that could prevent us from keeping that promise, such as closing an office or business unit, but we have not had to confront any of those problems as of yet. In fact, in the over two years of this support program's existence, we have not needed to return a single employee. The one person who could have exercised this benefit decided they would rather join another incubation team instead. That said, just because we have not needed to exercise the program often does not mean it is not valuable. As we mentioned, the threat of job loss often has a bigger impact on an employee's mental state than an actual transition. That means even just the promise the program provides, even when it rarely needs to be exercised, is extremely valuable to improving how employees view a potential role on an incubation team.

As we mentioned, there are tradeoffs to make and each company will evaluate those tradeoffs differently. We could have chosen to only return an employee after six months, but we felt there was still a substantial amount of uncertainty at that point in the business and it would not alleviate enough of the fear for the employee. On the other hand, we could have promised 24 months, but then the larger business may have problems placing returning employees; too much may have changed over that time period. How you balance these conflicting priorities will need to reflect your specific operating environment and workforce plan.

In the end we felt, for our company, 12 months struck the right balance. We made this decision in partnership with out Chief Product Officer and his team to make sure it would work for everyone. Initially, we were worried they would look at this as a large burden on their team, but quickly everyone realized that the program was valuable, and the actual cost was extremely small. This program is only for existing employees that transfer onto an incubation, not new hires to the company. For us that means that at any given time, we typically have under 20 employees on Incubation Rotation out of a population of over 10,000—just a drop in the bucket. As our program pipelines projects instead of bucketing them into cohorts, typically only one or two people are ending their rotation period at any given time.

In addition, as we mentioned, we have not needed to return anyone to their original positions. When we do need to, it should not be hard for an organization that large or absorb one or two people a year. This is especially true given that these employees have just gained incredible experience attempting to build a new business from scratch. These are skills and experience that the established business should welcome back enthusiastically and that are hard to recruit for.

# The Bench

Quickly the next question comes: What happens if the business pauses after the 12-month Incubation Rotation has expired? What happens to an employee hired directly into an incubation team? Again, we look toward the theoretical ideal world for inspiration. Ideally, if the larger business is not able to immediately find meaningful positions for impacted employees, and there are not currently available positions on other incubations teams, you would simply wait until a new position was created somewhere in the company. After all, there is always a need for talented people, and if your incubation program is running smoothly, you will regularly be starting up new incubations that will have a need for those talented people. On the other hand, you have a responsibly to ensure the long-term viability of the larger company—your employees need to be working on meaningful projects and not sitting around indefinitely collecting a paycheck without contributing to the company's success.

To solve this problem, we created a program we call "The Bench". Every employee on an incubation when it is paused, except those still within their Incubation Rotation period, moves to The Bench for a period of roughly 90 days. We say "roughly" because the exact timing will depend the exact circumstances and on local employment regulations, such as when their final paycheck must be delivered should the employee not find a new position.

During this bench period, the employees are given assistance to find a new job internally, and they are given the opportunity to contribute to short-term projects in the interim. In addition to contributing meaningfully to the company, these projects may give the employee additional experience and visibility that can help in their job search.

Some of those temporary projects may be just tying up loose ends on the incubation that was just shut down. In other cases, members of The Bench will find short-term work on another team within the company. It could be a temporary role on a different incubation team, or a team within the established business. It is often not too hard for them to find these positions since, from the business unit's perspective, they are a source of free labor—the incubation program covers their costs while they are on The Bench. This temporary work gives The Bench employee the opportunity to demonstrate how valuable they are and that can help them negotiate a permanent position within the 90-day window.

At the end of the 90-day period, if an employee has not secured a new position, they are given a generous severance package, including outplacement services. While it may seem harsh to eliminate someone's job, 90 days' notice and a generous severance package is certainly more than you would get from most failing startups. But this balance does more than that. It allows us to make sure we find the best fit for an employee and not unnecessarily keep people who no longer have the right skills for a position within the company. Over a span of many years, we have seen dozens of projects where a team of engineers is simply given to a manager. This "donation development," as it is called, is often done without the manager's agreement and without regard to the skillsets or level of experience of the employees. Having the right team is often one of the most critical aspects of building a new business, and force-fitting a team is only going to cripple their forward progress.

There are other models here that could work if you had the right conditions. The most obvious is that, if you had enough time and budget, and if the skillsets and physical locations of your employees did not vary or were not as important as they are in our situation, you could extend The Bench time—perhaps indefinitely. We could imagine a model in which because there were always enough new incubations needing generally the same skills, The Bench was something you hired for as a full-time position instead of a temporary holding area. Indeed, this was our original intent when we were initially developing the program, but our particular set of circumstances made it unworkable.

For example, we have many development centers around the world, and it would be difficult to be successful with a program that only allowed one set of employees around the world participate, or force those in other locations to relocate halfway across the globe. Instead, we set up The Bench program as this temporary holding area and we try to bias teams to hire in a location that has enough critical mass that their team can find new roles if their incubation is not successful.

Given our constraints and objectives, this Bench program has worked well for us. The majority of employees leaving paused incubation teams find new roles within our company in fewer than 90 days. Team members know they can drive toward success up until they decide the business is not working, and not get distracted by looking for a new job in the final months of an incubation; they will have roughly three months to do that afterward. Of course, we will not stand in the way of those who want to take their new skills elsewhere.

Another important factor is that an incubation being paused is rarely a surprise to the team. If they are being open and objective with their data, they already know if the business is working or not well ahead of an eventual funding decision. Think back to Chapter 2 and our example of the intrapreneur recommending her project be paused. She did not wake up one morning and decide things were not working. She saw evidence for months and tried multiple experiments to see if she could find a way to make the business work. She also did not do this in secret. In each monthly review meeting, she would update us on her progress and struggle—giving the Angel Team foresight that a pause was a real possibility in the coming months. This is several additional months of time for her to prepare and to prepare her team, which is exactly what she did. By the time her decision was brought in front of the Angel Team, she had already secured new positions for each of her team members.

Another measure of success is that we have been able to estimate the costs of our bench program well enough to fend off operational problems. To make our program work, we use statistical modeling that is regularly updated to estimate our bench costs. We use metrics such as the average length of time the average employee spends on The Bench at the end of an incubation, their average pay during that time, and the percentage of those employees who do not find work and are given severance packages. Using the results of this modeling, we are able to budget for what in most business would be looked at as an unplanned and unforeseen event. As we recommended in Chapter 2, you should embrace the uncertainty of building a new business and not ignore it—instead you should plan for it.

Finally, an important detail in our program is that we use a dedicated cost center to account for The Bench spending separate from the cost of actually incubating a business. This allows us to compare to other benchmarks, such as external startups, and look for improvements in our ability to incubate separate from our ability to make The Bench program operate more effectively.

## Making It Safe to ~~Fail~~ Learn

The inevitable will happen—a large percentage of your businesses will not succeed. For our type of businesses, we believe one out of ten will meet their minimum success criteria, and perhaps we will also have the occasional minor successes along the way. Time will tell, but if you are not careful, this looming failure will take a toll on your employees and could bias them further toward assuming their business is working when the evidence should be leading them the other way—that is how some committed bets are born. Programs such as Incubation Rotation and The Bench are important and help, but eventually it comes down to culture.

In many, perhaps most, established business, risks are explicitly avoided, and failure is a sign of poor performance. However, building a new business is different. You need your employees to take calculated risks and a business failing is often a sign of good performance, especially if it fails quickly. If you search the Internet for "fail fast," you will see many articles touting the practice, but many others saying that failing fast is just hype. Like many aspects of culture, it comes down to language. How you talk about something will set the tone for how your teams will think about it. While I often forget and occasionally still use the term "fail fast," we try instead to use the term "learn fast" to convey what we really mean.

We want our teams to learn absolutely as quickly and cheaply as possible if a business is viable. The faster we can learn a business will not work, the quicker we can reapply that time and money into a business that might work—whether it is a small pivot or an entirely new idea. This idea of "learn fast" is what you want your employees to embrace and what should permeate your culture. In addition to how you talk about "failure," there are two other concrete ways you can help build and maintain this culture.

First, when decisions are made to either pause a business or persevere onward, you need those decisions to be as open, objective, and data driven as possible. Yes, being data driven is important to ensure you are making the right business decisions but being transparent about that how and why you made those decisions will be key to your culture. If an incubation team believes they are being singled out, or that another team is being favored, it can easily create an us-versus-them culture that can be toxic. Instead you want teams to know they are being measured by the data they bring, not what you think of them personally. If you can do that successfully, then your teams will naturally bias themselves toward bringing objective data.

We learned this lesson first-hand early in our program's history. When we first started our regular 3P reviews, at the end of each review of an incubation, the Angel Team would privately deliberate, draw some conclusions, make decisions, and write up notes. That feedback would then later be summarized and passed onto the Founder—sometimes as long as a few days later. When there was anything incorrect or controversial in those summary notes, it was incredibly frustrating to the Founders. This went on for a period of months until finally one Founder spoke up and asked, "can we just make these decisions with the Founder in the room?"

It was an obvious solution to making the program more transparent, and it did make a big difference in the morale of the team and culture of program. To correct this, we simply started to have the Angel Team deliberate in an open session with the team and the various other attendees. We soon learned that this approach too had its drawbacks and seemed to lead to more confusion than help for the incubation teams. We found as the Angel Team verbally explored options, the Founders were often confused as they listened to the various positions each Angel Team member held. We also found that Angel Team members would sometimes hold back from raising criticisms that they felt might not be appropriate for an open forum. We realized that we had swung the pendulum too far the other way and we needed a good middle ground.

Rather than deliberate at the end of the day and inform the Founder the next day, and rather than have the deliberation with the Founder present where it served mostly to confuse them, we now have a short, private, deliberation immediately following the review. We then return straightaway, minutes later, with a decision that includes the reasons for the decision and any additional advice or context we feel will help the team. Doing it this way lets the Angel Team deliver it with a single voice to avoid confusion and while it is still fresh to avoid any loss of fidelity.

Once you have a culture of openness and objectiveness, you need a way to make sure the Founders bring the *right* data. To do that, you do not just reward teams for bringing data that proves their business is working, you also reward them for bringing data that shows their business is not working. It is amazing to watch confidence grow in a leader when they systematically and objectively look at data and present results that do not support their initial hypothesis.

Rewarding this learning sets the right tone for all the other teams, and there are any numbers of ways you can do it. For example, to make sure the individuals know they are doing the right thing, we have at times given out significant spot bonuses to those people who really exemplified this learning culture— one more advantage of incubating in an established organization. To make sure the entire company knows what we value, we often publicize the pausing of an incubation, for example with a companywide internal news article. We have also started the practice of publicizing these pauses on our company's external blog[9], where we can talk about what we learned from attempting this new business[10].

---

[9]Jin Zhang, "We're Shutting Down—Time to Celebrate!," *Highlight* (blog), December 12, 2016, https://www.ca.com/en/blog-highlight/were-shutting-down-time-to-celebrate.html

[10]Ankur Agarwal, "Startup Success Doesn't Always Mean Building a $1B Business," *Highlight* (blog), March 9, 2018, https://www.ca.com/en/blog-highlight/ca-accelerator-qubeship-successes.html

We continue to look for other ways to reward and recognize teams whose businesses have not been successful (see Figure 5-2). At the time of this writing, we are considering options such as custom desk awards, cash bonuses, or an innovation wall with plaques for all the teams or team members who made it through the program—regardless if their business was successful or not.

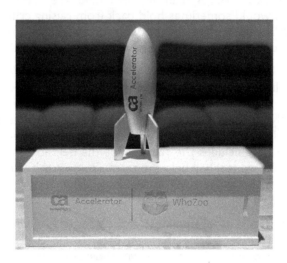

**Figure 5-2.** Awards given to exiting incubation teams, regardless of success

# A Supportive, Innovative, Environment

Having the right support system is critical to making your incubation program work and giving your new businesses the best chance of success. Not only having a safe place to experiment and learn, and not only having the right rewards, but also making sure you are taking advantage of your company's domain expertise will lead to success. That success will be hard won, but you already have all the pieces you need right there in your existing company. Regardless if they are something as complex as a revenue sharing bonus plan, or as simple as recognizing your employees when they learn a business will *not* work, these pieces are each critical to your success. You need to stitch them together in the right way, but once you do, you will reap the benefits, which can go well beyond innovation and new sources of revenue. Companies come down to people and a successful incubation program can help you attract, develop, and retain your best employees.

# Benefits Beyond Revenue

## An Incubation Program Can Improve Your Entire Business

*"The difficulty lies not so much in developing new ideas as in escaping from old ones."*

—John Maynard Keynes

Building a new business from the ground up is hard, and you need to effectively use everything you have at your disposal to make your incubations successful. However, just because most of your new incubations will not be successful does not mean that your incubation program is a failure. If fact, even if every incubation were to end in a failed business, there are many benefits to the larger company that go well beyond these new businesses and the additional revenue they may or may not ultimately bring.

You might not realize it at first, but while trying to build these new business, you are simultaneously changing your company from within. You are improving your company's processes, people, and image. You are making the company faster, leaner, and more innovative. You are building not only new businesses,

© CA 2019
G. Watt and H. Abrams, *Lean Entrepreneurship*,
https://doi.org/10.1007/978-1-4842-3942-1_6

but also the true business leaders your company needs for the future. You are showing your employees as well as your customers what an innovative company looks and acts like. Beyond revenue, what could be more valuable?

# The Hardest Job They Will Ever Have

Your intrapreneurs have a tough job. It may not be a stretch to say they have the toughest job in your entire company. While they may only be responsible for a single product, and they may not have as large of a budget as the other senior leaders in your company, the breadth of the required skillset they need is enormous. Engineering, user experience, operations, finance, support, sales, product management, project management, product marketing, event marketing, business development... the list goes on and on. Finding someone deeply proficient in each and every one of those domains to lead an incubation team is hard. Finding 20 people to lead 20 of your incubation teams will be nearly impossible.

An often-repeated piece of wisdom about venture capital is that you should invest in a team, not an idea. The theory being that even if the original idea turns out wrong, a good team can pivot to a business idea that works. A corollary is that ideas are cheap, the point being that a good idea is nothing without good execution—therefore, again, you need a good team. If a team is *the* key piece to a good incubation, and finding good leaders, and by extension good teams, for each of your incubations within your company is nearly impossible, then how can you possibly succeed? Simple—you need to systematically build both great leaders and great teams.

## Minimal Viable Teams

Building a great business comes down to the people who build it. Although any given incubation team will be small, and everyone on the team must contribute in multiple ways, the leader does not need to be the most proficient at absolutely everything. They need to be just proficient enough in some areas of the business and self-aware enough to know who to hire to compensate for their own short comings and complement the rest of the team. A successful startup, even an internal incubation, needs to have the right set of skills—at least a minimally viable set—to get started. This is the idea behind the concept known as the "minimal viable team".

Without this well-rounded skillset, teams will struggle, be blind to potential opportunities and problems, and will likely not be able to live up to their business' full potential. We have seen this situation many times, unfortunately, often catching it once it was too late. We've seen teams work like crazy without making any forward progress. Unaware of what they are missing, a team can have blind spots in fundamental areas such as Marketing or Sales.

Therefore, to be successful, you must start an incubation by forming this minimal viable team. The team will be made up of individuals who complement each other without any significant gaps in their combined skillsets. In an blog post on minimal viable teams, Charlie O'Donnell[1] does a great job breaking this down. In it, he shows the logic behind taking a broad set of skills you will eventually need and how turn those into a simpler set of the right set of skills for the initial core team. Think of skills in engineering, marketing, finances, sales, etc., and bucket them into three general areas each covered by a person—an outside person, someone to focus on customer experience, and someone to make the product.

Exactly which specific skills you need to cover and assemble will all depend on your business. For example, for a software-as-a-service business, you will need a team who can understand software subscription businesses, can write software code, and can design web-based user interfaces. In his 2012 South by Southwest talk, Rei Inamoto coined these three personas the "hacker," the "hustler," and the "hipster"[2]. In that presentation, he also pointed out the problem with large, deep, organizational structures and how scale in an organization can reduce its ability to innovate. His answer is much like our solution: solving this problem by creating "smaller, nimbler teams within this larger context without creating this vertical hierarchy".

We have intentionally moved away from using the words "hacker," "hustler," and "hipster," as some people found them offensive, and instead we use "developer," "deal-maker," and "designer"—but the intent is the same. Getting the right initial mix of skills is critical. This trio provides *just* enough coverage and focus to be able to begin to design, build, and market their new product. While these individuals must have specialized skills, they must also be generalists enough to overlap and cover each other's areas. A three-person team doesn't afford the flexibility for someone to say, "not my job".

Then, as the business expands in scope and complexity, specialists are needed to fill in skill gaps and add bandwidth to the team. For example, a good founding Chief Technical Officer working on a software product can probably code an initial prototype all by themselves. Once the product expands beyond that prototype—as they define their minimal viable product and approach Series A—additional software engineers, with expertise the CTO might not have, will be needed to build the product in a reasonable amount of time. It is a delicate balance between ramping up too slowly, which prevents the team

---

[1] Charlie O'Donnell, "Minimum Viable Team," *This is Going to be Big* (blog), August 22, 2012, http://www.thisisgoingtobebig.com/blog/2012/8/22/minimum-viable-team.html
[2] Rei Inamoto, "Why Ad Agencies Should Act More Like Tech Startups," SXSW 2012, March 13 2012, audio, 57:13, http://audio.sxsw.com/2012/podcasts/13-INT-%20Why_Ad_Agencies_Should.mp3

from moving at full speed and ramping up too quickly, which could risk turning the project into a committed bet. Ideally the team will hire just barely ahead of what they need.

A good question is, "where to start"? If you are building a technology-based business, do you hire a technical founder who in turn hires a business person? Or should you hire a business person who in turn hires a technical person? Although likely not a hard and fast rule for every business, Martin Murmann answered this question in his 2017 *Harvard Business Review* article, "The Startups Most Likely to Succeed Have Technical Founders Who Quickly Hire Businesspeople"[3]. His research showed that companies with technical founders create disproportionately more profit than those with business founders, or even those that have business and technical co-founders. They theorize that while it is likely a technical-oriented founder has enough basic business knowledge, it may be unlikely that a business-oriented founder has deep enough technical skills.

## Founder Fitness

It is not just general business or technical skills you need to worry about. The skills required to fully round out an initial minimal viable team are very broad, and as we mentioned, it would be unrealistic to expect every founder to enter the incubation program with every one of these skills. Understanding where a founder, and their founding team, has gaps and what to do about those gaps is key. Together with our Human Resources team, we created an internal training program we call Founder Fitness to address this challenge.

Founder Fitness starts as soon as a new business idea has been accepted into the incubation program—prior to the initial team members transitioning into Seed 1. We ask each member of the founding team to do a bit of self-reflection and complete a straight-forward self-assessment. This introspection is used as a tool to help them stop and take a critical look at themselves.

As they evaluate themselves along the dimensions shown in Figure 6-1—Intrapreneurship, Talent Management, Agile Product Development, Business Execution, and Relationship Building—they take stock in what they already have experience in and where they will need help. Each section currently has between 7 and 24 competencies or behaviors they measure themselves against. If their current manager has insights into any of these areas, we ask them to evaluate the team as well.

---

[3]Martin Murmann, "The Startups Most Likely to Succeed Have Technical Founders Who Quickly Hire Businesspeople," *Harvard Business Review*, November 6, 2017, https://hbr.org/2017/11/the-startups-most-likely-to-succeed-have-technical-founders-who-quickly-hire-businesspeople

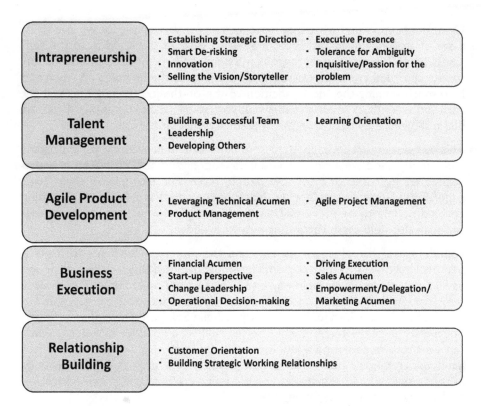

**Figure 6-1.** The five dimensions of Founder Fitness and their associated skill areas

This data is then used to look at the overall team to identify strengths and gaps. Next, the Angel Team uses this analysis to conduct an interview with the business leader. The interview is not a job interview, although it probably feels a bit like one to them. We use this interview process to validate the assessment data from the entire team and to identify blind spots the leader might have. For example, the business leader may feel it is okay that they do not have product marketing skills, because they are going to depend on their co-founder in that area. That is a great plan, as long as the co-founder actually has sufficient experience in product marketing. If not, the problem is not necessarily that the co-founder lacks the right experience, it is that the leader has a blind spot and a skills gap on their team.

The outcome of the interview is a set of recommendations for the team: what they should train up on versus what they should hire for and when. In the most extreme case, when the founders simply lack enough combined experience, we could recommend they hire a new business leader to run their team. The goal is to either find the right founding members or help build them into a minimal viable team.

Once the team knows what they want to train for, versus hire for, we give them a set of recommended resources aligned to each of the areas from the self-assessments. These resources range from a simple book or video recommendation, to instructor led in-person classes. We leave it up to the founders on when and how much training they do in addition to the on-the-job training they will get each and every day. We will give them support, guidance, and occasional direction, but in the end, they must own their personal development plan.

This self-directed approach to assessment and improvement is important because we need our leaders to be independent and self-motivated. It is also backed up by research into how people learn. For example, in their 2012 paper, Todd Gureckis and Douglas Markant showed that self-directed learning enabled people to be more efficient by focusing on what they do not know and may also help them retain this new knowledge.[4]

Founders use this initial assessment and the interview feedback to make a personal build-versus-buy decision. They must decide if they will hire someone to fill a skill gap or grow their way into fulfilling a need over time. The choices they make will all depend on the skill, the size and scope of the gap, and the timeframe it is required in. A deficiently in Agile Software Development might not matter until the team reaches Series A. If so, a Founder may decide they can wait to hire someone a few months later to fill that need. On the other hand, understanding how to interview customers is crucial and a deficiency in those skills would require finding someone to fill that gap immediately— perhaps even prior to beginning Seed 1.

## Learning from Other's Mistakes

One area we see many founders struggle with is executive presence. The ability to present their learnings and to answer questions in a concise and persuasive manner that gives the Angel Team confidence that their investment will be well spent. In addition to specific skills training, Founders can leverage coaches and mentors to help them on their journey and help them improve their executive presence. We regularly give Founders feedback from 3P meetings on how they could have more directly answered the question that was asked or how they could have structured their presentation in a way that was more persuasive. Since we encourage incubation teams to watch each other's 3P presentations, they can look at a 3P from the viewpoint of a reviewer instead of a presenter. From that vantage point, they can see the mistakes that are made and learn how to avoid those pitfalls. They can use these lessons themselves, as well as offer advice back to other founders.

---

[4]Todd M. Gureckis and Douglas B. Markant, "Self-Directed Learning: A Cognitive and Computational Perspective," *Perspectives on Psychological Science 7,* no. 5, (2012): 464-481, http://journals.sagepub.com/doi/pdf/10.1177/1745691612454304

As we described in Chapter 4, our program uses a pipelining model instead of grouping incubations into cohorts like many external incubators do. There are many pros and cons to these different approaches, but one benefit to pipelining is that there is always a set of businesses and leaders who are one step ahead of another given team. Founders get to learn from the other founders who operate more mature businesses and mentor and advise those who operate less mature businesses.

The Founder Fitness program along with this more ad hoc peer-based mentoring helps us tactically by building minimal viable teams that continue to learn the skills they need to be successful with their incubation. However, strategically it is much broader and more impactful. These programs are building the future general managers of the company. Leaders who can have broad and deep enough skills to understand customers, lead the development of products, and build new businesses. While that may not mean when they leave their incubation they are ready to be instantly promoted to run a large chunk of an enterprise, they might be ready to run a smaller part of the business or a small company while they continue to gain experience.

Founders who are successful growing as leaders, capable of building new businesses from the ground up, are invaluable to the mature business. Finding and recruiting these types of leaders is both difficult and expensive. Few people have this experience, and those who do are often entrepreneurs who would not likely be interested in joining an established organization—they want to build new ones. Using your incubation program to not only incubate businesses, but leaders as well, demonstrates additional value they may not find anywhere else. In the CA Accelerator, we pride ourselves on driving innovation by nurturing ingenuity. As we have said, building new businesses comes down to the people building them. That means you cannot simply focus on the "innovation". Instead, you need to focus on nurturing your people so that they can be innovative.

# Improving from Within

While building and improving your own internal leaders is certainly a compelling additional value that an incubation program can provide, the changes and enhancements go beyond people. If done well, your incubation program can also improve your company's internal processes. As we mentioned in Chapters 1 and 2, mismatched internal processes can kill innovation before it has a chance to start. These heavy-weight processes permeate throughout an established business, and can not only harm your new incubations, but they are likely already harming your established businesses as well.

As a company matures over many years, and as it looks to comply with more and more laws and regulations, it will work to streamline its processes. Unfortunately, that streamlining often results in one-size-fits-all processes that are designed for the least-common-denominator. Yet, at the same time, companies know they must compete with faster and more Agile startups who have near zero formal processes—they just get stuff done. The difficulty comes in how to balance the two: the need for legal compliance, or just overall general governance, and the need to move as quickly as possible.

Nitin Nohria, William Joyce, and Bruce Roberson spent 10 years trying to determine which processes and approaches really work[5]. Over the 10-year period, they examined more than 200 different management practices at over 160 different companies. In the end, it turned out that there was no direct relationship between specific techniques and stronger business performance. Instead they found that strategy, execution, culture, and structure were the top four reasons businesses succeeded, followed by talent, innovation, leadership, and mergers. The researchers found that the best companies were roughly twice as productive as their peers in their industry, and the most successful companies removed unnecessary layers of management, bureaucracy, and process.

Your intrapreneurs will quickly discover first-hand the unnecessary bureaucracy hiding in your organization. Because they have such a broad role, your intrapreneurs will see the bigger picture of where process problems arise from. While employees in the rest of the company may occasionally complain, many of them have likely become despondent and now simply accept and follow the processes and procedures put in from of them. In fact, many will feel like they have no control over the current situation and therefore will lack the motivation to try to effect change. Your intrapreneurs, on the other hand, will not be content with the status quo. They will want to move as fast as possible, but as soon as they try to circumvent standard procedures that get in their way, they will hit the corporate antibodies.

Just as we saw in our Brand Marketing story from Chapter 5, intrapreneurs will be told "you can't do that" or "that's not how our process works" whenever they attempt to go against the grain or skip bureaucratic process that gets in their way. In these situations, it is important to recognize that it is not the people getting in the way. In our experience and generally speaking, we found that people are well intentioned in how they do their jobs. These antibodies are typically not trying to defend their turf. They are trying to defend their process, because that process was based on sound reasoning—governance, limiting risk, and legal compliance. But how those reasons are turned into process are based on assumptions that most likely do not apply to your incubations.

---

[5]Nitin Nohria, William Joyce, and Bruce Roberson, "What Really Works," *Harvard Business Review*, July 2003, https://hbr.org/2003/07/what-really-works

That said, there will be cases where the reasoning is based on sound rationale and the processes do apply. Not only will your incubation need to follow some of these painful requirements, but their startup counterparts may not. For instance, there will be legal requirements or governance rules that public companies must follow and that private companies do not. In other cases, startups are either unaware or choose to ignore some laws.

For example, most small startups will happily take payment from any customer with a credit card. However, they may not be aware of the fact that there are sanctioned parties and denied persons with whom the United States government has said companies are not allowed to do business with. Most startups either ignore these requirements or choose to accept the very small risk that a sanctioned party may try to do business with them. Larger businesses are not willing to take these risks, and each and every potential transaction must be checked to make sure the company is not doing business with the wrong people.

In other cases, the red tape your intrapreneurs will encounter are because these problematic processes were created to cover every possible situation or designed for high dollar value contracts. For example, it may make sense to have a 10-person committee review and approve a royalty agreement for a $1 billion business, but the same type of agreement for a $1000 business will need a lot less scrutiny. It may make sense to require your contractors to carry $10 million liability insurance policies if they are allowed to access your building unescorted, but you probably do not care how much insurance coverage your t-shirt vendor has.

As mentioned in Chapter 3, we have found that things can change when you can explain the problem from your perspective and let the person in charge of the process help craft a better solution. Explaining how your incubation teams operate differently from the established businesses, and why it is important that they move quickly, can give a group in the established business the mental permission to think outside the box. You will also need buy-in from your company's leadership (we will cover that in the next chapter), but with that in place and this new starting position of "how can I help achieve your goals?," you will find that you can collaborate with teams to accomplish a new, faster, way of working.

This business process improvement will help your incubations move faster, but it also helps the rest of the company move faster as well. When process and procedures change to better suit faster moving new businesses, it can often enable the established business to move faster too. This is precisely the type of "unnecessary bureaucracy" that Nohria, Joyce, and Roberson pointed out, and it needs to be rooted out from your established business to outperform its competitors.

In addition, when other parts of the company see your incubations move with this greater focus and speed, the company as a whole becomes less complacent. Other departments start to innovate differently and use the lighter-weight tools and processes that your incubation program uses. We go into some of these details in Chapter 8.

In short, your fast-moving internal startups will drag the established company into the 21st Century, inducing internal change and improvements that not only make the incubations successful, but also in turn help other parts of the business just as much.

# Being Seen as an Innovator

You have improved your processes and now your company is leaner and more agile. You have trained and built the future leaders of your company and they now act with a greater sense of purpose and speed. People will notice. Employees, prospective employees, and customers will all notice; and that is a very good thing. Being seen as an innovator in your industry, versus a laggard, is like a tide that raises all boats. It will make it easier to attract and retain both employees and customers.

## Employees Will Notice

Employees will be the first to notice the changes. They will hear about interesting new products that are taking advantage of industry trends, working with new technologies, and approaching problems with a fresh perspective. Unlike the projects we describe in Chapter 2, these incubations will be out in the open, not hiding behind the scenes. Employees will hear about them directly from the CEO in town hall meetings, not from rumors or complaints.

There is a huge untapped potential in the employees within your company. Every day they see the pain customers have to overcome, and in each one of those problems lies a potential product to solve it. When employees here about how much freedom the incubation teams have to explore their product ideas, when they hear about support and training programs like Incubation Rotation and Founder Fitness, they will want to be part of it.

The result is they will pitch. They will get their ideas down on Lean Canvases and attempt to get into the program—but many of their pitches will not be accepted. In our experience, less than 20 percent of pitches make it into our program, but this number has fluctuated greatly over the years. However, the good news is that this low acceptance rate does not seem to negatively impact the view employees have of the program.

At least anecdotally, it appears that when employees' pitches are not accepted, they often walk away with an even greater appreciation of the program. Employees notice when you treat them and their ideas with the respect they deserve. They feel good when you listen to what they have to say and ask difficult, but thoughtful, questions instead of making them fill out 70-page presentation templates. They appreciate that the most senior people in the company—such as the CTO and Distinguished Engineers—are carefully considering their new business ideas.

As we mentioned in Chapters 3 and 4, they also value that we personally follow up almost immediately after the pitch and give them direct feedback on what we liked and did not like. Even when telling people that we will not be accepting them and their idea into the incubation program, their enthusiasm does not wane. In one recent instance, the employees said, "We are really grateful, it was a super project to work on and we really gained a lot from going through this process. We really enjoyed preparing the pitch!" In another instance, an employee told us how he believes the Accelerator program gives him better insight into how the company thinks, and then he said, "Accelerator was one of the reasons I decided to come to CA."

## Prospective Employees Will Notice

Since the company is now internally perceived as innovative, when your managers are hiring and conducting interviews with prospective employees, their enthusiasm for your internal innovation will shine through. They will use the incubation program as a selling point and talk about how the company values innovating and innovative ideas. Most importantly, they will explain that every employee has a place for their ideas to go and potentially be invested in.

As an employee looking for a new role, startups can be attractive. In a 2012 *Fast Company* article, "8 Reasons to Choose a Startup Over a Corporate Job,"[6] Kerrin Sheldon highlights why there is a lot to like about startups. The article cites more responsibility, better opportunity, unmatched learning, and personal recognition, among other reasons. We could not agree more with how attractive these aspects are, but there is no reason they should be exclusive to startups. Indeed, for each of the eight reasons highlighted in the article, and many others, our incubation program is a great place to work. We combine the best attributes of a startup with the those of an established business. This attracts people who want to do innovative and entrepreneurial work, but tire of the downsides of working for a startup such as more risk and uncertainty, less reward, and constant stress.

---

[6]Kerrin Sheldon, "8 Reasons to Choose a Startup Over a Corporate Job," *Fast Company*, March 13, 2012, https://www.fastcompany.com/1824235/8-reasons-choose-startup-over-corporate-job

We use the attraction to these startup attributes as part of our positioning of the company on our recruiting site, *Life at CA*. In addition to highlighting diversity and work-life balance, we highlight the employees that work within our incubation teams and they talk about what it is like to work for a virtual startup within a big company. This message works.

One success story was the hiring of the marketing lead for one of our more mature incubations. The team not only posted the job on CA Technologies' job site, but they also intentionally and specifically looked for employees from startups who already had significant entrepreneurial experience. The person they hired was the Chief Marketing Officer of a venture capital backed startup, who was looking for a change. This experienced entrepreneur said they deliberately were looking for an environment like our program. The way they describe it:

> "When I joined the CA Accelerator fresh out of leaving a venture backed startup, I was burned out on the lifestyle. I was eating Ramen twice a day as a necessity to chase my startup dream. The reason the CA Accelerator was so appealing to me was because it was all the benefits of a corporate job: market salary, great healthcare, etc. but also came with all of the freedom and creativity of a startup."

Even if the particular incubation they join is not successful and does not exit into a business unit, these intrapreneurial-oriented employees will have other opportunities. They could move into another incubation or move into the mature line-of-business and bring their startup experience with them. It can be a win-win for everyone.

Similarly, it goes beyond recruiting for just a few open positions on incubation teams. Yes, we run online advertising campaigns that specifically target incubation jobs. And yes, when a candidate clicks on one of those ads, we take them to an accelerator specific job page. But the surprising fact is not that this is an effective tool for recruiting and filling incubation jobs, but that it is also effective at recruiting candidates for non-incubation jobs. We get a noticeable number of people who find CA Technologies through the Accelerator page, but then ultimately apply for jobs elsewhere in the company.

## Customers Will Notice

All this innovation will not be lost on your customers either. They may hear about it first from the sales people or account managers assigned to them. Sales professionals will want to show thought leadership by sharing the innovation going on inside the company. Sometimes that will be a new incubation product that might be useful to a customer. Other times it may be a more general conversation with the goal of sharing how the company approaches innovation—a topic every executive has interest in understanding. Customers appreciate this sharing of how we approach innovation and walk away knowing that we are continuing to invest in the future, and in turn, their future.

In Chapter 5 we shared a story about the corporate antibodies that came out in force when we tried to create a separate brand for one of our incubations. Once we gave the branding and marketing teams the right context, they became some of our biggest champions and helped us build a better program. Their change in stance was due to two important reasons.

First, having new products that, from a branding perspective, appear to be part of CA Technologies' general portfolio, come and go—and fail—on a regular basis could cause confusing messages in the marketplace. Customers could find themselves not understanding what was a new incubation that might not survive and what was an enterprise product, what was a new direction for a product line and what was an experiment. Having incubations publicly available and marketed, but in a way that makes it clear they are separate from the products of the core business, allows incubations to experiment and fail without impacting or being impacted by CA Technologies' existing branding and marketing. Making it clear that, although this business is part of a larger company, it is still an incubation that helps protect our customers and our partnership with them.

Second, we created an approach to use these incubations to help CA Technologies' brand. Our approach was to externally brand our internal incubation program, CA Accelerator[7]. This overarching brand is used as a gateway between our incubation and the larger established business. While incubation teams are given the freedom to market to whomever and however they feel is best, they never mislead customers about who they work for—an established business—and their web pages, t-shirts, and other marketing material always refer or link back to CA Accelerator using its logo.

A great example of this in practice is how the program has been showcased as part of CA Technologies' annual customer event, CA World. Ahead of the event, press releases went out highlighting some of the innovative products, including those from the accelerator, that would be on display during the show. In the opening keynotes, the incubation program and some its products were mentioned, and attendees were encouraged to go check them out on the show floor. When they did, they found not just one or two, but 10 or more incubations all strategically positioned near the entrance to the exhibit space. Throughout the week, meetings and interviews were scheduled with

---

[7]"CA Accelerator," CA Technologies, accessed August 23, 2018, https://www.ca.com/accelerator

press and industry analysts, and as a result, articles and reports were published highlighting the program, how it works, and some of the people involved. In other words, they talked about how and why CA Technologies is being innovative, and not just a throwaway blurb about a new product or feature.

By associating these innovative new businesses with CA Technologies' overall brand, we associate CA Technologies with innovation. We are demonstrating to the market and our current and future customers that we take innovation seriously and therefore we are a company you can partner with for the long term. This type of brand-level marketing helps to transcend the natural lifecycle of any individual product. Instead of customers thinking about their relationship with a single product, it enables customers to think about their long-term relationship with the overall company.

In a 2016 article in *Harvard Business Review,* Denise Lee Yohn highlights six reasons companies promote their master brand in addition to individual products[8]. When it comes to retaining customers, the article highlights that companies can reduce customer attrition, that stand-alone products geared toward specific customer stages or maturity face, by promoting the overall brand. That way, customers see a natural progression from one product to another—all under the overall portfolio brand. In other words, using an incubation program to help build an innovative brand can lead to better overall customer retention.

We should also point out that these approaches—talking with customers directly about how the company innovates as well as having innovation as part of your overall brand message—can have a multiplicative effect. As customers take notice, so will industry analysts who will further reinforce their view of your company with your customers. At least in one case, we saw a label of "not innovative enough" removed from an analyst's product report as a direct result of our incubation program.

# The Benefits of Being Innovative

In this chapter, we described just some of the benefits of your incubation program and how those benefits go well beyond revenue. Remember that it takes years to build a meaningful new business from scratch. That means even if (when!) you are successful, it will take years before you can show your CEO and board members tangible evidence of value—all that new and meaningful revenue. The result is that you will need to convey these additional benefits to get the full buy-in you need to bootstrap the program.

---

[8]Denise Lee Yohn, "Why Companies are Advertising their Master Brand," *Harvard Business Review*, March 28, 2016, https://hbr.org/2016/03/why-companies-are-advertising-their-master-brand

# Bootstrapping an Incubation Program

## Leveraging Existing Resources to Accelerate Your Accelerator

*"Don't loaf and invite inspiration; light out after it with a club."*

—Jack London, American novelist (1876–1916)

Before you can build an incubation program within your company, in addition to great ideas, you will need at least two things: Buy-in from stakeholders across the company and enough funding to be successful. Incubating new businesses is not something you can rush—there are no quick wins. This means the commitment you get must be sustained for a long enough period of time to build demonstrable value from your incubation program before you lose the hearts and minds of your executives. These two fundamental requirements are intertwined. You will need buy-in to get funding and you will need funding before the broader company will be willing to buy in. In other words, you need to bootstrap the program.

© CA 2019
G. Watt and H. Abrams, *Lean Entrepreneurship*,
https://doi.org/10.1007/978-1-4842-3942-1_7

# Getting Buy-In

Incubation will operate differently than the product development going on in established parts of your company's business. The incubation teams will take shortcuts around unnecessary process and the sheer pace of innovation will be disruptive to the slower parts of the business. While getting top-down commitment is critical to stay incubating for years, to even get started you will need to get buy-in from a fairly substantial and broad set of stakeholders across your company—many of whom you may not initially think to consider.

To accomplish this, you will need to be able to use the learnings from Chapter 6 to explain the value and importance of your new program, but at the same time, set realistic expectations. Incubation can take longer and be more chaotic than the work done within the established business, with a low likelihood of any given individual incubation being successful. Once you set those expectations and can acquire and sustain buy-in from across the company, these individuals can become your biggest fans and allies—paving the way for you to accelerate your program and leverage the true potential of the established portions of your company to its advantage.

## Setting Realistic Expectations

There will be a large percentage of your company that will hear the term "internal startups" and envision instant Silicon Valley style billion-dollar unicorns[1]. In reality, venture capital firms that invest in startups take on a lot of risk. They know going into these investments that there is a good chance that many of their individual investments will not yield any return. Of course, more risk means their investors will require more return. Straight-forward financial math can show this feast or famine investing results in the need for these firms to look for one-to-two thousand percent returns on each investment just to stay in business. There is a great explanation of why this is in blog post by venture capitalist Jerry Yang. In the post, he shows that because of this risk and reward scenario, venture investors will steer clear of investments that *only* yield two or three-hundred percent return[2]. On the other hand, your investors—your executive management and your stockholders—would

---

[1]Aileen Lee, "Welcome to the Unicorn Club: Learning from Billion-Dollar Startups," *Techcrunch*, November 2, 2013, https://techcrunch.com/2013/11/02/welcome-to-the-unicorn-club

[2]Jerry Yang, "30% IRR—a primer for first-time entrepreneurs," *The Conscience of a VC in Paris* (blog), June 26, 2014, http://www.jmyang.com/blog/2014/6/24/30-irr-a-primer-for-first-time-entrepreneurs

probably be extremely happy with three-hundred percent individual returns and lower risk. This is both achievable and acceptable because, unlike in external startup investing, you do not need to swing for the fences and, as we discussed in Chapter 6, you can get value out of the program in more subtle ways.

## Value Migration

Even when wildly successful, incubations that are acquired by a business unit may not yet have a meaningful impact on revenue. After acquisition new businesses will need time to be scaled to the point where they are meaningful to the company's bottom line. You and your many stakeholders will need to take the long view of building new businesses. The challenge of course is that many of these stakeholders can have a short attention span. Think back to the lessons from Chapters 1 and 2 and how the established business expects meaningful and impactful results in quarters, not years. This is the exact opposite of what you will need for an incubation program to be successful.

In his book, *Value Migration: How to Think Several Moves Ahead of the Competition*, Adrian Slywotzky introduces the concept of Value Migration—how what customers value will change over time and therefore a company must change their products to stay ahead[3]. While the problem is similar to Clayton Christensen's Innovators Dilemma, the Value Migration approach takes into account that this is a constantly evolving process that changes continuously. While Slywotzky's book is targeted at the value you bring to *external* customers, we also use this style of analysis to illustrate how the value of an incubation program changes over time to *internal* customers—setting expectations of where, how much, and when your stakeholders should see value.

In broad terms, there are three different types of value we have discussed throughout this book. First and foremost, this method of incubation is ultimately designed to build new businesses that are meaningful to your larger company. While you are building those businesses, you can leverage this approach to innovation to improve how the company operates internally. You can also improve how the company is seen as an innovator both internally and externally. Unfortunately, you do not get all this value upfront and all at once.

As we also mention throughout the book, it can take several years to build a meaningful new business and you will not be able to rest after starting just the first one. Building up this pipeline of successful businesses will take time, care, and attention. Value will not come quickly from one place but spread out and from multiple directions simultaneously.

---

[3]Adrian J. Slywotzky, *Value Migration: How to Think Several Moves Ahead of the Competition* (Boston, Harvard Business School Press, 1996)

Ultimately, in three or four years, you should be able to point to your first early successes. While not as long of a lead time as building a new business, improving how the larger company operates is also not something that happens overnight. In addition, over time the additional operational improvements will diminish in number and impact. Instead, much of the initial value you will be able to get out of an incubation program is likely around the value it brings to your company in branding it as an innovator both internally and externally. Being known as an innovator will help with recruiting talented individuals as well as with finding and retaining customers.

If you plot the value of these three contributions over time, you get a chart similar to an illustrative example you see in Figure 7-1. There you can see in the first year we predict most of the value from this hypothetical program will come from improving the brand, while a much smaller percentage will come from operational improvements—your new businesses will not bring any value your first year or two. This mix of value slowly changes year after year. In the third year, the operational improvements that were discovered and acted on in previous years start to take root and provide more lift to the established business. By the time you get to the fifth year, roughly two thirds of the value is derived from the new businesses that are generated, with the remainder come from smaller contributions around brand and operational improvements.

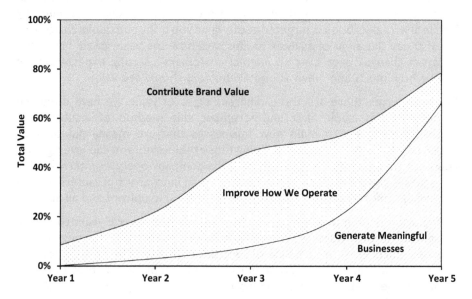

**Figure 7-1.** Illustrative example of how the value that an incubation program generates changes over time

While the substance will differ for your company and program, we have found simple tools, like the chart in Figure 7-1, can be powerful communication devices. Explaining in detail, as we do in Chapter 6, is necessary to understand where some of this value will come from. That is excellent if you need that level of detail but may not be appropriate in a short conversation with your CEO. As the saying goes, "a picture is worth one thousand words". When we used this visualization of value to set proper expectations with our senior executives, they tended to understand the diagram more or less with little or no explanation. We also keep this artifact up to date; updating it every year as part of our annual strategic planning and pulling it out whenever someone asks what our goals our for our program.

## Plan for the Worst

Very few of your incubated businesses will become a meaningful success. You have read it over and over again in this book so by now you are already expecting it. While you will be focused on *learning* fast, not *failing* fast, from the outside that can be a nuance that is easy to miss. So, while you may be expecting to learn fast, so should everyone else—all the stakeholders, partners, and participants.

While the exact numbers will vary based on your business domain and experience, as we pointed out in Chapter 4, many more business will be paused than exit successfully. In the external startup world, a one-in-ten chance of success if often anecdotally cited. While you may be able to do better as you mature and take advantage of your established business' expertise, a ten percent chance of success is a good place to start. You will need to set this expectation with everyone. Not just the CEO, but everyone in the company will need to know this is the expectation; otherwise, when they see an *individual incubation* be unsuccessful, they will quickly jump to the conclusion that the *entire program* is unsuccessful. If that happens, the company's mood and tolerance will turn on you. People will not want to waste their time and be associated with a failing program, and in turn, they will no longer want to commit resources or pitch ideas. In our experience, we found that describing the program as a way to create a startup-like environment can help people relate to how the program works and have the one-in-ten type expectation in mind.

In addition to just setting expectations of learning fast—learning, as quickly as possible, that a business will not be successful—you should also plan ahead for that lack of success. If a large number of your incubation teams will not be successful, you will need to plan for the operation and expense of the type of support programs we discussed in Chapter 5, such as "The Bench". This means coordinating with multiple teams—Finance, Human Resources, Communications, and more—and each and every person you work with on each and every team will need to be bought in for you to be successful. To keep that buy-in, they will need to have realistic expectations.

## Take Small Wins Where You Can Get Them

While only a small percentage of incubations will result in a successful business, that does not mean that every unsuccessful case will result in zero tangible value. Of course, there are the softer benefits of the program that we highlighted in Chapter 6, but there are other ways incubations could result in something meaningful and tangible. For example, an incubation could create a business that does not meet your bar of minimum success, say a $10 million a year business, but it might provide a conduit to sell additional established products. Imagine a free smartphone app that can optionally connect to one or more of your established business' products. While the app would not earn any money directly, its connection to other premium products in your portfolio can make customers aware of your other, paid, offerings. That might not count as a success statistics-wise, and the value may sometimes be difficult to measure, but it could still be very worthwhile.

In Chapter 2 we told the story of a founder who requested that the Angel Team pause her business. It is a great anecdote, but that chapter left out half the story. As that incubation progressed, we discovered that the incubation team had created an extremely solid technical foundation—a scalable analytics platform—for the product. We were not certain if the business would be successful or not, but separately we saw a lot of interest in the analytics platform from our products organization. We had to choose if this incubation was an analytics platform, or if it was a product that used an analytics platform. We chose both. We split the project into two separate incubations: one that would pursue a product built on the existing technology platform, and one that would focus on building an analytics platform that could be use by multiple established products within the company.

While, as you have already read, the product was not successful even after multiple pivot attempts, the underlying technology the product was built on was successful. It moved into our products group and became the basis for a central team that helps share technology across our business units and products. While we would not call it an "acquisition" as we describe it in Chapters 4 and 5, and it was not a $10 million business, it was a meaningful and tangible success that has helped drive meaningful revenue in the established business.

## Plan for Disruption

Innovation is messy and chaotic. While your incubations will have a framework to follow, hypotheses to test, and a team of people to help them, they do not have a long-term and upfront plan they are executing to. They are experimenting and learning, and as they are learning, they will change directions and tactics. By definition incubation will not be a direct line between idea and outcome. If you are finding that it is, then perhaps you are building committed bets.

Think about the operation of your program. New projects will be created and staffed. Eventually, those employees will either be successful and move into a business unit with their new product or learn fast and move onto their next career opportunity. Either way, the people will move to new teams or companies and will be replaced with new teams and new people as part of the next incubation. If you are pipelining your incubations, they will be spaced out so that the start of new projects and the completion of old projects will happen with regularity. Imagine moving out one team and bringing in a new team every other month. Now imagine how disruptive that will be to a company that would typically ask for your staffing plan a year in advance. As we mentioned, planning for this chaos can change the nature of these events—they are no longer disruptive, but instead, they are just part of the natural flow of the program.

When it comes to the human side, it is important to point out that this disruption does not have to be bad. Think about what it would be like to move into an incubation program that has the support and backing of established business. Think about what it would be like to take advantage of some of the programs we discussed in Chapter 5 and 6—programs like Founder Fitness or Incubation Rotation. These are opportunities that participants could find in few other companies. Making sure both the participants as well as the stakeholders understand what will eventually happen and the benefits and opportunities that come with these changes can help alleviate fears—think back to our discussion of value migration. Making sure participants understand the value they can get out of the program, and keeping them engaged during these difficult transitions, can help retain your top talent.

## Internal Disruption Can Be a Good Thing

Unfortunately, the disruptions are not limited to the comings and goings of projects. While incubation projects are underway, there will sometimes be conflicts with your company's existing and established businesses. Sometimes a conflict will be based only on perceptions or due to inaccurate product messaging.

Imagine you work for a car company, and your established business is known for building and selling family cars. Your automotive engineers see an opportunity to extend beyond the family market, so they start an incubation to build and sell a new race car. In hopes of true transparency and cooperation, the incubation team presents their product plans and marketing messages to the established product team. They get great feedback and insights from a mature team that understands the established business. Unfortunately, things can get confusing quickly.

If the incubation is positioning their new race car simply as "The best car on the market," your established business' customers may think the race car is competing against the family car and wonder, "Is the company saying the family car is no longer the best car?" Additionally, the established business may think they have a hole in their product line and begin to position their car as being able to "go really fast," even though that is not going to attract the demographic that will be interested in their family cars. Although not intentional, these two products—the existing established business and the new incubation—are now competing for customers. This artificial competitive situation, due to incorrect positioning of what should be non-competitive products, will result in no winners—only losers.

Less often, but still occasionally, the competition and conflicts between products will be real. This type of competition can be beneficial if it is good spirited, and it can also be disruptive and confusing for customers. A 2017 article, "The Pros and Cons of Competition Among Employees"[4], highlights some things to think about when it comes to internal competition. Some of the takeaways are that, on one hand, there is a lot of value to competition if employees can find new or faster ways to solve customers' problems. On the other hand, some competition can cause fear or anxiety, can lead to people misleading customers—just like in the example. The authors of the article argue that a key difference is in how to frame the competition—being based on excitement versus fear, rewards versus punishment.

You may get complaints from within a business unit that your incubations are competing with the established business. If that competition was unintentional, you should investigate and confirm that it is not simply a perception or messaging problem. Sometimes, however, you may want to intentionally compete with an existing business. You may have a new approach or be using a new technology that can help leap over the established business and, more importantly, its competitors. When you are intentionally competing and you get this complaint, the discussion you need to have with the established business is relatively straightforward: If an incubation with 10 or 15 people can disrupt your established business, what is stopping an even better funded competitor from doing the same? It will take careful planning to eventually integrate the incubation back into the established business, but it is much better to have that competition come from within. That way, the larger company wins regardless of which product is ultimately more successful. Approaching this disruption in that way, where both teams are openly working toward the same goal of helping the company and are not intentionally trying to sabotage each other, can help frame the competition in a positive way.

---

[4]Anna Steinhage, Dan Cable, and Duncan Wardley, "The Pros and Cons of Competition Among Employees," *Harvard Business Review*, March 20, 2017, https://hbr.org/2017/03/the-pros-and-cons-of-competition-among-employees

# Go Broad and Go Deep

To get buy-in throughout your company, along with setting proper expectations, you will need to use upfront planning to describe the value you can bring to the company over both the short and long term. You need to convey this value not only to the CEO, but to a broad set of stakeholders and partners that you will need to work with on an on-going basis from this point forward. Relationships with these stakeholders and partners will be worth their weight in gold if they are formed early and built on trust, or they will be lead weights pulling you down with every step if they are ignored, abused, or neglected.

You will need agreement and alignment from each stakeholder and colleague as they not only control functions important to your program, but many can be true partners and participate directly to help you improve the program over time. As you work your way through the organization, go beyond simply getting agreement—get participation and shared ownership where it makes sense. There are multiple ways you can involve leaders or their team members from different functions. For example, you could ask for help from the finance team modeling your budget forecasts. You should also be on the lookout for key experience or skills that you will need to build your program. When talking to these leaders, ask them to nominate an Angel Team member who can also be a communications conduit back to their respective groups on how the program is progressing. That is not to say that you should find new Angel Team members from each and every leader you speak to. You will need diverse representation from across the business, but too many people will make your pitch and 3P meetings unwieldy.

It is also important to never stop looking to find new facets of your company to recruit. If you recall our story from Chapter 5, we hit many roadblocks when we tried to market an incubation product using an off-brand name. This was because we had talked to members of the Marketing team about our program, but never anyone from the *Brand* Marketing team. This mistake was a huge lesson for us. Once the Brand Marketing team understood what we were trying to accomplish and why, they did not simply get out of the way, they became a huge help and champion of the program. The moral of the story: once you think you have found everyone you need, keep looking, because you have not found *everyone*.

Unfortunately, there is no set recipe for finding everyone you will need to be successful. Every organization is structured differently, and every incubation program should be tailored to a company's needs and culture. In the next sections, we present an overview of some of the people and areas that we found to be important, but your organization will likely be structured differently and may be more or less complicated. These are presented top down, not necessarily in the order you will want to tackle them in—that will depend on the personalities involved as well as corporate politics. In reality, you will want to tackle many of these conversations in parallel.

## Chief Executive Officer

When it comes to getting buy-in and approval for a program of this breadth and scale, it may seem intuitive to start with the top of your organization, typically your Chief Executive Officer (CEO) . However, you cannot simply march into their office, tell them about this great book you read on incubation programs, and expect to walk out with approval and millions of dollars in funding. Before they will be willing to spend money on a new program, they will want to see a plan that has already had the necessary vetting, approvals, and buy-in from various groups within the company. Unfortunately, those other approvals and buy-ins can sometimes be difficult or impossible without buy-in from the top. It is a bit of a catch-22.

To make this work, you will need to make progress in steps. First, you will need a sponsor, and for a program this broad, it makes sense for that to be an executive who reports to your CEO. In our case, if you recall the story of our program from Chapter 3, it was our Chief Technology Officer (CTO). In other companies or situations, it could just as easily be your Chief Marketing Officer or Chief Product Officer—it will all depend on how your company is organized. You and your sponsor should put together a sketch of the program you want to build, pointing out, for example, some of the benefits we highlight in Chapter 6. This sketch serves as a plan for a plan. It is something your CEO can buy into conceptually without yet committing any funding. You are looking for a, "Yes, this looks good in theory—come back to me when you have a complete plan and we can talk about money."

With this conceptual buy-in, you can work with the teams we highlight in this section, as well as others you discover along your journey, to build up enough support and enough of the details to come back and ask for specific funding and be able to commit to specific metrics or deliverables. You will need to come back with a complete solution—including how to fund it—and only then ask for your CEO's support and buy-in.

If it was not done as part of getting the conceptual buy-in, this would also be a good point in time to build awareness with C-level and other top executives. Some of whom you will need to go deep with and get help from their teams to build out the plan or garner support from once the program is up in running. Even those you do not need to dive deep with will need to be aware of this effort when it comes up in meetings—you do not want to leave an executive out of the loop just because you do not *currently* need their help.

## Products Team

Your incubation program will be creating new and innovative products, so it would be counter-productive to do that without the help and support of the person leading your products organization. In our case, that is our Chief

Product Officer (CPO), but it will be your company's equivalent. Even better, it may be that your CPO is your sponsor. If that is the case, keep in mind that your business units and product teams are focused on the current quarter and are measured by near-term tangible metrics like profit. As we mention several times throughout this book, building a new business is different. For that reason, it is not recommended to build your incubation program within a business unit or even within the general umbrella the business units operate within. You will need your incubations to have the space and freedom to experiment and learn fast without getting distracted by or impacting the established portions of your company.

That does not mean, however, that you can forgo your CPO's support and assistance. While still a small number of the overall product organization, a large percentage of your founding teams will come from the that the established products organization. This means that you will want to closely coordinate and collaborate on programs like Incubation Rotation and The Bench.

The same goes for the business unit leaders. Not only will they need to understand and buy into programs like incubation rotation, but most importantly, they will be the eventually purchasers of your successful business. Also, like we discussed in the previous section, you may be competing against your company's established products—either conceptually or actually head-to-head. Similarly, there are likely already innovation programs underway within the product organization. You will need to get agreement with the general managers and their operations team on how to differentiate between the types of innovation that are appropriate for the products organization versus those appropriate new incubation program.

In Figure 7-2, we show how we can differentiate between innovation that should take place within the established business, and innovation that should be kept separate until it matures enough to move into a business unit. There are many aspects to take into account, and the answer to where something belongs can often rely on interpreting shades of gray. However, if you were to summarize the distinctions, it comes down to where the risk is. As we point out in Chapter 4 and Figure 4-3, if the risk is primarily around execution, it most likely belongs in a business unit. If instead the risk is primarily around the business itself—if the market actually exists and if the opportunity large enough—then it is better structured as an incubation that is free to experiment.

| Product Line Innovation | New Business Incubation |
|---|---|
| External Environment | External Environment |
| Established market | Rapidly emerging/evolving market |
| Known market size | Unknown market size |
| Clear customer segmentation | Unproven customer hypothesis |
| High-to-medium competitive intensity | Low-to-no competitive intensity |
| Established or emerging market leadership | Lack of established market leaders |
| Proven business models | Unproven business model hypothesis |
| Project Context | Project Context |
| High-confidence revenue targets | Unproven revenue model, no target |
| Well-defined product requirements | Incomplete product requirements |
| Extends a current product or line | New business or distant adjacency |
| Pivots likely on product only | Pivots on any business model aspects |
| Primary risk is execution | Primary risk is product-market fit |
| | High risk of failure irrespective of execution |

**Figure 7-2.** Example criteria to differentiate between ideas that should be innovated on within the established business versus separately as part of incubation program

## Marketing Team

It was not obvious to us when we first started to build our version of an incubation program, but buy-in and collaboration from your Marketing team will be one of the most critical pieces to your success. As mentioned in Chapter 6, much of the value of the early program will be in forming positive impressions of your company for your customers, employees, and future employees. Many of the concerns about the program will be on how the market will view internal competition and immature products and the possible brand confusion and dilution that could follow. All these areas will take collaboration with different functions of your Marketing team to take advantage of the program benefits and overcome potential roadblocks.

One lesson we learned early on was that we needed to go broader and deeper into the Marketing organization when kicking off the program. While obvious in hindsight, we should not have viewed "Marketing" as a single entity with just one or two people we needed to coordinate with. As we pointed out in our story from Chapters 5 and 6, there is a large difference between Corporate Marketing, Brand Marketing, and Product Marketing. When building a program of this scope, two out of three is not good enough—and you may find that there are many more than three parts of many different corporate functions, including Marketing.

For our situation and because of how critical the various flavors of marketing are to our program, we found it necessary to go deep and broad. This includes functions that we have only more recently started to closely collaborate with. For example, Field Marketing, Product Marketing, Event Marketing, Brand Marketing, Internal Communications, Public Relations, and Analyst Relations. Every organization is different, and you will need to explore exactly how responsibilities for different functions are carved up across teams and people.

## Human Resources Team

When coordinating with the Human Resources team, you will want to make sure the key people in that organization understand the potential impacts and benefits the program will have on the employee base. You will need your Human Resources team's buy-in, and more importantly, their help in creating and implementing programs like Founder Fitness, The Bench, and Incubation Rotation. Your incubation teams will be transferring employees to and from other parts of the established business, as well as recruiting new employees externally.

Similar to the Marketing team, there are many different facets of Human Resources that you will want to coordinate with and leverage. For example, working with the benefits team to create a custom bonus plan to reward successful incubations, or working with the recruiting team to both make sure they are leveraging the branding potential of the incubation program, as well as helping you source talented people with start-up mindsets. The Founder Fitness program is essentially a custom training program that we built with help from our Human Resources and Employee Development teams.

Here is another important tip: When it comes to large and diverse teams, a great tactic is to find someone to be your point person within that organization. Someone to support the incubation program and help you navigate to the right person for any particular need or sometimes to insulate you entirely from needing to know the details of how that team works internally.

We learned this model from our partnership with Human Resources. We already had a Human Resources Business Partner dedicated to the CTO team, but she saw helping our incubation program, with all of its distinct people needs, as a natural expansion of her role—and it paid off. Having champions like these can really make the difference between a marginal program and a great program. Whenever you can function in this model, we recommend it, but it requires finding the right person who can take on this role. We have been less successful with this approach in other teams precisely because we could not find the right person who would fully embrace and embody what are trying to accomplish with the incubation program. Be careful with single points of contact that are simply middlemen to the larger organization. While they can sometimes help, other times they become a bottleneck to getting things accomplished quickly.

## Board of Directors

At some point in your quest to bootstrap your program, possibly after it has been approved but before it has been widely discussed, you will likely need to brief your company's Board of Directors or equivalent. They will want to understand how incubating new businesses will benefit the company and how you will be measuring the success or failure of the program. As with other executives, you not only need to make sure they understand the broader context of what you are doing and why, but they also need to have realistic expectations around how infrequently incubations will be successful and how long it could take to build a new meaningful business. This is an approach to innovation that they may not have seen, so you will need to explain why this approach will be more successful than past attempts at creating new businesses.

In your preparation to present to the board, it will be important to talk with your corporate strategy team. They set the overall direction for the company and help it make smart high-level investment decisions. They also know how to properly package information for board-level consumption, so getting both their input and buy-in will be extremely helpful. This may also be a good point to loop in the Investor Relations team. While it will still be some time before your program comes up in an investor call or analyst day presentation, making sure the Investor Relations team understands what you are planning and the value it will bring—both in terms of new businesses and also the image of the company—will be important for the longer term. Once the incubation teams start to speak publicly, a financial analyst could ask about the program and your Investor Relations team will need to know how to answer.

Assuming your presentation goes well, this will not be the one and only time you need to present the program to the board. Just as with getting buy-in from other executives, you will want the board to be your champions. This can be especially important over the long term. As executives are replaced throughout the years, having commitment for the program at the board level can help smooth out transitions in leadership. To keep their commitment to the program, you will need to periodically update the board on the progress you have made and keep them excited about your continued and demonstrable value.

## Legal

With buy-in from the top, you can now go broader in deeper into the company's organizations to build the relationships you will need to be successful on a day-to-day basis. Since the products you will be building within the incubation program should not pose any more of a risk to the company than its established products, you likely will not need to closely coordinate with the Chief Council as much as you will with some other executives.

However, the broader legal team can still help the incubations with tasks like patent protection—something a small startup might not be able to afford or do quickly. In addition, since the incubation teams will be pushing boundaries, and many may not be aware of some hard lines they are not allowed to cross, you will need support from your legal team to keep your risk to an acceptable level.

Having a Product Lawyer assigned to each incubation can help keep teams from unintentionally straying out of bounds. Regulations like the European Union's General Data Protection Regulation can be difficult to navigate for the newly initiated, but having a lawyer on call for the incubation team can turn that regulation from being a huge risk in to a straightforward piece of work. The Legal team will need to understand that the dollar amounts involved in incubation are very small, so they can balance how to let many of the incubation-specific risks go, but yet still protect the larger established business. You want to avoid a $10 thousand business causing a lawsuit that crashes your billion-dollar enterprise, but you also want to avoid inhibiting innovation because you are worried about the risk to a $1,000 vendor contract.

## Procurement

Procurement, similar to Legal, comes down to balancing risk tolerance with the need for incubations to move quickly. You will want to have partners in the Procurement team to help streamline processes and approvals. Again, much like you did with the Legal team, you will need to make sure the Procurement team has the proper context to properly balance risk and speed. You are not asking them to break their own rules, but instead putting them in your shoes and asking them to help craft a solution to your problems. Like other teams, Procurement is multi-disciplined, and you will need contacts into different parts of the Procurement organization, for example, vendor negotiation or corporate purchasing cards.

In this chapter, and throughout the book, you have read how we try to "set the context" with teams or "help them understand," but it is important to remember that you do not have all the answers and likely never will. You are on a journey of continuous learning that, in addition to discovery through the creation of new business, you will learn a lot about your established business and the way it works. Often times, it will be you who needs to understand and have context of the needs and requirements of the various backend functions of your established business.

For example, for far too long, we did not understand the role the Legal team played when it came to procurement contracts. An incubation team would send their assigned product lawyer a vendor contract to review, and the lawyer would say "this looks fine," but then the procurement team would find out about the contract after it had already been signed and baulk at its terms. Not simply because they had not been involved, but because while the contract had been fine from a legal standpoint, it did not include important business requirements—for example, the proper payment terms that the Accounts Payable team could commit to.

Notice in the example, we started with a simple purchase from a new vendor, but quickly moved to needing support from Legal, Procurement, and eventually Accounts Payable. As you hit these type of situations, you will discover who to build important relationships with as you follow the chain of people required to get something, seemly simple, done quickly. These relationships will be key to helping you not only navigate existing processes but also build new processes that make more sense for your incubating businesses.

## Finance

The Finance team is another area that requires broad participation in your incubation program. Not just financial planning and budgeting, but functions like Sales Accounting for proper revenue recognition, and Accounts Receivable to route that revenue to the proper internal profit center accounts.

In addition to the more detailed finance functions, higher up in the organization there will be questions around return on investment. The Finance team will be taking a critical look at how much money you are investing into these incubations and how much revenue you are bringing in—remember, they have the established business as their frame of reference.

Early in our program's history there was a revenue forecast review meeting that had, for some unknown reason, included our incubation financial projections. Of course, in those projections our new businesses were forecasting $0 in revenue. After the meeting, a key finance executive in the company happened to see one of our founders in the hallway and asked, "Why don't you have a revenue target?" to which the founder quickly replied with a smile, "I do. It's zero." The executive paused for a moment, and then simply said, "Oh, OK." It was at that moment when this executive finally understood what we were doing. We were not sandbagging forecasts to try to make us look better. We were undertaking deliberate innovation that did not have known outcomes and avoiding the creation of works of fiction or building committed bets.

Remember that most teams, like Finance, are highly aligned to the established business—after all, that is who they support day-in and day-out to make sure the company is financially stable and meets financial regulations. Once they understand how you do business, these advocates and partners can be a huge advantage, but periodically they will need to be reminded that what you are trying to accomplish, and the way you are trying to accomplish it, is different than within the established business. Incubations are about experimentation, not straight-forward execution.

# Securing Funding

Now that you have buy-in and support from the top—your Board of Directors and CEO—you have your money in the bag, right? Not so fast...

Our company has a strong commitment to innovation, including incubation of new businesses within our accelerator program. While from outside the program that can appear to be a blank check, it is not quite so simple. Periodically, someone will come to us and say, "It must be nice to have unlimited budget!" to which we reply, "Not really. Our unlimited budget comes with unlimited strings attached." The truth is that while we certainly could ask for increased funding for program if we had a compelling need, we would first need to demonstrate that we were spending our current funding wisely and that any additional investment would be worthwhile. Just as the Angel Team would evaluate an individual incubation project, our CEO and CFO would want to see our plan—how we spend our money today and how we would spend any increased investment. They would want to know we were spending our money efficiently and on projects that could eventually be meaningful to the company as well as have a reasonable chance of success. They would ask deceptively simple question, such as, "How much are we spending on the existing incubation portfolio and are those current investment levels justified?" and "How much additional investment is needed?" and "What will our return on investment be?" and "Where will this new funding come from?"

This was exactly the situation we faced as we were initially building our incubation program. I (Howard) was having a discussion on the overall uncertain nature of the program with our CTO—who is our program's sponsor—and as the call was wrapping up he added a parting request, "How much is this all going to cost?" We hung up and I opened up a blank spreadsheet and just stared for a few minutes. How was I to determine how much it would cost to run projects that were by their very definition uncertain? These were true experiments. How was I to know if they would last a week, a month, or a year? How was I to know how many resources they would need a year or more in advance without even knowing what "they" were?

# Build a Solid Financial Plan

To answer financial questions, you need a solid financial plan. A plan that puts you in a position to answer any financial question at any time, even on a moment's notice. By mathematically modeling how the program works and keeping that model up to date over time as you learn new information, you can answer these and other hard questions with some certainty even though the program by its very nature is uncertain.

You will need a model that not only helps you understand the cost and risk of executing on a single incubation, but the cost and risks to run the entire program. It must cover all the moving pieces for the full pipeline of activities—from sourcing pitches from employees to exiting scalable businesses into business units. All the different types of incubations in different phases; the risks at these different phases and the costs for other items such as marketing and travel. The costs and overhead of administration and running programs like The Bench. Of course, let us not forget to include the expected success and failure rates along with the time frames involved. If that sounds like way too many unknown variables combined with even more unknown variables, it is, but that does not mean you cannot model the program effectively.

## Incubation in the Extreme

In July of 1945, Physicist Enrico Fermi was on hand to witness the world's first nuclear weapon test—the ultimate incubation project. The team building this new weapon had confidence that the device would work but could not determine ahead of time the strength of the resulting explosion. After the impressive demonstration, Fermi is said to have thrown several pieces of paper in the air and, from that and blast he had just witnessed, concluded that the strength of the explosion was ten kilotons. It turned out he was close—the actual strength was approximately 21 kilotons[5]. Never before had a weapon like this been tested—up until this point it was completely theoretical—so being off by a factor of two is quite a good estimate. (Keep this in mind as you try to predict the outcomes of your individual incubations.)

Fermi became legendary for the problems that he used to challenge his students with while teaching at the University of Chicago—for example, estimating how many piano tuners work in Chicago given only the city's population.[6] The solution to these problems, often known as "Fermi Problems," is to estimate each variable the best you can and then apply simply arithmetic to arrive at an estimated answer. Given Chicago's population, how many pianos are there in Chicago? How often does each piano need to be tuned on average? How long does it take to tune a piano and how many hours a day would a piano tuner work? Just like in our situation of modeling an incubation program, answering each of these questions precisely would be difficult, but it is not hard to make simple, rough, guesses that when combined, result in a reasonably accurate estimate.

---

[5]Margaret Burgess, ed., "A Backward Glance: Eyewitnesses to Trinity," *Nuclear Weapons Journal* 2 (2005): 45. http://www.lanl.gov/science/weapons_journal/wj_pubs/11nwj2-05.pdf
[6]"Fermi's Piano Tuner Problem," NASA Glenn Research Center, accessed August 23, 2018, https://www.grc.nasa.gov/www/k-12/Numbers/Math/Mathematical_Thinking/fermis_piano_tuner.htm

The reason why this type of analysis yields results that are reasonable is because the overestimated guesses when combined with underestimated guesses tend to cancel each other out. However, one challenge in approaching our model this way is that even if the model is completely accurate, it will only model averages. Individual incubations could vary widely and therefore the model will often only be accurate in aggregate as the number of incubations running simultaneously grows.

## Modeling Your Program

Here we present a simplified financial model for a hypothetical incubation program. As we point out repeatedly throughout this book, you should not blindly copy our program—each company has a different culture and different goals. Take this model, along with its general approach, and then modify and expand it to fit your needs.

---

**Note**   The values presented in this model are fictitious and for illustrative purposes only. Do not use them directly in your model.

---

We approach this model in a bottoms-up fashion. Modeling the costs and chance of success of an individual incubation project at each of its phases, and then use those results to model a continuous pipeline of incubations to determine the costs of the overall program, as well as other important statistics; all assuming your specific goals.

In Table 7-1, the model starts with some assumptions about an incubation project for each phase of its lifecycle:

- The number of people on a team in a given phase.

- The total annual cost of those employees, including their salaries, bonuses, and benefits. You could expand this by modeling the salaries of individual team roles, based experience and skills needed in a minimally viable team, but we will not go that deep in this example.

- Other expenses the team will have. For example, equipment, travel expenses, and marketing spend. As with the people costs, you could build something finer grained, but here we will just lump these all together into a single simple guess per phase.

- People and other costs are added together into a single Annual Costs column to simplify future calculations.

- How long each phase will last, in months.
- The odds of a given phase being successful.

**Table 7-1.** Illustrative Inputs to the Financial Model

| Phase | People | People Costs | Other Expenses | Annual Costs | Phase Months | Odds of Success |
|---|---|---|---|---|---|---|
| Seed 1 | 2 | $400,000 | $15,000 | $415,000 | 2 | 95% |
| Seed 2 | 3 | $600,000 | $50,000 | $650,000 | 4 | 85% |
| Series A | 7 | $1,250,000 | $75,000 | $1,325,000 | 15 | 25% |
| Series B | 12 | $2,500,000 | $100,000 | $2,600,000 | 12 | 50% |
| Series C | 15 | $3,000,000 | $120,000 | $3,120,000 | 6 | 99% |

Simple arithmetic and the initial inputs from Table 7-1 are used to derive intermediate calculations that will be needed to understand a pipelined model and how all the moving pieces work together. These results are calculated and placed into Table 7-2:

- The cost of each phase is calculated by taking the average phase length and multiplying by annual cost (both from Table 7-1) and dividing by 12 months (e.g., $415,000 times 2 divided by 12 = $69,167).

- The column entitled Number Until Success is more complicated to explain and a bit abstract, but in short, you want to know how many incubations you will need to run of each phase before you will find one that meets your success criteria. To calculate that column, starting with Series C, divide by the odds of success for each corresponding phase (Table 7-1) and work backward to Seed 1. (e.g., 1 successful project divided by 99% success rate = 1.01, 1.01 divided by 50% = 2.02, etc. Please note that the values in the table have been rounded for simplicity.)

- The cost of success is calculated by simply multiplying the previous two columns; the cost of a phase and the number required until success is reach (e.g., $69,167 times 10 = $691,670).

**Table 7-2.** Intermediate Calculations of the Illustrative Financial Model

| Phase | Cost of Phase | Number Until Success | Cost of Success | Simultaneous Projects | Pipeline Cost |
|---|---|---|---|---|---|
| Seed 1 | $69,167 | 10.0 | $691,670 | 0.83 | $346,082 |
| Seed 2 | $216,667 | 9.5 | $2,058,336 | 1.58 | $1,029,906 |
| Series A | $1,656,250 | 8.1 | $13,415,625 | 5.05 | $6,6691,919 |
| Series B | $2,600,000 | 2.0 | $5,200,000 | 1.01 | $2,626,262 |
| Series C | $1,560,000 | 1.0 | $1,560,000 | 0.23 | $787,878 |

Now we build the pipeline—the number projects, and their costs, operating simultaneously in a perfectly balanced pipeline. In order to calculate that we need to pick a goal. In this example, we assume you want to have one successful incubation—a meaningful new business—every two years. Continuing where we left off in Table 7-2:

- To know how many teams of each type we will be operating simultaneously within our pipeline, we use the cost of success of each phase and divide it by the corresponding annual cost of each phase from Table 7-1, then divide that by the two-year goal (e.g., $691,670 divided by $415,000 divided by 2 = 0.83; rounded to two decimal places).

- Finally, to calculate how much the pieces of the pipeline will each cost, we multiply the number of simultaneous projects in each phase by their respective annual cost from Table 7-1 (e.g., 0.83 multiplied by $415,000 = $346,082).

Note that, as you can see in Table 7-2, the number of projects run at any given time do not work out to be whole numbers; instead they are fractional projects. As an example, 1.58 Seed 2 projects means that if you were to count all the Seed 2 projects running each day of a given year, they would average out to 1.58. While all this modeling may seem complicated when written out in book form, there is very little actual math involved, and the payoff is worth it.

From the inputs and intermediate calculations, we derive answers to meaningful questions. We can use people, salary, and success rates to estimate bench and severance costs, and make some high-level estimates of the cost for the fixed staff and overhead. You can see the results of our theoretical model in Table 7-3:

- The total costs of all the projects is simply the sum of the last column of Table 7-2. It represents the direct costs of running all the simultaneous incubation projects.

- The three-month bench cost can be derived by inverting the odds of success and using the cost of people and the number of projects. For brevity, we have not included this calculation in this example.

- The summary includes a cost for fixed staff, just to remind you to include your fixed program overhead, but the value included here is completely arbitrary—use your actual costs.

- The number of Simultaneous Projects is the sum of the second-to-last column of Table 7-2.

- The number of new projects that need to be accepted into the program each year to keep the pipeline full is calculated using the "Number Until Success" for Seed 1, divided by the number of years between success—in this example, we said 2 years between meaningful successes (e.g., 10.0 divided by 2 = 5).

- To give you a sense of size for our theoretical program, total project staff is calculated by using the number of people per phase from Table 7-1 and multiplying by the corresponding number of simultaneous projects from Table 7-2 and then summing the results.

**Table 7-3.** Summary of Financial Modeling Results in the Illustrative Example

| Summary | |
|---|---|
| Incubation Projects | $11,482,050 |
| Three-month Bench | $1,726,452 |
| Fixed Staff | $1,000,000 |
| Total Cost | $14,208,502 |
| Simultaneous Projects | 8.73 |
| New Projects per Year | 5 |
| Total Project Staff | 57.68 |

Altogether, in this example, you would spend just over $14 million per year to create a new, meaningful, business every other year. That cost not only includes all the overhead of running the program, but also the cost of unsuccessful business you will incubate along the way. To generate the successful businesses at that one every-other-year rate, you will need to run about eight to nine businesses at a time and take on five new businesses each year—about once every ten weeks. Overall, once the program was fully ramped up, you would expect approximately 58 people working on incubation teams at any given time.

If $14 million per year seems like a lot of money, that is because it is. However, it is not a question of size, but a question of value: could these businesses be incubated more economically? At the size and cost of this hypothetical program model, including overhead the like bench and fixed staff, it costs roughly $1.6 million per incubation per year. In our experience, it is not uncommon for committed bets to cost two or three times that much—or more. In that sense, assuming your actual program matched this hypothetical performance, this approach is objectively more than twice as economical as the committed bets within the established business. That does not even count all the additional benefits we discussed in Chapter 6, but you can do even better still.

Just as we have, you will learn a tremendous amount from hands-on experience running an incubation program. And just as your businesses need to use the data they have to pivot when needed, you must do the same at the program level. The $14 million figure was based on the assumptions used as inputs to the model, but as you learn fast what works and what does not, you can improve these assumptions, which in turn can greatly improve the programs efficiency.

For example, imagine over time you learn how to improve the likelihood that teams in Series B will be successful in making it to Series C, from 50% to 75%. While the average cost of each incubation will remain around $1.6 million, the total cost of the program will drop to under $10 million—a 30% improvement! That is just one example of a way you can improve the program. By continuously measuring these inputs and looking for underlying drivers of cost and success along with ways to improve those drivers, you will continuously improve the cost effectiveness of the program and your stakeholder's return on investment.

These examples were calculated using a fixed number of exits as a goal, but you could invert this and instead model how often you would exit something if you had a specific limited budget. You could also go as detailed or fine-grained as you are comfortable with and update the model as you learn more—breaking down one assumption into multiple sub-assumptions to help you accurately predict different aspects of your program.

Another direction you could expand into is to include revenue estimates and use this model to show theoretical returns. If you were to compare this investment to an external acquisition, the total amount invested to get a success is the upfront cost that must be returned over time. By setting criteria on revenue potential and pausing incubations that do not meet a specific bar, you cannot guarantee success, but you can guarantee that when you have success it will be of a certain scale.

If all this math is a little overwhelming and it seems like all this modeling is a leap of faith you do not want to blindly rely upon, the good news is it will take time to ramp up a program like this. Assuming you will be following our pipeline-based approach, and not using cohorts, you will want to space out any new incubations that you bring into the program. If you were to use the model in our example, you would want to bring on a new team once every 10 weeks to build that pipeline, and even after the first two years, the program would not yet be at its calculated capacity of eight or nine projects.

All this ramp-up time will give you the opportunity to refine your model and work out the kinks in your processes. As you progress, you will be able to track actual values—how long it actually takes to move from Seed 1 to Seed 2, how much it actually costs to run a Series A project—and use these averages to feed back into your model. While still only predicting averages, over time the model will become more and more accurate. We will spare you additional math, but a property of Fermi Analysis is that if your individual inputs have a standard deviation of one, the entire analysis will be within one standard deviation. In the model we use internally to manage our program, we calculate the standard deviation of some of our inputs and use those to estimate the standard deviation of some of our model's outputs to understand how much variability there may be year-over-year.

With that simplified model to work from, you can figure out how the program can contribute to the larger goals of the company. How many incubations do you need per year to be successful? How much *should* you spend on incubation versus the established business or acquisitions? The model also gives you a way to determine, in concrete terms, where there are opportunities to improve and how to measure those improvements. You can play with the inputs to the model—lowering the time or cost for a specific phase—and see what effect that has on the cost to build a successful business.

## Initial Budget

Once you have a solid starting point for a model, the next challenge will be to figure out where the money will come from. You need a source of funding, and unless you are lucky enough to work for a company with unlimited capital, the money has to be taken from somewhere else.

Luckily, there are a confluence of forces that together can help bootstrap your funding. First, as we mentioned, building your incubation pipeline from a cold start will take time. You will want to make sure to space projects out appropriately and avoid starting more than one project at the same time. This is needed, partially, because you want to focus on getting projects off on the right foot, especially when you are new at it. In addition, if you are following the pipeline approach versus creating cohorts of teams, you will want to have your funding requirements smoothed out and avoid many projects all needing their peek funding at the same time. Because of these factors, it could take as much as two years or longer to fully build up the pipeline, and along with it, your need to consume your eventual full funding target.

Second, finding the right projects will take time—this is a situation where it pays to be a little bit picky. Initially, when we first started our program, we were accepting roughly one-in-five ideas into the program, and now that we have matured in what we look for, it is closer to one-in-ten. Regardless of the actual success rate, to get enough pitches to feed your program, you will need to get the word out throughout your company and those prospective intrapreneurs will need time to build canvases, pitch them successfully, and transition into their new roles.

Together this additional time means you need less money at the start of your program. It will give you the ability to ask for a much smaller amount of budget your first year, with the promise that you will come back with measurable results and a larger ask the next year.

## Round-Up Rogue and Disparate Projects

While smaller, the initial funding still needs to come from somewhere, and that brings us to the third force at play: rogue and disparate projects. If you recall from Chapter 2, one of the consequences of treating your new business ideas like you do your established businesses is that they are operated using the wrong set of processes and measurements. They are often overfunded for their current state—large, committed bets—and there is an overall lack in their governance and transparency. A great way to wrangle all these misfit projects that do not fit in a business unit is to pull them into your new incubation program. You offer to take them in, give them proper oversight and visibility, promise to right-size them based on their actual needs, and overtime figure out if they make sense to continue to invest in. Of course, if these projects come with budget, and as they are eventually rightsized, shut down, or successfully exited into a business unit, it will free that budget up for you to invest into new incubation projects. Ta-da! You have just found your initial source of funding.

In other words, these disparate projects check three boxes all at once: a source of ideas, a source of funding, and a way to help the established business in the short term. This is exactly the approach we took when bootstrapping our incubation program. If you recall our origin story from Chapter 3, in September 2015 we pulled in four pre-existing projects that had each been incubating their businesses in different ways. By the end of October, we held our first 3P review of these businesses and continued to manage those projects within our new framework from that point forward. We learned a tremendous amount from incubating those four, initial, business—many of those lessons are found throughout this book.

Having an incubation framework and model made all the difference. We were able to use these tools as a yard stick to measure the progress the teams had made and activities they were currently engaged in. As we discussed in Chapter 2, often innovation in an established business takes the form of a committed bet. Teams would be staffed and working on activities as if they were in Series B, but in reality, their businesses only had the maturity of a Seed 2 project. In these cases, right-sizing the team—putting them back in Seed 2 and taking away time and resources—can get the team focused in the right direction.

Eventually, two of the four projects were paused, one pivoted to an early exit back to the established business, and the fourth recently exited to a business unit earlier this year. As the projects were paused, right sized, or exited, we repurposed their funds to bring in our next incubations. In fact, because of this savings combined with the long ramp-up time, we actually underspent our initial budget in both of the first two years of operation. If you think about what that means in reality, we drove multiple innovation projects to conclusion, took on new incubation projects, and still came in under budget. This provided evidence that our methodology was working and gave executives confidence in our program.

# No Time Like the Present

As the old Chinese proverb says, "The best time to plant a tree was 20 years ago. The second best time is now." Building a program of this scope is never easy, and there will never be a "best time" to start. You simply have to start your bootstrap by beginning to plan out your program and develop the buy-in you will need to fund and operate it. There is no magic bullet that will make everything just happen, but there are some pieces that are more key than others for long-term success. Most importantly, setting realistic expectations with partners and stakeholders while getting their commitment to support and participate in your program for the longer term.

During his SXSW 2018 panel, George Watt, one of the authors of this book, was asked about the keys to building a successful accelerator program. In his answer, George confirmed that C-level support is an absolute necessity, but there was more to his answer than you might think. As he put it:

> Certainly buy-in from senior leaders is key. But it is also critical to set their expectations correctly. For example, they need to understand the time it takes for an incubating business to become successful—and it's not going to be weeks, or even a quarter, which is a common expectation. It is also critical to remind them of those expectations from time to time. They have a lot going on, so don't assume they will remember everything you told them. In addition, they need to know you are being good custodians of capital, so they need to know the right level of detail about your model.
>
> That kind of C-level support is key, but if you can get at least one person at that level to lean in and become an active participant in the program, the benefits can be magical. We are fortunate to have a CTO who participates very actively in our program. He is an active member of our investment team—we call it the Angel Team—and he participates in our pitch events and retrospectives. What's great about that is that he is always, "in the room where it happens," to borrow a phrase from the musical "Hamilton". He attends board and C-level meetings, so if the Accelerator comes up during those he is able to answer questions they may have or engage us if necessary. He can also bring feedback from those groups back to us, so we can respond to it, or tell us it's time to schedule an update for the executive team. And since he participates in our planning and retrospectives, he brings context from our most senior executives directly to those discussions, so we can better understand their objectives and help our program better support and align with those.

Only with true buy-in and deep engagement across the company can you get the alignment and continued commitment you will need for your incubation program to be successful over the long term. In the process, you will also learn a tremendous amount about how your company works top-to-bottom and places where it can improve. The incubation program you are putting in place, along with all the thinking and modeling that has gone into it, is like a small experimental slice of your larger company. The lessons you learn and the processes and tools you use to be successful can also apply equally to the overall company—sometimes in unexpected ways.

# Inspiring Lean Innovation

## Stimulating Lean Innovation Culture in an Established Organization

*"The greatest ability in business is to get along with others and to influence their actions."*

—John Hancock, American merchant, statesman, and
prominent Patriot of the American Revolution (1737–1793)

In Chapter 6, we mentioned some of the benefits a program like our accelerator can have beyond bringing innovative new ideas to your company, such as employee development and improving your company's reputation. In addition to those more obvious—albeit sometimes hard to measure—benefits, your program can have a more insidious positive impact on your corporate culture. In this chapter, we share some examples of how this manifested itself in our organization.

The specific ways in which this impact manifests itself in your company may differ slightly. Though being deliberate about capturing and leveraging these opportunities is an important aspect of ensuring its value and impact are maximized. Furthermore, capturing these benefits will help you demonstrate the value of your program to your sponsors, executives, and stakeholders, and may help drive increased participation.

© CA 2019
G. Watt and H. Abrams, *Lean Entrepreneurship*,
https://doi.org/10.1007/978-1-4842-3942-1_8

# Innovation Everywhere

We have no illusion that innovation occurs only inside, or because of, our program. It is obvious, but worth stating, that we strongly believe we do not have a monopoly on great ideas. Nor do we believe our Accelerator is the only place ideas can, or should, be nurtured. To the contrary, we believe that innovation happens everywhere in our company every day, and that most of it will happen outside the constructs of our Accelerator. We also believe that many of the approaches and techniques we use in our program can be beneficial elsewhere, and that our program can benefit from the learning of others.

> *"Alone we can do so little; together we can do so much."*
>
> —Helen Keller

# Inspiration Through Collaboration

We are intentional about our collaboration and do our best to involve people from other parts of the organization in key activities and roles. This includes their serving in influential roles in our Angel and Advisory Teams, and participation in "off-site" retrospectives where we inspect and adapt the program and those roles themselves. Diversity is the rocket fuel of innovation, so this has been enormously beneficial to our organization and our program. Being intentional about diversity, transparency, and inclusivity has resulted in another fantastic benefit to our company.

People who have participated in our program have adopted various aspects and approaches of it—including both those we created, and those we have adapted or borrowed from Lean and Agile best practices—in their own teams. This has happened not only in the organizations you might expect, such as engineering, but also throughout various other groups. For example, early on our Human Resources Team adopted aspects of how we run our Instant Agenda style meetings following one of our off-site events. In addition, many organizations have adopted, and adapted, tools such as the Lean Canvas having witnessed our use of them. For instance, teams outside the Accelerator have developed a Customer Experience Canvas, an Idea Challenge Canvas, a Scientific Research Canvas, and a Microservices Design Canvas, to name a few.

This adaptation, even of tools and techniques that stand alone as Agile or Lean best practices, is a critical aspect of our program. As was mentioned in Chapter 7, becoming a viral example of how a modern Lean/Agile organization should operate is an important and deliberate program objective. Introducing people not only to these tools and approaches, but also to how they can be used, is a key element of that.

# Lean Research

Perhaps one of the most complete examples of bringing this culture to other domains can be found in the new approach to scientific research that has been adopted by our Strategic Research Team. The Strategic Research Team is responsible for conducting scientific research in partnership with world leading universities and other research partners. They were having a very difficult time justifying and obtaining funding for new research projects. As we explored the root causes it became clear that there were many similarities with the challenges faced by teams trying to innovate in established organizations. Foremost among them, for example, was that people outside the Research Team were having difficulty understanding the research project ideas that were proposed, why they mattered, the problems they were intended to address, and whom would benefit. That was almost too familiar to believe. Time for an experiment!

I (George) worked with the Strategic Research Team to design a Lean approach to scientific research proposals. In brief:

1. A scientist or team prepares a Research Canvas that captures the heart of each research proposal on a single sheet of paper.

2. We assemble a team, similar in purpose to the Accelerator's Angel Team, to review research proposals (a smaller team subject to similar, though much simpler, quorum rules).

3. A researcher is given 10 minutes[1] of uninterrupted presentation time to present their idea and its rationale to the Research Angel Team, using the style and artifacts of their choosing.

4. A 10-minute dialog with a Research Angel Team follows to ensure the Research Angels understand the proposal and its impact on the research portfolio and funding pool.

5. Immediately following the dialog, with the people who pitched the research idea present, the Research Angel Team holds a fist-to-five vote to determine whether the proposed research should be added to the portfolio and delivers a final assessment to the team.

---

[1]Research pitch and dialogues are sometimes extended to 15 minutes in duration when methodologies or other material items differ significantly from standard procedures and may require additional explanation or context.

This new approach has reduced the time required to make research funding decisions dramatically, from months (or more in extreme cases), to as little as 30 minutes. This reduction is possible largely because the new format ensures research teams focus on, and are able to communicate, the most important elements of a research proposal in a way people unfamiliar with the research can clearly understand. In the past, more lengthy research pitches often resulted in researchers confusing participants with unnecessary detail resulting in redirects, rejections, and multiple pitches for the same research idea. Lack of a regular cadence for the reviews made scheduling difficult, exacerbating the issue. This format works whether the research team intends to use internal employees to conduct the research, is recommending a donation of their own budget to a third party (usually a university) who will conduct the research on our behalf, or is requesting approval to bid for research funding from external source (e.g., government grants).

Not only has this new Accelerator-like approach to research resulted in faster decisions regarding our research portfolio, the research is also much better understood by the members of the Research Angel Team, our Leadership Team, and others throughout the company. This better understanding has resulted in people outside the Research Team developing an interest in, and in some cases contributing to, the research projects, which had not previously been the case. Furthermore, this new approach has made the Strategic Research Team a better research partner. This type of scientific research almost always requires collaboration, and this streamlined approach has made it possible for our Research Team to respond quickly when invited by partners to join projects that have a short deadline for acceptance. Even when we decide not to participate in a project, we are able to inform our partners rapidly so they can pursue alternatives. This responsiveness has given rise to even more opportunities coming our way.

## Supporting Personal Growth

The Accelerator program's benefit to the Research Team did not end there. In addition to taking the pulse of our people throughout the course of work, we conduct regular employee opinion surveys in order to ensure we are aware of what is going well and where we can improve. During one of these surveys we discovered a very unusual and confusing combination of responses to some key questions. Several questions on our survey had always been correlated and would normally be rated either positively or negatively together. However, on one survey some of those questions were rated very highly, while others were rated very low. It made no sense at all.

During an open retrospective of the survey with the entire team, we discovered the reason was that the team members valued mastery of their domain and continuous learning extremely highly, and their concern was that they would not be able to maintain their learning culture. Fortunately, our company has a number of programs and benefits targeted directly at this. We made the team aware of those programs, though some of the unique requirements of this team of scientists were still not satisfied. What now? "I need your help!"

We approached the person on our Human Resources Team (we call them our "People Team") who designed our Incubation Rotation program and explained our needs. She worked with our scientists to get at the root cause of the issue and created a new, company-sponsored, program not unlike our Incubation Rotation, which enables our researchers to upgrade their degrees while remaining employees of the company. Two researchers enrolled in the program immediately, were accepted into post-graduate programs by the University of Barcelona, and were engaged in studies there at the time of this writing. This is another example of how a program like our Accelerator can drive value into a company beyond its more obvious benefits such as revenue from new, innovative businesses that incubated within.

# Synergy Through a Portfolio of Initiatives

It has been our experience that a program such as our Accelerator can be even more impactful when it is part of a larger portfolio of initiatives aimed at supporting innovation and nurturing ingenuity. We have over a dozen such initiatives. Key among them are:

- A Scientific Research Team that is focused on longer-term challenges and opportunities

- An Applied Research Team that bridges the discoveries made by the Scientific Research Team and makes them consumable by the Accelerator incubations and our mainstream business teams

- An Accelerator program to nurture innovative ideas and new, breakthrough business opportunities

- An Inner Source program that enables companywide collaboration and sharing of knowledge and code[2]

- Video vignettes and detailed point of view position statements regarding emerging technologies from our technologists and thought leaders to help share knowledge, identify collaboration opportunities, identify people with "hidden skills," and spark open dialog and discussion

---

[2]InnerSource takes the lessons learned from developing open source software and applies them to the way companies develop software internally. For more information, visit http://innersourcecommons.org.

- Companywide technology summits to address emerging opportunities and threats

- A patent program to help innovators in every role in the company capture their innovative ideas, reward them for their effort and inventiveness, and identify ideas with the most potential for a significant future impact

While each of these initiatives has value on its own, we have found the combination of these drives even more value. For example, though much of the outcome of our research projects is usually too far ahead of the state of the art to be of immediate benefit to a mature product team, now and again the scientists discover something (e.g., an algorithm) that can be of immediate use to a mainstream product and potentially drive market leadership in a domain. When that happens, the scientists are not always able to translate their learning into consumable code for a product team. That's where the Applied Research Team steps in. They create prototypes, proofs of concept, and working code that mature product teams can leverage and understand.

There have also been cases where the scientists have developed ideas that have become incubations inside our accelerator. In one case, the scientists realized that a discovery of theirs might have an application that could find product-market fit in the mid-term (e.g., 2-3 years). They recruited a founder for the idea, and it was accepted into the Accelerator.

Not only does this portfolio of complementary innovation initiatives provide value through its inherent synergy, it also creates many opportunities for collaboration among people who may not otherwise know of the existence of others whom they could—and should—collaborate with. This is especially true in the case of initiatives such as our technology summits and InnerSource program, which bring people together by design. However, those are not the only areas in which this portfolio has a broader impact on companywide collaboration. For example, because our scientists tend to focus on things that might be of benefit to mature product teams 3-5 years from the present and beyond, they often develop "specialized" skills far ahead of the mainstream organization. That team has been developing skills in artificial intelligence and machine learning for decades and can assist mature product teams to adopt those technologies now that they are becoming mainstream. In turn, this collaboration often results in one—or both—teams developing new ideas which they may bring to the Accelerator, and the virtuous cycle continues.

# Lean Innovation in the Mature Business

It has long been our assertion that the techniques and approaches we use can also be adopted by mature, mainstream businesses in order to nurture the great innovative ideas that arise within them every day. Even teams building solutions that have value in the near term can fall victim to some of the challenges discussed earlier in this book. Mature businesses need to exercise maniacal customer focus when building adjacent solutions or new features, or they risk building something nobody wants. We've seen it. More than once. They need to avoid committed bet trap, which is commonplace in mainstream organizations. They require minimum viable teams that cover every aspect of their business from design, to development, to delivery in order to accomplish this.

Though these things may appear beyond obvious as you read this, that is not always the case during the day-to-day operation of a mature business. Consider, for instance, minimum viable teams in an established organization. As businesses mature and grow, they tend to optimize their operations for scale. That often involves things such as acute organizational specialization, which puts everyone with a specific type of skill in a single team (e.g., marketing, sales, product management...). This type of structure often hinders the progress of teams who are pursuing new, innovative opportunities which would benefit from leveraging a broadly skilled minimum viable team. The organizational structure simply cannot support it.

Fortunately, there *are* ways to address the potential roadblock to minimum viable teams even within an organization that is optimized for scale (e.g., temporary secondment of specialized resources, matrixed management...). Though care must be taken if approaches like temporary assignment are to be used, since a matrixed or seconded employee will often—frequently unconsciously—still operate based on the priorities of their parent organization, sometimes even in opposition of the team they have been assigned to help.

There are countless other examples of established organizations missing opportunities that other facets of a Lean approach could have helped deliver. There are also countless stories of avoidable waste. We have seen large engineering investments essentially wasted because mature teams did not iterate on a minimum viable product in order to find product-market fit. Furthermore, since established organizations evolve over many years, onset of these roadblocks can be very insidious. The impact can often be seen in other functions of mature businesses as well. For example, we have seen mature businesses over-investing in things such as marketing for a mature product that is near the end of its lifecycle, when extensive marketing is not necessary. Those over-investments are lost opportunities for investment in new, breakthrough ideas—or, at a minimum, they are simply waste.

While our colleagues in the mature organization have created companywide initiatives to drive these concepts into our mainstream businesses, you can approach mainstream adoption in several ways. Whether your mainstream organization develops a single program, a common approach, or each organizational unit creates an initiative directed at its unique needs, those who are not familiar with concepts like those discussed in this book can use the incubation program we described as a model for their own initiatives.

Those who are already familiar with those concepts can leverage their own incubation program—or this material—to help explain the concepts to others and build support for their departmental, or companywide, initiatives. We have also found that the presence of a program focused on breakthrough innovation like ours makes it less politically risky for those who are interested in starting their own program, or can be used to help justify their department's own innovation initiative.

What may be most important in this context is that, through our program we have sent a clear message to everyone in our company that it is not only safe to innovate, it is strongly encouraged. We have found that, even when senior leadership of a large organization wants their employees to innovate, and even when they say it often, employees can still believe it is innovation is too risky to their career. A commitment to a program such as our accelerator is strong, visible evidence of high-level commitment to innovation, ingenuity, and employee development.

# Taking It Outside

We have been experimenting with ways in which to bring our accelerator concept outside the company, both to give back to the community, and to identify new business ideas. Our results are still inconclusive, but one experiment is seen as having been very successful.

We partnered with ESADE, a highly-respected business school, and Universitat Politècnica de Catalunya, a highly-respected technical university, to develop a business challenge contest as part of their master's degree curricula. The university faculty created several teams of five to six people, with as equal representation from each school as possible on each team. We presented two challenges to these teams related to real-world problems our customers currently face. The teams each developed an idea regarding a possible solution, built a case for the solution, and—like our aspiring intrapreneurs—captured that solution in a Lean Canvas. Teams then pitched their ideas to several of our Angel Team members using the same format we use. The only difference was that we also used the discussion time following the pitch to provide challenge-related feedback and coaching for the students and faculty.

The pitches were all very good, and each team managed to clearly and successfully communicate their idea in the 10 minutes of uninterrupted time. Every team was then welcomed to pitch their ideas to the full Angel Team if they so desired. If the Angel Team was interested in the ideas, teams were to be given the option of being hired into our Accelerator to pursue them. To be clear, the students were under no obligation to join our accelerator, even if we made an offer to them. Though, we were so impressed with some of the students we may make them employment offers regardless of the outcome of their pitch. Two of the four teams decided to pitch their idea to the full Angel Team, and one idea showed so much promise the students were brought into the Accelerator to refine it.

# Measuring Impact

Though there are some simple things that can be done to measure the impact a program of this nature has on the mainstream business, such as calculating pitch pipeline statistics, the number of ideas received by the program, and consumption of program artifacts, measuring its true impact can be very challenging. The very size of an established business organization can make it difficult to even discover that others are adopting the program's techniques and approaches. In addition, as is the case in our company, there will be people in the mainstream business who are aware of Lean startup and Agile approaches, so it can be difficult to determine the origin of the application of a tool or technique. Though, we *are* often informed by those who implemented an approach or tool based on our program and we do our best to capture that. Sometimes even people who had already been familiar with some of the concepts we use inform us they adopted a style of implementation or a tool based on our program's use of it.

# Transparency Is Paramount

We have learned that transparency is the key to success on all fronts. Our bias toward sharing information makes it easy for people to find us, and easy for them to adopt and reuse what we prepare. The more open we are, the more feedback we receive regarding not only the impact of our program outside the program itself, but also regarding how we might improve our program for aspiring intrapreneurs or those who pitch successfully.

We have also learned that reinforcement of this openness and transparency is critical. People outside a program of this nature can easily feel the program is "elitist" or "not for me," and they must be frequently reminded that they are welcome. People supporting a program like this often need this reminder, as they can develop a closed posture if they get caught up in day-to-day operations, and that will reinforce any perceptions that the program is closed or elitist. That perception alone can kill an incubation program, causing an "us versus them" culture to develop and the idea pipeline to dry up.

# Conclusion

## Don't Delay, Act Now! Intrapreneurs are Standing By!

> "Would you tell me, please, which way I ought to walk from here?"
> "That depends a good deal on where you want to get to," said the Cat.
> "I don't much care where—" said Alice.
> "Then it doesn't matter which way you walk," said the Cat.
> "—so long as I get somewhere," Alice added as an explanation.
> "Oh, you're sure to do that," said the Cat, "if you only walk long enough."
>
> —Lewis Carroll, *Alice's Adventures in Wonderland* (1865)

Thank you for reading our book.

If you have ever tried to innovate in an established organization, you have likely encountered one or more painful obstacles. If you did, we hope you were able to overcome them. Whether or not you have already done so, we hope that sharing our journey will help make your future attempts at innovation easier and more fruitful.

We believe that understanding the obstacles you are likely to encounter is essential to preparing you for the journey you are likely to face. That is why we began there. Whether you are an innovator or starting an incubation program of your own, we also believe understanding the unhealthy behaviors that evolve as a result of those conditions is essential for your success. Even if you can avoid those behaviors yourself, you may be acutely impacted if others do not.

© CA 2019
G. Watt and H. Abrams, *Lean Entrepreneurship*,
https://doi.org/10.1007/978-1-4842-3942-1_9

We shared our journey, our program, some of our missteps, and some of our successes. We discussed how an established organization can create an unfair advantage over garage-based startups by leveraging their much larger and more diverse pool of resources and talent, and we examined how a program like ours can deliver benefits far beyond revenue generated by successful incubations such as talent attraction, development, and retention. We also explored the absolute need to build strong support for a program like this with executives at the highest levels from the outset—and regularly reinforce it with them—so your program has the runway it needs to get off the ground, and the support it needs to remain airborne. Finally, we explored how, when you do that, your program can have a profound, perhaps even viral, impact across your entire company's culture and execution.

You might be wondering why we wrote this book. The answer is simple. Both of us are fortunate to be in a line of work that enables us to frequently meet with new people who have a very broad variety of experience and responsibilities. As we discussed our journey with them, we learned that many of them faced obstacles similar to ours and were working to surmount them. Many of them asked us to share additional information regarding our program and our journey. We wrote this book in response to those requests. We also hope that by sharing our journey we will be able to learn from you. So, if you have something to share, please let us know.

## Inspect and Adapt

We do not believe our program is perfect, nor that it started with perfection. We don't always get things right, but we always do our best to make them right once opportunities to improve are discovered. Though we have stated it earlier, we believe inspection and adaptation is the key to success of any program like this. Even if it were perfect today—and we are confident that's not likely—the world is ever changing, and rapidly so. Thus, a perfect program today will be imperfect tomorrow. We have "learned fast" on many occasions. We believe that makes us stronger, and we are transparent when that happens. We hope this transparency demonstrates to our intrapreneurs that we are motivated by their success, and we are listening to them.

We would also like to remind you that awareness alone is not enough. We, at times, fell victim to some of the root causes and resulting behaviors that we actually designed our program to address. This usually happened when we got too caught up in the day-to-day routine of operating the program and forgot to take time to check in with those we serve—our founders and their teams—or lost sight of the bigger picture. That is how we discovered some of the more cunning pitfalls such as the insidious committed bet, seagull management, and undetected founder bias.

That is why we remain extraordinarily committed to inspecting an adapting at all levels. We continue regular introspection and retrospectives of the program teams, the Angel Team, and the execution of our businesses. Our founders regularly share their learning with one another through routine online chat, detailed presentation of their learning, and short articles and blog posts; some of which are publicly available.

> *"The greatest obstacle to discovery is not ignorance—it is the illusion of knowledge."*
>
> —Daniel J. Boorstin

We also want to remind you that, while we have created a structure and provided guidelines and tools, these are not intended to be used rote. Our program was designed to be implemented with brains fully engaged. We rely on our incubating teams, founders, Accelerator Program Team, and Angel Team to identify when a new approach to something is required and speak up. There is even room for some variation amongst teams within our program. That is, in a sense, the point of the program—to give those intrapreneurs the freedom they need to innovate and evolve their breakthrough ideas.

We believe flexibility and the ability to learn fast in this context will also be important to the success of your program. Please adopt the spirit of the program, use as much or as little of the framework as makes sense for you, borrow any tool, approach, or technique, and adapt them all to your needs and culture. Then build upon it and share something even better with others.

# Act Now!

There is no better time to begin your journey than right now. Do not wait for the perfect time; there isn't one. Do not wait for the perfect program design. Most importantly, do not worry about perfection or anything that closely resembles it, as you begin. When we held our first 3P review our program was quite rough around the edges and definitely was itself a minimum viable product. But it *was* viable!

> *"It is better to be vaguely right than exactly wrong."*
>
> —Carveth Read, *Logic, Deductive and Inductive* (1898)

As we discussed, we started rough and went through many iterations. We started by bringing existing incubations and committed bets into the program. We then began filling our incubation pipeline with what was likely a much less shared understanding of our evaluation criteria and objectives than we have today. This enabled us to learn. Based on that learning, which occurred inside our program, elsewhere in our company, and outside of it, we have evolved immensely since then. None of that would have happened if we had not decided to run our first experiment. The looming deadline of our first 3P review was the impetus that resulted in our first complete program definition, artifacts, and ceremonies—months ahead of schedule.

So don't delay, act now!

Good luck!

# Index

© CA 2019
G. Watt and H. Abrams, *Lean Entrepreneurship*,
https://doi.org/10.1007/978-1-4842-3942-1

CPSIA information can be obtained
at www.ICGtesting.com
Printed in the USA
LVHW082336051119
636426LV00006B/57/P